# Practical Enterprise Risk Management

## A Business Process Approach

### GREGORY H. DUCKERT

WILEY

John Wiley & Sons, Inc.

*Library of Congress Cataloging-in-Publication Data:*

Duckert, Gregory H., 1949-
  Practical enterprise risk management : a business process approach / Gregory H. Duckert.
      p. cm.
  Includes index.
    ISBN 978-0-470-55985-7 (cloth); 978-0-470-89251-0 (ebk); 978-0-470-89252-7 (ebk); 978-0-470-89253-4 (ebk)
  1.  Risk management.  I. Title.
  HD61.D85 2010
  658.15'5—dc22

                                                        2010016278

Printed in the United States of America

10  9  8 7 6 5 4 3 2 1

*To Dina,*
*my best friend,*
*my soul mate,*
*my heart mate,*
*my wife,*
*my everything.*

# Contents

# Preface

THIS BOOK IS INTENDED to be a handbook of *how to* establish a highly effective enterprise risk management (ERM) environment that is actually a business tool that yields real business value. This book is a definitive guide for members of the Boards of Directors, the C Suite, Chief Risk Officers (CROs), and those charged with ERM, as well as all levels of management. In addition, this book is a must have for any shareholder who owns stock in any publicly listed corporation and should be read cover to cover to understand why she should be concerned. This is a how-to, hands-on guide, not a generic framework scenario.

With the advent of corporate business catastrophes such as Enron, WorldCom, Lehman Bros., General Motors, and so on it behooves corporate executives to get better connected with their businesses. In addition, the government has now initiated a number of regulatory activities, including Sarbanes-Oxley, which further complicate the lives of the auditors and the corporate executives. The only way to be truly in compliance with Sarbanes-Oxley is to be well aware of what is going on in your corporation, virtually daily. To accomplish this, it is necessary for corporations to establish a highly effective information-centric risk assessment methodology. Without such a methodology intricately woven into the fabric of the organization, it is virtually impossible to guarantee any type of compliance in a realistic fashion. Enterprise-wide risk assessment is much more than simply a catchy phrase or the latest in a string of failed corporate initiatives. If properly constructed, it can be a highly effective governance and oversight tool, which becomes almost irreplaceable in the arsenal of tools necessary for progressive organizations today.

Of interest is that the Chairman Emeritus of the Committee of Sponsoring Organizations (COSO), Larry Rittenberg, PhD., CPA, CIA attended the session I presented for the Madison, Wisconsin, chapter of the IIA on Enterprise-Wide Risk Assessment in 2001. The entire discussion was focused on the concept of using data to evaluate risk throughout an organization. In the presentation, real-time triggers, key process indicators, key risk indicators, Metric Oversight Monitoring Systems (MOMS), and numerous other concepts were discussed for consideration by the participants. I have used these and other similar tools during 30 years of data-centric risk assessment. These tools and methodology will be discussed in this book.

Dave Coderre, a very talented ACL practitioner and author, published the GTAG (Global Technology Audit Guide) on Continuous Auditing in which he presented a very convincing argument for the necessity of continuous audit tools, continuous monitoring, and continuous risk assessment. All of these advanced methods, of course, revolve around the utilization of data. I had the great pleasure of having Dave Coderre as a participant in one of my risk assessment sessions discussing the use of data-driven risk assessment a number of years ago. It is excellent to see that the subject matter is finally getting some serious discussion at these levels.

This book is meant to be a reference point for all organizations that are engaged in or will be engaged in the exercise of establishing an enterprise-wide risk assessment and management oversight system for their organization. It presents an alternative approach to the models that are most commonly seen. In keeping with the underlying thought process of this book, it is straightforward and to the point. This book is not an exercise in overcomplicating a straightforward issue. There are many people who believe that complexity adds value to a process or a methodology. I am not one of them. The whole premise of the book is that complexity in most cases adds nothing to a business process but complexity.

A risk model is no exception. The reality of the matter is that when a risk model becomes overly complex it also becomes unusable. Therefore, as we proceed from this point forward, everything will be clearly expressed and understandable. There will be no complex theories to entangle endlessly what is actually a very commonsense subject matter. Under no circumstances will there be any abstract theories or unattainable methodologies employed.

The approach to risk assessment undertaken in this book is based upon fact, common sense, and practical methodologies for implementation. The model also eliminates subjectivity and guesswork as much as possible. The model presented parallels the normal operation of the business, be able to be effectively utilized at all levels of the business, and can be truly used to create an all-encompassing risk model.

In Chapter 1 I discuss the subject of corporate governance and what is wrong with it in its current format. In addition, I call attention to one of the major shortcomings of most corporations and one of its biggest risk areas, which is systems implementation.

In Chapter 2 I address what I believe to be a significant misunderstanding relative to the subject of risk and risk management. Essentially every model that is out there to perform any type of enterprise risk management is based upon the premise of subjective scoring to arrive at a conclusion. Subjective models are always time and space dependent, and therefore inconsistent. In other words, the same exact situation will always be viewed differently by the exact same person on a different day in a different environment or on a different hour in the same environment.

In addition, when dealing with the subject of risk, you must be prepared to estimate probability and impact or exposure; these models attempt to deal with the subject matter via scoring and unexplainable calculations. Anybody that is the least bit familiar with risk or risk management knows that probability and impact can only be calculated using cold hard facts and data.

Chapter 3 is centered on the business, which is what risk assessment and risk management is all about. I discuss how to go about this and how to create pictures of the enterprise to ensure that effective risk management is put in place and becomes a must-have business tool.

In Chapter 4 I discuss what true business risk is, how it can be categorized, the fact that risk is not a one-off occurrence, and how to establish a risk universe for evaluating all risk.

In Chapter 5 I talk about one of the most critical issues in risk management—the ability to do it objectively not subjectively. I talk about utilizing a data-centric approach, why it is necessary, and why doing risk assessment and management any other way really does not track logically.

In Chapter 6 I begin the discussion of how to build a fluid dynamic risk model that is designed to flow with the movements of the enterprise and to keep pace with changes as they occur. I also discuss options that can be utilized to drive the model.

Chapter 7 is an extensive discussion of how to actually build a model with all of the various components included. It talks about how to construct an ERM environment that is absolutely centered on the organization in its day-to-day operations. There are extensive examples given throughout the chapter relative to the concept of enterprise risk management and key risk indicators (KRIs). There are examples for the administrative areas of the organization as well as operational areas.

Chapter 8 discusses the future evolution of the ERM model and why this is absolutely essential to keep the ERM environment vibrant and connected with the business. Also, the subject of how to make systems self-monitoring from a risk perspective, utilizing advanced tooling, is discussed.

In Chapter 9 I raise the issue of special risk situations and related topics that presents significant exposure to the organization. The two key topics that are discussed in this regard are outsourcing and mergers and acquisitions. In addition, I discuss significantly reducing external audit fees through the utilization of twenty-first-century approaches.

Chapter 10 is the last chapter of this book, and we talk about ownership of risk, extending the impact of the ERM environment, and summarize how to build an automated environment to handle all of your governance concerns.

Another subject that is addressed in this book is the prioritization of risk and risk management relative to internal controls. Internal controls can exist separately and distinctly from the business; however, business risk and the business are inseparably intertwined.

I have finally tired of listening to a bunch of supposed experts pontificate on what they believe enterprise risk management to be, while clearly demonstrating they have not the slightest notion of how it should be done in a manner that yields real business value. This approach actually evaluates and manages risk truly on an enterprise basis, and provides a highly effective business tool as well, while many of the others are financial or administration-centric.

Therefore, do not be surprised or alarmed when I take issue with common practices that have been espoused by very large and well-recognized organizations. I am not trying to be hypercritical nor implying that they are not competent nor unethical. I am simply trying to speak the truth regarding those situations that I believe to be counterintuitive or in some cases unacceptable business practice and a poor use of business resources.

Also, be prepared as the approach used here is different from the norm and as such you will have to expand your thought process and allow yourself to accept something other than the same old recycled ideas, not that recycling is bad, but in this case it is. Keep an open mind and shift your thought parameters and I believe you will find a much better approach to ERM at the end of the day.

I now undertake the task of clarifying once and for all what a common-sense, logically structured, ERM environment should look like and why if implemented properly, it will create a singular, highly effective overriding governance infrastructure.

Thank you for coming along on this journey!

# Acknowledgments

I N CREATING THE METHODOLOGIES that underlie this book, even though they are my concepts, I have been fortunate to have the support of some key people. The first person I would like to acknowledge is Joel Kramer of MIS Training Institute, who believed in my talents and my thought processes and never once wavered in his support of me as I worked at honing my skills in the seminar business. This helped me greatly in expanding the tools in my arsenal of risk assessment/management and gave me the opportunity to attain the success I have worked very hard to achieve.

Another is Dave Coderre of Canada who had the vision and courage to take my concepts, implement them, expand on them, and standardize them in his professional career. In addition, he also is an author in his own right and gave me the encouragement I needed to undertake this challenge.

I would also like to extend my sincere thanks to Phillip J. Hatch the president of Ventoro who generously gave of his time to talk with me and his permission to use his data often cited in this work from his in-depth study of offshoring and offshore outsourcing.

Most importantly, my beautiful wife Dina and my children Andrey and Vera who are absolutely critical to my success in every way; I could not do what I do without them and their undying support.

Last, but not least, I want to thank Stacey Rivera of John Wiley & Sons for all of her patience and help in bringing this book to reality.

# CHAPTER ONE

# Corporate Governance: A Gut Check

 ## THE GREAT SOX FALLACY

One of the key corporate undertakings that undermined and will continue to undermine the success of enterprise risk management (ERM) is Sarbanes-Oxley (SOX). The most amazing thing about the SOX effort was how few of the so-called knowledgeable practitioners that were giving guidance on the subject matter actually understood the salient issues relative to why SOX evolved in the first place. I authored and taught an auditor training class entitled "Sarbanes-Oxley: A Road Map to Compliance." It was astounding to see how misguided the compliance efforts were that were being sold to these client companies as the panacea for all of their problems. It was even more astounding to hear how little people really understood about what the act was intended to do and how their whole focus in life was on Sections 302 and 404 of the act. Some of the key points I tried to explain to the seminar participants were the following:

- The problems that gave rise to SOX in the first place did not start nor would they end in finance.

- The real issues were centered on ineffective operations and the inability to generate a profit.
- When the risks that were present in operations that undermined their ability to operate effectively were not mitigated, then the risk of financial ineptness was imminent.
- This would leave the financial people with no other alternative but to manipulate the numbers to meet analysts' expectations.
- Implementing an overabundance of controls in finance for financial reporting would not solve the problem.
- There were many more sections to the act than just Sections 302 and 404, such as Section 409 on real-time disclosure.
- The gathering up of a bunch of control information and then trying to test them inadequately with archaic methods was going to be of little or no use.
- The preferred method of compliance (a top-down risk assessment approach that would be data driven and holistic to the enterprise) was the only effective way to deal with these problems.
- When the risks were identified, the root causal events had to be addressed, and that would be the first step for resolving these issues.
- I also informed them at that time that they had just seen the tip of the iceberg and that there was much more to follow.

The top-down risk-based approach was supported by the pronouncements from the Securities and Exchange Commission (SEC) and the Public Company Accounting Oversight Board (PCAOB) in 2005 when they too observed that the "check the box mentality" of the compliance approach used by virtually all of the large consulting houses had missed the mark of satisfying the requirements of the act.

The subsequent gigantic meltdown of the banking industry brought on by significantly undermanaged risk in the real estate markets speaks volumes about the ineffectiveness of the act and gives us a glimpse of another piece of the iceberg starting to surface.

Sarbanes-Oxley was a noble effort in its intent to protect shareholders' interest; however, the message was lost on the practitioners in their zeal to generate quick profits in catastrophic conditions, which they had had a great hand in creating. The first catastrophic mistake was to embrace the Committee of Sponsoring Organizations (COSO) model as *the* framework for compliance—not because COSO is a bad framework; but since it is internal control-focused, it is clearly audit centric. What was required was a business model, not an audit model. Instead of performing a knee-jerk reaction to the circumstances, cooler heads should have prevailed and waited for the COSO ERM model (completed approximately two years later), which would have yielded a much more beneficial governance structure.

Unfortunately, so much money, time, and effort was put into the Sarbanes-Oxley exercise, with mixed or less than satisfactory results, that it soured senior management in many organizations from taking on any other major corporate initiatives, which would have included ERM, of course. So now there is great resistance to adopting another environment that appears to be an add-on to the already fractionalized compliance efforts of the organization. Therein lies the tale of woe for ERM and the significant reluctance to embrace it.

##  THE VISION-CHALLENGED LEADING THE EVEN-MORE-VISION-CHALLENGED

Absent the few independent practitioners (like myself) who are crying out in the wilderness against the multiheaded monsters of the world who keep espousing the same old tune, you don't see many fresh ideas coming out of the large-scale consulting groups. It is the same old process for evaluating risks that has literally been around for years. The process is based upon scoring methodologies, such as one-through-five, or zero-through-three or some other convoluted number combination that is applied to risks, control effectiveness, impact, and other such subject matter.

At the end of these exercises, some type of generic "risk-based" conclusion is inevitably reached, which is normally comprised of a band of green, a massive band of yellow, and a band of red. This is normally followed by some other gyration for refining the process, which involves discarding the high and low scorers, tweaking this, and tweaking that in order to justify an already preordained conclusion. Worse yet, the whole exercise must be repeated every time risk needs to be evaluated on an enterprise basis. This will, of course, be necessary because unlike these static models, risk is not static at all. Talk about the application of AI (artificial intelligence)—these exercises are a classic example, in a very different sense of the phrase.

Why in the world do we have all of this massive computing power, generating terabytes of data that supposedly drives everything in our organization and yet not one of the supposed visionaries from these large consulting consortiums has ever thought, *You know what, maybe we should use data as the basis for risk assessment?* What are they thinking? Or even a more puzzling conundrum is that maybe they're not thinking, and therefore where is their vision?

I cannot possibly imagine a bigger risk than spending millions or billions of dollars being led by supposed visionaries who have no vision.

## GOING BACK TO THE FUTURE? HOW *NOT* TO RUN IT

One of the greatest risks plaguing organizations in the past, today, and certainly into the future will be the inability to implement successfully progressive, highly advanced risk-centric systems. The following observations are meant to highlight some of the key areas of concern. I originally conceived "The Dirty Dozen Critical Shortcomings of Application Systems Implementation" as an article for publication. These observations came into existence after years of my own audit experience and reverification of its accuracy with thousands of my audit constituents.

I discussed it with Professor Larry Rittenberg, the current COSO Chairman Emeritus, and we tossed it back and forth with modifications. With all due respect to Larry, who is an extremely busy person, since the results of our discussions were never published, I have reverted back to my original content for the purposes of this book.

In the continuing environment of voracious systems implementation, it is perhaps time to step back and learn some lessons from history. Many of these are not new lessons, but neither have they been learned. In the following sections I will visit some critical shortcomings that continue to hinder our progress in real utilization of the vast systems capabilities that our organizations possess.

## SYSTEMIC FAILURE: CRITICAL SHORTCOMINGS OF APPLICATION SYSTEMS IMPLEMENTATION

The "dirty dozen" shortcomings are listed and expanded upon in the following pages. They represent my views of significant risks and areas of failure that are all too prolific in this discipline.

1. Moving to a New Application Platform: What's the Business Reason?
2. Inaccuracy of the Financial Projections and Committed Costs of the System (OOPS!)
3. Failure to Establish a Realistic Timeline That Incorporates All Critical Aspects of Implementation

4. The Phase 2 Syndrome—Never Happens!
5. Failure to Do a Total Systems/Personnel Impact Analysis
6. Implementing a Platform Contrary to the Established Design Criteria
7. Back to the Future
8. ACE (The Awful Consultant Experience)
9. Data, Data Everywhere, but I Can't Answer Your Question
10. SCORE (System-Centric Oversight and Risk Evaluation) AWOL
11. The Dog and Pony Show
12. Getting Cooked by the Boilerplate Contract

## Moving to a New Application Platform: What's the Business Reason?

One thing that will guarantee failure to achieve the original objective of a project is when no original objective was established. One of the key questions that the system sponsor should be able to address is the primary business reason for the change.

It is not appropriate to change system platforms just for the sake of change or because everybody's doing it. Each organization is unique in its needs and requirements. As a result, because our primary competitors are moving to a client/server platform does not necessarily mean that the client/server platform is appropriate for us. If a financially viable business reason that necessitates the change cannot be specifically identified and justified, there is no reason to change environments.

The business reason must be critical to the overall success of the organization. It must be clearly justified by returns on investment that warrant the capital expenditures, and it must be vital to meeting the needs of our customers, or carving out a larger share of the marketplace, to name only a few.

Migrating to new systems for no apparent reason is a consummate example of following the crowd no matter where the crowd is going. If the crowd is rushing into a burning building, should we all follow along? A new system is not the panacea for all business ills. In fact, it is probably dealing with a symptom instead of the real cause.

## Inaccuracy of the Financial Projections and Committed Costs of the System

If you have ever seen the acquisition and implementation of a large-scale system from start to finish you have almost assuredly seen OOPS, the Overspending Our Project Scenario. This can occur in different forms, some of which are detailed in the following list. The always popular "let's soft sell the original financial estimates to justify the project to senior management or the board." Simply stated, all of the costs are not included that will be required to make the system a reality. Factors that will be "overlooked" include:

- Long-term technical support
- Specialized consultants or contractors required
- Ancillary hardware that becomes necessary due to primary platform inadequacies
- Additional software that will be purchased by the users to plug the "gaps" in the system (real or perceived)
- Future technological upgrades required, which are inherent to the software (turnkey environment—hardware and software)
- Moving beyond Vanilla when it really needs to be a 40 scoop 30 topping banana split to deliver the baseline requirements of the users
- The *real* life cycle of the system before it requires significant changes to keep pace with business changes
- The business interruption that occurs when new releases of the software are installed and the associated costs
- The hidden costs never accounted for when the users are so dissatisfied with the system that is delivered that they have to buy computers and software to build workarounds that have the desired functionality
- The cost of application support when the flood of user requests for modifications materializes because the system misses the mark so badly
- The cost estimate is simply wholly inadequate and poorly prepared, and fails miserably in contemplating all of the cost that will be necessary

Think about it. When was last time you saw a system of any magnitude come in under its original financial and time projections?

## Failure to Establish a Realistic Timeline That Incorporates All Critical Aspects of a System

Where do these implementation dates come from, anyway? It appears that they are rarely in touch with reality and what is required for the system to be fully operational and functioning as originally envisioned. Every implementation date should be grounded in some legal or regulatory issue, or in a defined and justified business requirement.

If the required date is known and cannot be achieved—when exploding the timeline backwards given the resources available or essential lead times required—another course of action should be explored. The common practice of pulling an implementation date "out of the air" and then tying the CIO's and other related party's bonus compensation package to it runs totally contrary to sound business logic.

The objective of the exercise is not to see how fast the system can be implemented, but how well it meets business needs. Half-baked implementations tied to timelines that have no basis in reason or logic always fail to achieve the key objectives: increased productivity, lower operating costs, better information, and ease of use. In fact, in most instances productivity takes giant strides backwards resulting in more hidden cost to the company or organization.

## The Phase 2 Syndrome—Never Happens!

Doesn't it seem that the key features that the business requires or that were critical to the overall satisfaction of user community are never in Phase 1? Why is that? It doesn't really do any good to purchase the most powerful and feature-packed system available, and then fail to implement its primary functionality. The standard phrase that is normally heard when the users ask about the features is "It will be implemented in Phase 2."

Unfortunately, as many disgruntled users and overoptimistic senior executives have learned, Phase 2 is a figment of IT's imagination. By the time this event is raised as an issue, new releases of the base software are out, and the hamsters are trapped on the same hamster wheel for all eternity. If the original intent of purchasing the system was to implement minimal functionality, then save a lot of money, buy a cheaper system with far fewer features, or better yet do nothing—it will be a lot less risky.

## Failure to Do a Total Systems/Personnel Impact Analysis

Prior to implementing any system, there should be a total inventory performed of all of the systems and personnel that will be impacted by the new environment. This says by definition that IS/IT is only part of the landscape. The users should, of course, be the primary drivers of the system, though IT normally dominates the project, even though it's a staff function and not a line function (another failure point), and as such the analysis should identify all affiliated and peripheral users of the system.

Failure to perform the appropriate impact analysis on both systems and personnel will virtually guarantee a technological or human rejection of the system once implemented. When the project is first anticipated, it should be mandatory that a thorough and complete impact analysis be performed.

Communication and feedback loops should be established to ensure that vital information is available as necessary to everyone who will experience the impact or, more likely than not, suffer the negative fallout of the project.

## Implementing a Platform Contrary to the Established Design Criteria

As we have progressed across the spectrum of systems implementation theory, today we've achieved 180 degrees of separation from traditional viewpoints. The problem is that contemporary theory is rarely, if ever, followed in its purest state, therefore issues arise on a postimplementation basis.

The traditional theory of systems implementation was essentially that the organization would purchase a system that most closely approximated its operations and then modify the system to fit the business. As we know contemporary theory—as advanced by Systems, Applications & Products in Data Processing (SAP) and other similar platforms—is to reengineer the business to fit the software. The unfortunate reality is that most organizations want to embrace the new technology but not the new implementation theory.

As such, new platforms are implemented with old theory. Today's systems are self-contained, highly integrated information flow systems, and they are meant to be implemented in their entirety, a pure state of existence. However, in practice only portions of the new platforms are implemented, instead of in their entirety. And then these partial systems are interfaced to other existing systems in the business. Some of the negative results of mixing the two competing theories include the following:

- Potential loss of data integrity and mistrust of the resulting information that is generated by the system
- Excessive maintenance costs on interfacing
- Customization cost to the original software, assuming it can be performed
- The necessity to update the customized environment at great expense each time a new release of the software is brought out
- Potential need for conversion tables or other intermediate steps to convert the data for use, which are subject to error and extremely expensive to maintain

## Back to the Future

How many people do you know who would acquire a brand-new $300,000 house with four bedrooms, three baths, and a two-car garage, and then rip out one bedroom, two baths, and tear down one side of the garage? Perhaps they would do this so it looked like the house they grew up in as a kid—an example of the "comfort zone theory." Obviously, no one in a sane state of mind would do this. However, how many times have you seen organizations buy brand-new systems and then modify the reporting, functionality, and overall design of the system to make it look like the system that was in existence before?

Why is this done—simply because it makes people feel more comfortable? Clearly what has occurred here is a horrendous waste of organizational resources, and instead of positioning ourselves for the future, we have slipped neatly and quietly into the past. When was the last time that someone actually reviewed the outcome of a system implementation to ensure that it met the fundamental criterion of financial return or efficiency gains relative to the original assumptions? Every system that is implemented should move the organization forward, not backwards. We have got to run the organizations that we have today and will have in the future—not the ones we had yesterday. No enlightened executives should be encouraging the "chase yourself around the block theory" because you always end up at the same old house, only unfortunately much poorer.

## ACE (The Awful Consultant Experience)

Normally when you hear the expression "ace in the hole" it is a positive thing that creates a competitive advantage. A more accurate interpretation of ACE as it is used in the context here is that an awful consulting experience can put you far in the hole financially and technologically. The awful consulting experience can occur in a variety of ways:

- You pay a lot of money for highly skilled consultants but end up training a number of recent graduates to be better at their next job.
- There is a lack of stability in the consulting team, where the consultants are going out of your business as fast as the revolving door can turn and moving on for bigger and better money.
- The consultant tries to do too much and simply is not equipped to handle it and doesn't have other resources to draw on.
- The consultant holds you hostage and becomes such an integral part of your business that you can't live without him; therefore you hire him at exorbitant cost.

- No knowledge transfer takes place between the consultant and your personnel, and therefore you are never allowed to own your system (the ransom event).
- Numerous other instances that due to lack of time and space I will not mention.

## Data, Data Everywhere, but I Can't Answer Your Question

Let's think back to what seems to be centuries-old logic. Recalling one of the fundamental principles of why databases were created in the first place would bring to mind the issue of data redundancy. One of the driving forces behind the creation of databases was to eliminate all of the extraneous data that seem to be in divergent locations around the organization. Well, looks like they have come full circle. Now in many major organizations there must be thousands of versions of relatively the same data in the form of spreadsheets, databases, and miscellaneous files to name a few.

We seem to have all types and kinds of data out there, but it does not appear to be structured in any logical fashion that makes it accessible. In literally thousands of situations where I have asked people (auditors primarily) how they would objectively assess risk in their respective organizations, the answer normally comes back as "I would love to do it" or "That would be great if the data was there."

It seems almost incomprehensible that in the twenty-first century, with computers having existed for decades, people would still advance that argument—except that it's true more often than not. We have had data scattered among several systems and databases for years, and now we want it to take up residence in data warehouses or data farms. That is a noble exercise that should yield tremendous benefits, assuming data integrity to the source system can be assured.

The issue of concern is this—is it data for data's sake or data for information's sake? The point being made is that in system development on very rare occasions is a targeted data analysis performed that will allow the organization to consistently oversee the critical aspects of its business with virtually little or no effort. In most organizations, we are nowhere near attaining that type of instantaneous feedback on the pulse of daily activities that drive our existence.

The fundamentals aren't even in place; an example would be a credit memorandum where the reason codes are not accurate. Therefore, the organization cannot even address the problem that caused the customer's dissatisfaction. There is an old axiom that still holds true: "You can't fix a problem you don't know you have." In this day and age, if you can't measure it, you don't know you have it. Therefore, by definition you cannot solve it and make it go away. There are all kinds of data out there, but there is a real dearth of valuable information to run the business. This is commonly referred to as the DRIP theory (data rich, information poor).

## SCORE (System-Centric Oversight and Risk Evaluation) AWOL

By this time in the systems evolutionary cycle it should be an accepted fact that every system has the ability to utilize tools and methodologies that provide for consistent and accurate oversight of the organization on a continuous basis. The fundamental problem is that although systems can perform these tasks, the systems implementers choose not to let them. System-centric tools should be standard in every system created and should utilize the data that runs the organization to provide a continuous feedback oversight mechanism.

Such tools and methodologies would allow management to have a continuous view of the world they are responsible for. They should be able to evaluate their risk on a daily or even hourly or minute-by-minute basis if they so desire, which would allow them to react to business hotspots as soon as they occur. These tools and techniques should be incorporated into the system and be keyed to the users, so that they will be able to fulfill their primary management responsibilities quickly and without having to go through significant data analysis.

As the title of this section implies, these types of tools are AWOL (absent without leave) or essentially nonexistent. The failure is that the data is for the most part there, the tools should be, and we are significantly underutilizing our IT resources, which we have spent billions of dollars to acquire. This is a classic case of mismanagement of resources. Unless systems implementation strategies change in the foreseeable future, this huge waste of organizational resources is destined to continue.

## The Dog and Pony Show

Everyone that has been involved in a systems implementation has been to the dog and pony show. The dog and pony show comes in different varieties, two of which are:

1. The software demonstration
2. The visit to customers of the software vendor to see an actual installation

The software demonstration is a bit of the dog and pony show in that it normally occurs in the vendor evaluation and selection stage. By that time the vendor has responded to the Request for Proposal (RFP) and stated with certainty that they can meet all of the requirements that your organization is looking for in a system. Conveniently when we see the demo, sure enough, all of the features are there.

At some point it would be prudent for the organization to verify that in fact they have seen a real-live system and not a vaporware version of how it would appear if the vendor got the job. Learning that the system is not all that it appeared to be in the demo is disastrous—especially if the problem isn't recognized before the postcontract phase.

The second show, the customer visit, should never be limited to the primary suggestions of the vendor. Clearly, vendors would select those successful implementations that would present their product in a favorable light. What needs to be determined is what is not so favorable. So the key is to determine how to get in contact with the primary regional and national user groups of the software you intend to buy, so that you can have in-depth discussions regarding the key issues they have with the software and vendor.

This is not to say that vendor-arranged site visits are worthless, but some very specific things need to be determined at the site visit. For instance, is this organization similar to ours; are they of comparable size; do they have the same business structure, same number of locations, and same transaction intensity—to name a few? Getting to the real gutsy issues with the system is the most critical thing that can be done prior to making any commitment with the vendor. Once you sign the contract, they have just become a partner in your business. For more on contracts, see the next section.

## Getting Cooked by the Boilerplate Contract

Without a doubt one of the worst things an organization can do is sign a boilerplate contract with the software vendor. Prior to signing any contract, the organization should have a trusted and knowledgeable representative in-house—or hired—that will visit the vendor's site before the contractual commitments are signed. The representative has to check for a number of things that may negatively impact the organization, some of which are the following:

- The ability of the vendor to technically support the system
- The financial viability of the vendor and their likelihood to continue to support the product
- The necessity of software source code escrow to protect the organization in the event of vendor failure

- The depth of knowledge regarding the product throughout the vendor's staff
- The operations of the vendor (to develop a sense of their strengths and weaknesses)
- Any discrepancy between demonstrated software and existing code
- The potential existence of multiple software vendors who have written individual portions of the system being purchased

In addition to this list, this person should receive in-depth training on the system to enable him to understand all of its key attributes and nuances. Without any type of contract protection for the organization, which can only come about if the representative thoroughly understands the system, the organization will have no protection, or it will only be obtained by costly litigation. In that case there are only losers.

These dirty dozen failures in systems implementation have only scratched the surface of the significant amount of waste that goes on continually in systems implementation. This is a huge continuing risk to the organization. It is imperative that some significant changes be made in software implementation before we go through another round of predestined failures. The future depends on IT—the time for change is now!

 ## WHAT IS GRC ANYWAY?

It always astounds me when I look at how certain terminology and/or "new" initiatives emerge. Take for instance Total Quality Management (TQM). That original science, fostered by such greats as Deming, Juran, and Crosby back in the 1940s, brought to business practice some extremely practical and useful tools for modifying and improving process. In addition, they championed the utilization of metrics and measurements to make a business better one process at a time. Most of their tools could be employed today in major corporations to solve many of the problems in their operating areas that have forced companies to seek the solution of outsourcing as their only way out.

Yet anyone who has read the "Ventoro Offshore 2005 Research Preliminary Findings and Conclusions," which can be located at Ventoro.com, will clearly see from the statistics presented that the largest cost savings coming out of outsourcing efforts by major corporations are from process improvements, not from salary and wages as is popularly believed. This subject is discussed in Chapter 9 in the context of risk.

All of that aside, TQM was not good enough. To give things just a little different twist, Reengineering was conceived, and Six Sigma made common ordinary individuals into black belts. (Karate anyone?)

Now we have people talking about GRC. So let's break it down and see what this means. G is obviously governance, which I believe everybody in this country would say we need a little more of. R stands for risk management, a nice concept but poorly done in many large, medium, and small organizations alike. And C is the dreaded compliance, which has been traditionally overseen by regulators of course, but some would ask how effectively.

The acronym implies that these are separate and distinct areas of concern, which they clearly are not. They are all interlocking and inseparable when viewed using any type of common sense. The key point being missed here is that all of these should be part of logical but interrelated subsets of ERM. That is, ERM should be the overarching umbrella under which each and every one of these fall. The classic mistake made by most corporations today is that they are treating these as separate and distinct areas of concern and in some cases like SOX compliance, creating a separate and distinct unit to oversee it.

There's no reason for any of this, as these areas should all be subsets of the larger ERM environment, which would unite them into one unified effort. Corporate governance will be fulfilled by a highly effective, well-structured, properly automated ERM environment.

Remember, the E stands for enterprise, which means that everything, by definition, would be governed highly effectively by a centralized methodology. R is the effective identification of and determination of risk and is inherent in ERM. Last, but not least, M stands for management of all risks. Compliance is just another subset that has to be effectively managed as a critical risk of the enterprise. My vote would be to get away from acronyms such as GRC that imply fractionalized corporate structures that are highly duplicative and cost-inefficient.

##  ARE YOU CUBIN'?

What I'm alluding to here is this: are you familiar with the two cubes brought to us by the good folks of COSO?

The cubes are, of course, the COSO framework and the COSO ERM framework. I think we are all painfully familiar with the origination of the COSO framework, which was brought about as a result of the savings and loan failures in this country. At that time COSO was working with the Treadway Commission in an attempt to keep the federal government from regulating the audit industry.

The audit industry was a subject of great scrutiny at that time as a result of the failure of approximately 600 different savings and loans scattered around this country. In essence, what we had was a total failure of the second tier of the banking system.

This was brought about by such inflated property values that everybody hung out a shingle in front of his house thinking he was a real estate appraiser. These "appraisers" supplied inflated values to the savings and loans, which then lent money on these inflated values to unsuspecting clients. Does this sound at all familiar? If you did nothing more than change the sign from property appraiser to mortgage broker out in front of the same quack's house, you would replicate a key factor in the massive financial meltdown we just went through. We just never learn, do we?

Yes, this has happened before, and it is actually what gave rise to COSO as an entity. COSO's goal was to keep the federal government out of the audit industry, which they successfully did. The argument was that they would create the COSO model or internal control framework, and this would fix everything.

The intention was to have all organizations embrace the model, and raise management awareness of the importance of internal control. The model and its framework were intended to lead to a higher degree of corporate governance and ethics resulting in the elimination of misstatement and malfeasance in the corporate boardrooms. Noble intent, that is for sure, but the question still remains: has the effort worked? I don't believe that you have to cogitate too hard to determine if it has or has not—clearly not.

Even more mystifying is that it became the standard of compliance for Sarbanes-Oxley when it was embraced in 2002. I will not speculate any further on this subject matter. I believe by applying a little common sense you can arrive at your own conclusions as to whether the outcome satisfied the mission.

All that discussion aside, in the fall of 2004 COSO created the COSO/ERM framework, and quite honestly I believe that COSO did an exceptional job in putting together guidance for embracing risk. As I mentioned before, Professor Larry Rittenberg attended a presentation I gave in 2001 on enterprise-wide risk assessment (EWRA), as I called it then, which addressed a lot of the subject matter that later came out in this framework. To his credit I feel that Professor Rittenberg has done an exceptional job in furthering risk as a key corporate initiative, which is personally very pleasing to me, and he should be commended for that work.

Figures 1.1 and 1.2 are the two cubes that are the products of COSO. They are presented here to make a comparison at least in the context of how I view them. I will not grind through each and every attribute of these models, but it is important to understand some of the key criteria that are being presented by them. It is

**FIGURE 1.1** The COSO Cube

*Source:* COSO.

important that corporate executives and board members understand what is being exemplified by these models and the subtle, but very important, differences between the two. Shown in Figures 1.1, 1.2, and 1.3 are the COSO cubes.

Three key questions need to be asked in reviewing the cubes:

1. How do they differ?
2. Why do they differ?
3. What is the implication of this?

My take on these questions is as follows. In viewing the cubes side by side what you start to notice are some fundamental differences in the contents, but the implications of these may not be clear-cut. On both of the cubes across the top are areas of corporate strategic concern. The thought process is that the five bands or eight bands below those levels, if properly included in the corporate governance structure, will ensure the accomplishment of the strategic objectives. A noticeable difference between the two cubes when you look at the strategic objectives level is the presence of four objectives on the COSO/ERM cube versus three on the COSO cube.

On the COSO/ERM, cube you can see a category of Strategic has been added. That is a very important category in that it can take into account such critical

**FIGURE 1.2** The COSO/ERM Cube

*Source:* COSO.

**FIGURE 1.3** Side-by-Side Comparison of the Cubes

*Source:* COSO.

corporate initiatives as outsourcing and mergers and acquisitions. Both of these areas are, of course, fraught with risk, a subject matter that will be discussed in Chapter 9. The other notable difference at that level is that "Reporting" has replaced "Financial Reporting," creating a much more business enterprise flavor as opposed to accounting flavor.

When you look at the COSO cube and its five original bands, it is clearly emphasized that controls are the main focus of that environment and that risk plays a very minor role. If you look deeper at the framework, you can see that control environment forms the foundation of the cube. Just as in a house, it is the supporting infrastructure that makes everything work.

You can also see that risk assessment is actually following, or appears to be an afterthought in relationship to control activities, as you come down from the top of the model. The implication is clear that controls precede risk assessment.

Think about that for a moment, and you'll probably start asking the same question that I did when I saw the model back when it was first issued. How can controls possibly precede risk in any type of thought process? That makes absolutely no sense from a logical perspective. If you don't know where your risk is or what it is, how do you know what to control and how to control it?

For example, what if I told you that one room on one floor of the 40-story hotel was filled with gold and all of the rest of the 600 rooms were standard hotel rooms. Then I said that I wanted you to design a control plan for the premises. You could do whatever you wanted in order to bring the hotel into an appropriate controlled state of existence.

What would you do first? Start running around and installing big steel doors on every room in the building, stationing armed guards at the front door of the hotel, screening all customers as they came in the door, and searching them? Clearly not, you would first take a tour of the hotel, locate the room where the gold is in fact located, the point of maximum risk, and secure that area appropriately.

That would be logical, that would be *common sense*! However, if you were to talk with any high-ranking auditor in most of the large auditing houses in 2010 they would tell you they are definitely looking at risk. In practice that is simply not true. They are only concerned about how many controls they should test and how big a sample they should take to justify their opinion. Risk assessment could not be any farther away from the process. They are still following the precedent expressed in the original COSO model, which is to put controls first, with risk assessment as an afterthought.

When you look at the COSO/ERM model, you start to see an entirely different picture. As has already been highlighted, right from the strategic level of the model there are distinct differences in the approach. The most important difference is the business feel as opposed to finance feel that the model starts to communicate. What am I saying? It is been my contention all along that the COSO model, as noble an effort as it was when it was created, was way too bean-counter–oriented to be of any value to a major business enterprise or large-scale organization of any type.

The eight bands on the COSO/ERM model are much more logically oriented toward business as opposed to finance and accounting. The order of precedence itself coming down from the top of the model is far superior to its predecessor and makes much more sense logically.

Some key differences are that you can see that "Control Environment," the foundation of the COSO model, was changed to "Internal Environment," giving it a much more enterprise feel. "Objective Setting" was injected as a new band for the purposes of establishing operating objectives that will help to attain the strategic objectives identified across the top of the cube. The next three bands ("Event Identification," "Risk Assessment," and "Risk Response") are all directly related to the mission of risk assessment and management. We'll discuss some of these components in a little more detailed fashion in this chapter.

The other key observations are the order of precedence and the foundation. You can clearly see where all three of the risk-related bands precede control activities. For the first time in history, somebody has gotten the logical thought process in the correct order. *It is always risk before controls!* Regarding the foundation of the COSO/ERM cube, you can see that monitoring has now become the point of focus. Just preceding monitoring, you see the band "Information and Communication." This has a logical and businesslike flow that is totally absent in the original COSO model.

The implication here is that the information and communication generated by the entity or enterprise can be utilized to evaluate the risk and the operations of the enterprise on an ongoing basis. This would be fed to the monitoring infrastructure in place in the enterprise to act as a feedback mechanism. The data and information gathered would be recycled back up to the top of the model to reset operating objectives and make necessary corrections where unacceptable risks are in evidence.

This would be in keeping with the logic that risk factors, organizational information, and data can be utilized on an ongoing basis to monitor not only risk and controls but also operational performance of the enterprise. This can be accomplished by implementing the data-centric ERM strategy detailed in Chapters 6, 7, and 8.

Illustrated in Figure 1.4 are the eight bands of the COSO/ERM model along with their detailed contents. I will not belabor the discussion. However there are some items worthy of note.

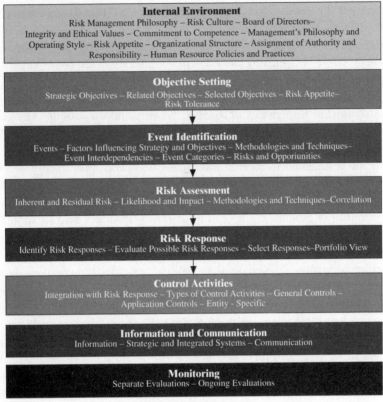

**FIGURE 1.4** The Eight Bands of COSO/ERM

To put in plain terms, the COSO model for auditors, and the COSO/ERM model is for business people. This makes all the difference in the world in how the frameworks will be perceived and whether they will be embraced or not. As important as finance may be to some people, it does not create one product or get one service out the door to be sold to a customer. This has been the rub all along. Easily 90 percent of corporate executive and operations management have nothing to do with bean counting. Don't care, *may* want to know.

The unfortunate reality of what has occurred is this. In a knee-jerk reaction to try and placate the American public and shareholders in general, the federal government jumped the gun. For political expediency and gain, they allowed a couple of politicians to create a law of the land prematurely, which was then thrust upon corporate America in a totally bizarre fashion. Without getting into all the sordid details, let's just consider a few fundamental and egregious errors that occurred as a result.

First of all, the supposed fix for all of the ills that was in fact supported by all the large accounting firms and consulting houses was to strengthen financial reporting controls. As observed earlier, that is not where the problem started and did not solve the problem. I am not Monday-morning quarterbacking here. I stated categorically back when the act was first passed that this approach was wrong in my seminar "Sarbanes-Oxley: A Road Map to Compliance," and I stick by that conclusion today. When I was critical of the approach and how many of the prime players who caused the events in the first place were now reaping billions while *not properly* fixing the situation, many people walked out. Could not stand the truth, I guess.

The second critical error is that the original COSO model was utilized as the compliance methodology for the act. Why would anybody do this when it had not stopped anything at all up to that point in time? I can only speculate, but one theory would be since COSO was never really embraced, all the tools that were created by the large firms and consulting houses for that purpose were never utilized. What better way to recoup your investment and make a massive profit than to lobby to make it the preferred compliance framework? It was actually mentioned in the Sarbanes-Oxley Act itself, and the big firms were off to the bank with the armored cars full of money.

Yet in 2005 the SEC and the PCAOB held a roundtable on the results of the initial compliance efforts. "Round" is the operative word here because the corporate executives all roundly lambasted the ineffectiveness and the cost of the effort. In fact, if you look at the actual language that came out of the session, the following observation was made:

> The feedback indicated that one reason why too many controls and processes were identified, documented and tested was that in many cases neither a top-down nor a risk-based approach was effectively used. Rather, the assessment became a mechanistic, check-the-box exercise. This was not the goal of the Section 404 rules, and a better way to view the exercise emphasizes the particular risks of individual companies. Indeed, an assessment of internal control that is too formulaic and/or so detailed as to not allow for a focus on risk may not fulfill the underlying purpose of the requirements. The desired approach should devote resources to the areas of greatest risk and avoid giving all significant accounts and related controls equal attention without regard to risk.

> (Source: Division of Corporation Finance, Office of the Chief Accountant, U.S. Securities and Exchange Commission, May 16, 2005)

Gee whiz, would that be a politically correct way of saying those wizards of the accounting world missed the point entirely, again? Yes, that is exactly what it is saying. The following observation to that, of course, was to direct that all efforts should be done on a top-down risk-based approach. That sounds very familiar, since that's what I was advocating back in 2002 and is what I am discussing now in this book. And yet today again they go down the road of controls irrespective of risk.

The other major fallout of this was that the billions of dollars that were "wasted" on the ill-gotten compliance techniques have now stymied the effort to install ERM in organizations today. What should have occurred is that no compliance should've been thrust upon corporate entities until the COSO/ERM model was completed in 2004. At that point, they could have implemented ERM as an all-encompassing governance tool as well as a business tool to run the entire enterprise. If this had been done, we would not be in the position we are today with fragmented corporate compliance—the SOX group here, the ERM group there, the compliance officer someplace else, and at the end of it all a convoluted, costly, and highly inefficient mess.

By invoking ERM early on, we could have set a pathway to corporate success by creating tools and methodologies that would have actually yielded a defined return on the investment for the business itself. Instead, what we have is a somewhat dysfunctional structure prevalent across virtually all corporate landscapes that only bring additional cost to overhead with no benefit to either the business or the shareholder. Is that what we had in mind when this act was originally brought into focus, or was it the protection of the shareholder and enhancement of value?

The upshot of this is that Sarbanes-Oxley consumed all corporate resources, and in tough economic times corporations simply cannot justify any type of large-scale expenditures to implement ERM. Unfortunately, if you were privy to a lot of boardroom conversations you would see that there is mass confusion relative to the subject matter itself. This stems again from a lot of misguided pseudo-knowledge on the part of large consulting houses who really do not understand the subject matter at all.

The only effective way to accomplish corporate governance is to design an ERM environment that is all-encompassing and not an accumulation of disjointed special-interest subsets of compliance. In Chapter 2, we will begin the discussion of what an effectively designed ERM environment should look like.

CHAPTER TWO

2

# What ERM Is and What It Is Not

 **DON'T BE MISLED: WHAT ERM IS NOT**

Before we can begin to design a successful enterprise-wide risk assessment model of a slightly different nature, we really have to understand clearly what a risk model of this nature is not.

There are a number of organizations today that are promoting their theory of what one of these risk models should be. In many instances the models that are being promoted are nothing more than extensions of what could be considered classical financial thought processes. In many cases the models are based upon financial internal control theory that has been applied or misapplied, as the case may be, to organizations for many years with mixed or no success. The reality of the matter is that "Financial" as a risk category is only one of numerous risk categories that need to be considered to build a truly business-focused risk model.

Unfortunately, a number of these organizations believe they can simply take the financial approach that has been used for years to establish internal controls for the business and transform it into an all-encompassing risk assessment model. This is, of course, not valid as a primary assumption, and it should be challenged as invalid on its surface as a method of assessing risk in the complex organizations that we have today.

The thought process that a risk model that is essentially financial in nature will accurately assess and/or manage all the risks in a business is fundamentally flawed. Anyone who looks at a business and thinks about it logically knows that the financial statements and the controls that relate to those financial statements deal with the business in a historical context.

What appears in the financial statements is simply the result of what has already occurred in the operations. It is viewing the problem backwards to assume that you are going to manage and/or mitigate risk at the financial statement level. By that time, the risk has occurred, and the exposure has been realized. The only thing that can be done at that point is to determine how big of a check is going to be written or to what account and for how much the journal entry should be made. This is not to say, however, that the financial statements cannot be effective tools in analyzing risk in a historical context. This concept will be explored in much more detail in Chapter 7.

Another interesting but certainly speculative feature of a number of these risk models is that they are based on subjectivity. There are a number of concepts that are subjective in nature and have regularly been applied to the practice of risk assessment. A theory that has been applied to risk assessment on a regular basis is that the model should be based upon weighting and scoring methods to somehow rank the risks in order of importance. The weakness in this thought process is that the scoring and weighting is based upon some individual's thought process at the time that these "risk exercises" are performed.

The problem in this is that any subjective-based model is time and space dependent. That is to say that if the same individual was asked to weight and score the very same situation at a different time, say the next day, the results of the risk assessment would be different. The reason for this obviously is that people's judgment is swayed by time and feelings unless it is done on a fact-anchored basis. As a result the very same person will arrive at a different conclusion absent specific data, information, or facts as a guide.

Another issue that comes into play relative to subjectivity is the terminology that is applied to risk assessment on a consistent basis. Examples of the terms would be the concepts of "low," "medium," and "high" relative to risk. In many cases, these terms are used freely and in combination with other interesting terminology such as "heat mapping," which sounds strangely military in nature. The interesting thing about this thought process is there are a number of catchy phrases associated with "low," "medium," and "high" with really no effort to define what "low," "medium," or "high" means.

The reality of the matter is that if pursued, a number of the proponents of this methodology would be hard pressed to distinguish the difference. In most cases absent any knowledge to the contrary, "low" would be defined as a little less than "medium," "medium" would be defined as a little less than "high," and "high" would be defined as little higher than "medium." The reason for this is the absence of an operational definition of each of these related to a specific risk circumstance. Absent valid and reliable information and data, no other conclusion can really be arrived at.

The third notion that comes into play is not related directly to subjectivity, but due to lack of specificity, it clearly implies subjectivity is the thought process that "one size fits all." The unfounded concept that a universal risk model can be applied to all circumstances, all companies, or all organizations borders on the ridiculous. This is not saying that similar risks do not impact a number of different organizations—they do. However, they have to be considered differently based upon the specific circumstances in effect at a particular organization.

A particular risk will not manifest itself the same in every circumstance, and the exposure will clearly be different based upon a particular fact situation in which the risk occurs. It is inappropriate at best to roll out a boilerplate approach to risk assessment for a number of organizations especially if the risk model is subjectivity based.

A fourth concept that gets a lot of attention is that of benchmarking. Benchmarking is a useful thought process if in fact it can be verified as a legitimate point for comparison. The theory of benchmarking is well and good; the problem is in the execution and validity of what is determined by employing the theory. The idea is to compare the organization to a valid baseline or to a similar circumstance. However, there are a number of questions that need to be asked relative to the basis for comparison, for instance:

- If comparing with the industry standards, is a straightforward and uniform method of information gathering enforced and adhered to? If not, then the obvious risk is that you are going to compare apples and oranges.
- How do you validate the data and/or information to which you are comparing yourself? There are numerous ways in which data can be presented by different parties lacking specific guidelines to the contrary and the enforcement of it. In addition, how do you protect yourself against puffing the numbers, overoptimism, or outright misrepresentation?
- How do you ensure that the results and/or basis of comparison are not combined in an incorrect way, duplicated, or in some other way lack integrity in the data?
- What is the assurance that the companies that you are being compared to have the exact same management team as your company?

- What is the assurance that the companies that you are being compared to have the exact same data or information systems?
- What is the assurance that all those that you are being compared to have the exact same business model, are centralized or decentralized, and so on?
- What is the assurance that the geographic locations and marketplaces for those organizations being compared to are exactly the same as yours?
- Finally, how do you ensure that your interpretation of the facts and/or information is correct? The same set of facts or data can be misinterpreted differently without specific guidance. For instance, data can easily be interpreted totally incorrectly if the type of data being reviewed is not known. The two primary types of data being referred to here are raw and blended data. This concept will be discussed in more detail in Chapter 6.

There is a great tendency today in business for organizations to compare themselves to their peers. Unfortunately, in many instances the comparisons are not made between true peers. In most instances if organizations were to look seriously at those to which they are comparing themselves, they would see the seriousness of their mistake. Different organizations operate under different management structures, policies and procedures, business models, and simple day-to-day operations abnormalities.

To make major decisions based upon the results without first legitimizing the comparison by answering the questions set forth could be a monumental mistake. It would be very similar to assuming that there are great synergies to be gained by combining two organizations in a merger only to find out that the synergies are never realized because they do not exist.

To summarize what an enterprise-wide risk assessment is not, it is not subjective, it is not one size fits all, it is not universally determined, and it is not the result of benchmarking on a generic basis things that cannot be validated. Possessing large generic benchmarking data sets is wonderful if your objective is to collect a lot of manure for the data farm (warehouse).

However, to utilize data and information derived in this fashion as the basis for assessing risk in your organization is a major risk in itself. The data must be refined and be specific to your business subset. As an alternative to the models presented, for the remainder of this book we will discuss how to build a data-centric globally integrated risk assessment model. This model is a business-oriented fact-based alternative to the speculative models that have been discussed earlier. The intent is to equip the organization with a tool that can be utilized today and carried forward into the future.

**KEY QUALITIES OF AN EFFECTIVE ERM**

The key qualities of an effective ERM environment are numerous and varied, and they must be strategically aligned with the organization in order to be highly effective. ERM must have all of the key fundamental components in place and functional if it is to be effective. These components are discussed in the following sections.

## High-Level Corporate Sponsorship

One component that is essential for an effective ERM environment is for the board of directors and senior executives to take it extremely seriously. That means that support for the initiative must be consistent and unflappable. All too often, these initiatives lack strategic thought process and are poorly implemented from the start. As such, they cannot maintain longstanding support from the critical levels of management and board.

An essential element is the presence of a strong and highly knowledgeable Chief Risk Officer (CRO). This person must be a visionary who is not locked into the antiquated practices of the current predominant thought processes. The CRO must take day-to-day responsibility for informing the senior executives, the Board of Directors disclosure committee, and all other interested persons on the status of risk throughout the organization. This position must have a direct reporting relationship to the disclosure/risk committee and the board to ensure that the position is not compromised from doing its job by corporate politics and improper structure.

## Well-Defined Risk Structure for Evaluating the Entire Enterprise

The ERM environment must be created around a well-defined structure for evaluating risk across all elements of the organization. This must include a thorough and complete mapping of the entire enterprise, physically depicting all key operating elements of the organization. One of the maps would include all of the operating subsets of the enterprise. A second map would include all of the administrative or cross-functional types of support mechanisms. The reason for this is to not overcomplicate the physical mapping exercise and to solidify the notion that the risks of the various parts of the enterprise are quite different and they need to be evaluated separately and distinctly from each other. I will provide examples of such maps in Chapter 3, as these are essential to effective risk management on an enterprise basis.

## Properly Determined Risk Appetite

Management must determine a proper risk appetite: in other words, how much risk can we take long before it is too much? This risk appetite must be in place for any and all events that may occur throughout the enterprise. This implies by definition that members of the organization must be involved to provide input to management on these key issues at every level of the organization. It is imperative that once the risk appetite is established, namely the amount of risk that management is comfortable with, the risk limit must be strictly adhered to. We have seen recently in the banking industry where the risk appetites were either not well established or were blatantly ignored.

One thing that is tricky about determining the risk appetite is the variety of risks that have to be taken into account. Normally we hear that the risk appetites in the mainline businesses are clearly established. However, this is a very, very small part of the entire risk picture of an organization. When establishing a risk appetite on a portfolio basis we must be sure to include all types of business risks, as well as specialty areas of physical and logical risk. Developing a portfolio of risk is no small task, but it is absolutely necessary to properly install any type of risk management methodology in an organization.

## Well-Defined Risk Language Used throughout the Enterprise

A risk language must also be developed that details terminologies and methodologies that will be employed universally in the organization. This risk language should be communicated to all persons in the organization and then utilized continuously to build an understanding of its meaning and content. If necessary, risk terminology should be published and distributed across the enterprise to ensure uniformity of employment. Once determined and understood, this terminology should be used consistently in all communications and become a part of mainstream dialogue.

An example of something that would be part of the risk language of the organization would be the risk categorization scheme that is employed. We will present some alternative schemes in Chapter 4; however, it should be noted that some type of categorization is necessary.

## Clearly Defined Risk Culture

Every organization that is going to effectively employee ERM must have defined a risk culture that they want to prevail within the organization. The risk culture can be highly conservative, highly aggressive, or essentially neutral. As we all realize in our own daily lives, any culture spawns subcultures; the risk culture is no different. For example, there may be very specific understandings of how the organization is going to deal with operational risk on a consistent basis.

What inevitably occurs is that an organization such as sales and marketing in their zeal to market and sell products makes promises that the organization cannot fulfill operationally. At that point, the sales and marketing organization has become a risk subculture. They create a situation in which promises are made, legal obligations are undertaken, and expectations are set. However, when we do not satisfy those obligations operationally, then we create a situation of great dissatisfaction for our customers.

These situations can be avoided if sales and marketing acts within the criteria of the risk culture that has been established. In other words, they will adhere to the established guidelines for promise dates and lead times. Whenever they depart from this pattern of behavior, they create a risk subculture that is unacceptable. When the risk culture is clearly established, everyone lives by the same rules, and no exceptions should be allowed.

## Highly Automated and Data-Centric Reporting Protocol

This protocol of reporting risk by utilizing systems and basing virtually all risk management in the context of data will establish any ERM organization as "top of game" (or whatever clever terminology you would like to use). As will be discussed in Chapter 6, the only effective risk management methodology that should be established must be data/fact based. Using data or facts will lead to rapid and accurate evaluation of risk and timeliness of reporting that cannot be achieved by any other means. A model of this type can provide for virtually instantaneous feedback depending upon the degree of automation employed in the organization for this purpose.

If you sit on the Board of Directors, the audit committee, the disclosure committee, in the CEO's chair, the CFO's chair, or the CIO's chair, or own their stock, wouldn't you want this type of information accurate and timely? This is the type of reporting methodology that every competent CRO should be building within her organization.

## Well-Defined Inventory of Key Risk Indicators

Key Risk Indicators (KRIs) are critical to the successful implementation of any type of near-time or real-time ERM environment. You may ask yourself, *So why do I need this?* The reason is that your business is changing literally every minute that it operates. The more current your information, the more ability you have to effectively govern the organization and prevent unwanted results from compromising your success. KRIs should not be confused with Key Process Indicators (KPIs), as in most cases they are not at all alike.

In some instances, they can actually be polar opposites. We will discuss the differences in Chapter 4, but be aware that a data-centric approach to ERM using well-defined KRIs is the only sensible way to establish it in the twenty-first century. Any other methodology will have little or no residual value as a business tool and, in fact, will be cost-intensive and cumbersome to maintain.

## Straightforward and Highly Usable System of Analytics

When employing data, it is imperative to use an effective set of analytics because data is only as good as your ability to use and interpret it. A lot of the large consulting houses believe that complexity contributes value, but in fact the only value it creates is value for them. It is not necessary, nor advisable, to develop analytics that are too complex (algorithms and logarithms and the like) to get a fix on fundamental business risk.

If you cannot explain the analytic, literally, it is too complex. Of course, that plays into the plans of consulting groups who like to take their clients hostage and charge them large ransoms, oh pardon my petulance, fees. We will talk about a number of straightforward, highly functional analytics that anyone can understand and interpret quickly and easily without the need for the great all-knowing consulting group. The best practice is of course the old KISS theory, Keep It Simple, Stupid.

## Effective but Uncomplicated Categorization of Risk Scheme

The categorization of risk is extremely helpful because it may help you see concentrations of risk. When utilizing risk categories, it is helpful to keep in mind a couple of fundamental concepts and facts.

- **Risk cannot be neatly categorized.** Risk is not something that can be neatly pigeonholed into nice and uniform little segments. Risk will virtually always flop over categories no matter what kind of scheme is employed. This realization will serve you well in understanding that perfect categorization of risk is not going to be possible.
- **More is not necessarily better.** In Chapter 4, I will present alternative categorizations of risk that are fairly straightforward. A much more complicated scheme with numerous subclassification schemes is contained in the COSO/ERM model.

The question that has to be asked is whether the complexity adds anything valuable to the exercise or simply increase the complexity of the exercise. When the scheme is too complex, it tends to drive the discussion off of the subject matter at hand. In other words, the discussion descends into a debate about the right category and subcategory instead of focusing on the risk and how it is going to be managed day to day.

A categorization schema should only be used for sanity checks and making sure we haven't forgotten something critical. Remember, it is the risk and the management of it that is the object of the exercise, not a perfect categorization scheme.

## Strategic Plan for Constantly Improving the Risk Management System

Complacency about enterprise risk management is the death knell for an organization. Even if you have created the greatest enterprise risk management environment to ever exist, you cannot rest on your laurels and hope that it's going to be sufficient for the future. As we are all well aware, risk is a dynamic process and never ceases to change.

When change is eminent in the area for which you are responsible, it dictates a requirement to stay ahead of the change and to constantly be improving the format of how you conduct your business. All ERM environments should have a strategic plan for constant migration of the risk management system to the highest plateau of performance. The strategic plan should constantly be re-evaluated to ensure that it is keeping pace with the movement of the business, the market, the technology, and the world.

The strategic plan for every ERM environment should include as much automation as possible. It should also be synchronized directly with the IT strategic plan of the organization for which it performs its functionality. As will be discussed in Chapter 8, there is no room for turf wars and corporate politics interfering with a strategic alliance like this. It is absolutely imperative that ERM and IT be very closely aligned as both of their futures really depend on each other.

## Ability to Eventually Migrate the Methodology to Facilitate Predicting the Future

The ultimate objective of any ERM environment is the ability to see the future before the future arrives and undermines the organization. It does absolutely no good to constantly be in a state of looking backward when you are trying to run a progressive organization. You must be in a position to stop undesirable consequences before they become consequences. In other words, see them coming.

This is what I will allude to later in this book as the concept of looking out the windshield instead of in the rearview mirror. The organization needs somebody to look into the future and start to take an inventory of those types of undesirable events that may be lurking in the darkness beyond. At the same time, executives should be trying to identify opportunities that may be present so that the organization may avail itself of these positive events.

An example would be an abrupt change in the marketplace in the offering that presents a risk to your competitors. However, since you recognize it early, it is actually an opportunity for you to gain a competitive advantage or perhaps dominate the marketplace. There have been a number of these that have taken place in recent history. One such example would be the significant impact on the newspaper industry of the Internet and its diversion of advertising dollars and loss of readership. Recognizing earlier on that there was an imminent shift in the technological savvy of the consumer, the tastes of the consumer, and the form of consumption would have bode well for the organizations still running the printing presses.

 ## PRIMARY COMPONENTS OF RISK ASSESSMENT

Regarding traditional "risk assessment" that is performed using subjective-based judgment, it is important to note that risk assessment cannot truly be done without data. To truly perform risk assessment, you must be able to address the following three conditions:

1. Identify the risk
2. Calculate the probability of occurrence
3. Determine the impact/exposure

It is clear that the second and third conditions cannot be satisfied without utilization of data. There is absolutely no way to determine probability accurately or estimate impact without using data. That is why all traditional "risk assessment" methodology that is subjectively based is not truly risk assessment. It is simply a listing of risks with some type of subjectivity applied to it. It is imperative that all risk assessment be objectively based to ensure that an accurate risk assessment is performed.

## NEED FOR A BRAIN (BUSINESS RISK ASSESSMENT INFORMATION NETWORK)

There are a number of issues that need to be considered and dealt with effectively to ensure the success of any risk assessment/management model. One of the issues is to be able to evaluate risk as effectively as possible. A primary rule that should be followed is to remember that you are managing your risk and not the risk of another organization. What that means then is the maximum benefit is gained by measuring your organizational risk utilizing your own data. By looking for points of comparison within your own organization, you will much more accurately reflect the risk picture, which you are charged with managing.

There is really no logical business reason to be looking at other people's risk pictures, through benchmarking, to understand the risks that are present in your organization. It makes much more sense to take an inward look, based upon known facts and data of the organization to determine where the real risk resides and what is the best way to manage it or mitigate it.

Many times organizations feel compelled to build primary business tools in the shortest period of time, instead of ensuring the quality of the tool. This issue is proven consistently in the area of implementing new information systems in organizations. In most of these situations, an implementation date for the system is determined from some mystic vision of when it has to be done. The fact of the matter, though, is that there is often no mandatory or regulatory requirement relative to that date. The result in virtually all of these situations is that a system is delivered that nobody wants, people are forced to use, and is actually contrary to productivity as opposed to enhancing it.

It would be ill advised to shortcut the process in building any risk model that you intend to be valid. It would be risky in and of itself to build a risk model that is ineffective. This should not be interpreted to mean that you must make the model complex to make it good. Great care should be taken to structure the model to maximize the benefits, which should be accompanied by a minimization of effort. As a result, a model that is multi-task–oriented must be built that not only accommodates risk assessment today but also facilitates a more efficient risk assessment in future.

The primary consideration in building an enterprise-wide risk assessment model is to make the model usable at all levels of the organization. It is inappropriate to make a model that can only be utilized at the higher levels of the organization, since most risk occurs at the baseline point of conducting business. The more utilitarian the model, the more effective it is. When defining the risk assessment model at the baseline of business, it is imperative to remember that simplicity will maximize the utility.

If the model is overly complex, it will simply not be employed on an effective and continuous basis. In order to fully appreciate and manage the risk, the model must be operational at the point where the risk occurs. If risk is to be properly mitigated, the responsibility for managing the risk must be distributed throughout the organization. In defining a risk assessment model within the context of this book, a number of clear rules will be adhered to:

- Any risk assessment model that would be built has got to be specifically designed for the business that is to be risk assessed.
- The model must parallel the structure of the business and its operation.
- The model must be logically organized and easily explained and utilized if it is to be effective.
- The minimization and elimination of subjectivity must be the primary rule governing the model.

As shown in Figure 2.1, the Business Risk Assessment Information Network (BRAIN) acts as the central clearinghouse of information for the

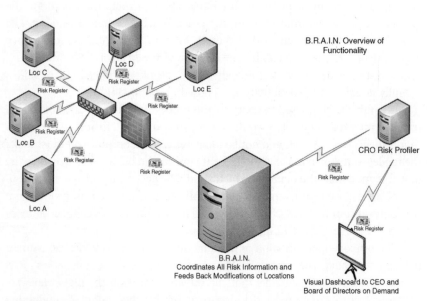

**FIGURE 2.1** The BRAIN

organization and establishes the connection point between the operating units and the CRO functionality.

 ## PROCESS OF CREATING A BRAIN

Before any type of risk assessment model is undertaken, it is critical to determine what the business is. The question that you must be able to answer here is: "What is the business?" The essence of the question is to make sure that when assessing risk we understand all the primary parameters of the business that influence its success or failure.

For example, a large bank that issues credit cards may make the mistake of assuming that their business is totally comprised of lending money and therefore is centered in credit risk. The reality is that the primary success or failure of their business will be determined by customer service, as would be true in many other businesses. Failure to realize this could lead the bank to invalid assumptions relative to what is necessary to mitigate or eliminate risk in its business operations.

One of the major indicators of risk for such organizations would be the churning of its customer base and the loss of those customers to competitors. The key then would be for the bank to not only focus on the financial aspects of credit risk in lending but also to prominently include in its risk model measurements of customer dissatisfaction, which is the primary precursor to churning of the customer base. A method of defining and understanding the business, to set the basis for the risk model, will be discussed in detail in Chapter 3.

The next key issue that needs to be addressed is to understand what *real business risk* is. The key to determining what real business risk is means to understand the various sources of risk and exposure that confront the organization. In order to do this, the business must be analyzed from the highest to the lowest level and in reverse. One of the mistakes that cannot be made is to equate all business risk with financial risk at the onset.

Only risks that are poorly managed or not mitigated will eventually become what are commonly mistaken as financial risks—at that point they are really exposures. There are some classic risks that start as financial and end as financial; however, they are only a small portion of the total risk picture that confronts businesses today. In discussing risk in this context, it is imperative that the organization consider all the various sources of risk that present themselves on a daily basis.

The sources of risk can be categorized very simply as everything. They are commonly caused by the economic environment, political/governmental environment, your customers, your vendors, your employees, your management, and the organization itself. The types of risk that need to be thought about and considered can be determined at the discretion of each individual organization and/or group. In building a risk model, we must be sure that we incorporate the appropriate types of risk and that these types are all-encompassing.

The model should be capable of incorporating all of the potential risks that could be experienced by the organization. In Chapter 4, some suggested risk types or categories will be put forth for consideration. Examples of each type of risk will be presented to get insight into how risk could be classified.

The third key step in building the BRAIN is to determine how to minimize subjectivity and maximize fact-based risk analysis. In Chapter 5, we will discuss how to use objective data and substantive information in maximizing the evaluation of risk in the organization.

The objective data that should be employed in analyzing risk would be the data created by the organization itself. The financial and operational data that it uses to operate on a daily basis should be the primary elements in the risk assessment model. Substantive information is a set of facts that can only be gathered from independently verifiable and reliable sources normally outside of the organization.

Examples of substantive information would be such things as information from outside legal counsel or from outside regulatory agencies that is deemed to be expert opinion or can be independently verified. A good example of this would be the latest critical interpretations of the HIPAA regulations as applied to the medical industry. This has now evolved into a major concern relative to the privacy of medical information especially in the area of electronic claims. This is a source of extreme risk and cost to medical organizations. The interesting part about this initiative is that the impact of it will not be confined only to the medical industry in the future, but will impact privacy concerns for personal information in all industries.

Being unaware of some of the intimate details on these regulations can pose a very serious risk to the organization. The critical functionality of protecting all information that is confidential is a key fiduciary duty, as well as challenging risk, for every organization. It must always be done well, without exception.

The last major concern for the risk model will be making it a fluid dynamic risk model. This will facilitate the movement from reactive to proactive, or virtually proactive, risk assessment and management. The reason that this is critical is related to the dynamic nature of the business world as we know it today and as it will evolve in the future. The fundamental philosophy to live by in business today is that the organization with the highest quality product, selling at the lowest price, possessing the best information *wins*.

This implies that the operating processes must be operating near perfection, costs must be tightly controlled, and your information systems and technology must form the critical underpinnings of the organization. The problem in most organizations even today is that their information systems are in such disarray and so poorly focused on the critical data they need that they cannot effectively analyze their operations and react in a timely manner. A strategy for rectifying this situation in existing systems and for preventing the same types of occurrence in new systems will be discussed in Chapter 8.

# CHAPTER THREE

# Understanding What the Business Is

 **DEFINING THE BUSINESS**

Before any type of risk assessment exercise is undertaken, the primary exercise that needs to be completed is to define what the business is. That may appear on the surface to be an overly simplistic question to ask, but it is truly critical. It is interesting to analyze what a lot of businesses perceive to be their primary functionality; however, what really drives their cash flow and therefore their longevity may be something entirely different.

 **A BANKING EXAMPLE**

The bank in this example is performing a risk assessment, and it is heavily committed to consumer lending. In particular, let us consider credit cards as the primary business line. If you asked most of these bankers what their primary business risk was, they would say that it is credit risk, because they believe that they are in the lending business. As a result they might tend to micro-focus their risk assessment on credit scoring and underwriting.

Looking at it logically, the risk that is inherent in their underwriting operation is blatantly obvious by their concentration of nonperforming loans and write-offs in their portfolio. It says, by definition, that the underwriting process is deficient; it is just a matter of degrees at that point. The other key component of credit risk is interest rates. Where is the risk there? The spread between the bank's cost of money and the financing charges and fees assessed to their customers is so massive that the risk is virtually nonexistent. In reality, any increase in the prime rate on most cards is simply a pass-through to the customer and simply requires an update of the system parameters that calculate the bills monthly. Making sure that this function is performed timely and accurately is actually the largest risk they have going, as regards to credit risk outside of the underwriting criteria.

If we were to analyze the business logically, we would quickly determine that a risk analysis of this nature is addressing only a part of a complex risk picture. We would likely determine that their primary business is not lending; it is customer attraction, servicing, and retention. Underwriting and/or credit scoring is only one element of risk in the grand scheme of their risk picture, which would then be incorrectly focused in most respects.

If you were to ask average consumers who use credit cards on a regular basis and possess two or more cards what lending institution's name is on the top of their cards, they might not even know. Actually why would they really care? The status, if any, is really associated with the type of card (regular, gold, platinum, titanium, liquid nitrogen). In many respects it has nothing to do with the name on the card. A primary concern of cardholders is that the card be accepted when they give it to a merchant. Another is that they be billed accurately and timely. Expectations also include the accurate and timely application of payments to their accounts and that purchasing capabilities not be impeded by errors in this process.

The final and most important concern is that when they have a problem, the card issuer reacts quickly and decisively on behalf of the cardholder and brings about a satisfactory resolution. It stands to reason that these are the major issues that are going to impact the customers and therefore the business. If the organization does not reach the same point of logic, the risk assessment will be flawed.

Therefore a much more effective method of assessing risk would be to concentrate on those indicators that are focused on customer satisfaction. The logical format of the risk assessment would then proceed on that basis. Credit risk will evolve as a natural component of the risk associated with maintaining a stable, quality-oriented customer base.

## ANSWERING THE KEY QUESTION: WHAT IS THE BUSINESS?

The key question that needs to be answered is this: What is the business?

First of all, segment the business into its primary functionality. What is its main purpose for existence? What does it do to generate cash? What must it do well to remain viable? This varies obviously between industries and business models, with each organization having its own unique characteristics. That is what requires that the risk model be specific to each and every situation and facet of the business. Without knowing what the business is, it is virtually impossible to assess risk. It is clear that no two businesses are identical. In fact, divisions or subsidiaries of a company that create essentially identical products or services are not going to be totally comparable; therefore they cannot be risk assessed in the exact same fashion.

In designing a risk model, we have to ensure that the basis for the risk model is in tune with the business. It is predestined that any attempt to assess risk without due consideration of the intricacies of the business is destined to fail. When determining what the business is we have to address the fundamental question of what it does and how well it does it. When we know what it does, we must determine what are the essential things required to do what it does. Once we have determined what it does and what is essential, then the fundamental questions of risk can be addressed:

- Is the business successful at what it does for a living, that is, its key outcomes?
- Does it efficiently employ the essential resources that support it?

## DETERMINING THE CORE BUSINESS PROCESSES

Core business processes are what the organization does to meet the demands of its critical stakeholders on a daily basis as it operates. The core business processes must be executed with extreme precision and attention to detail to meet the expectations of those customers, stakeholders, other key parts of the organization, outside vendors, and so on that rely on it every day to deliver.

Core business processes are those parts of the organization that are responsible for the generation of cash and/or the efficient utilization of cash. If the core processes of the organization are not operating effectively and efficiently, with minimized risks, the entire organization can be compromised.

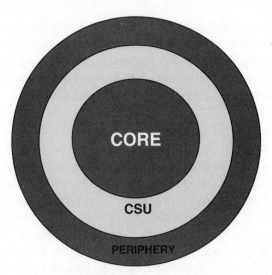

**FIGURE 3.1** Three Levels of Business Structure

Every organization that is going to employ ERM has to analyze its corporate structure thoroughly and what makes it successful. Without analyzing and determining where the key processes of the business are positively or negatively impacting the primary stakeholders on a daily basis, there can be no hope of minimizing or mitigating risk.

When analyzing core processes, it is imperative to understand what are the primary types of business risk that take place in the process, and who is going to own those business risks from a management perspective. A simple illustration of how an organization can be viewed is shown in Figure 3.1.

In Figure 3.1, you can see that the structure is divided into three circles. The outer circle is labeled the periphery. The periphery consists of all of those functionalities that exist and owe their very existence to the fact that a core business is fully functional and operational. Examples of these functions would be human resources, finance, tax, legal, and so on. In other words, it is a very simple formula: no core business, no need for peripheral functionality. Granted, it is imperative to have all those types of functionality when you have a well-established core business, but lacking this there is absolutely no necessity for these functions at all.

The CSUs are the critical support units that are absolutely essential to the functionality of the core business processes. The types of operations that would be included in this category would be IT, research and development, engineering, supply chain management, underwriting, actuarial, and so on. It is obvious to anyone who is familiar with fundamental business process models that to run the organization without these functions running at peak efficiency would be virtually impossible. Some of the most critical business risks that exist in the organization are those that could undermine these parts of the corporate structure.

Without properly mitigating or limiting risk in this category of functionality, the entire future of the core structure and/or business is in question. This will be discussed in Chapter 9 as one of the key problematic conditions of outsourcing many of these functionalities in any major organization.

The core obviously constitutes the center of the universe for any organization. The central issue here is that you cannot compromise the core in any way, shape, or form—or you undermine the entire enterprise. Should they not be mitigated properly within the context of good corporate oversight, the business risks in the operational sectors of the core can create problems that will flow from the lowest levels of the enterprise all the way to the boardroom. The fundamental maxim that must be remembered here is this: if you compromise the core, you compromise everything.

In recent as well as in not so recent history, we have all seen ample instances where major corporations have compromised the core business and have paid the ultimate price, by going out of existence.

 **SETTING THE STRUCTURE: CREATING A PHYSICAL MAP**

One of the critical features of enterprise risk management is to understand each and every part of the enterprise. This sounds extremely elementary, but without creating a physical map of the organization you cannot recognize the entire risk picture that you are confronted with as an organization.

It takes a high degree of discipline to spend the time necessary to create an accurate mapping of the organization, but without the mapping it is impossible to understand what types of risk exist, and where they exist. The discipline of creating a physical map will bring a number of advantages to the table such as the ability to create logical data pathways (LDPs) for tracking risks to their root cause, as well as the ability to determine the location of the risk of a global scale with pinpoint accuracy if properly established.

A mapping of the enterprise should not be confused in any way with an organizational chart. Mapping is the discipline of isolating each and every area of primary business risk and being able to address it systematically and methodically on a continuous basis. With properly automated processes, organizations of any size can be physically mapped using the appropriate level of discipline to allow for the evaluation of risk virtually in real time.

Of course, organizations with thousands of operations will not depict each and every one unless they can be strategically organized on some kind of global scale. There are many ways in which this mapping can be performed. It can be laid out in a simple hierarchical format, or if greater precision is required, it can be laid out physically in a global depiction and precisely accessed by location in the world. I will use examples from numerous industries throughout the book to explain the concept of risk assessment and the importance of the mapping exercise.

 ## A MEDICAL EXAMPLE: A HEALTHCARE SYSTEM

Even those that are not in the healthcare business will interact with or become intimately familiar with a healthcare system. A healthcare system consists of a number of individual components that provide a seamless pattern of care for their clients or patients. One of the key components of a healthcare system is a hospital, and the hospital in turn has a number of key core processes that make it successful or make it fail. This being the case, we will use a healthcare system, and in particular a hospital, as a key example of how risk assessment can be conducted throughout the entire organization.

Even if you are not in the healthcare business, a straightforward, common-sense 30-second review of the facts would clearly demonstrate the risk intensity of these facilities. Healthcare facilities are not just businesses in the classic sense of the word in that they have to raise capital, provide goods or services for money, and maintain financial viability. They also have many other risk dimensions to consider that standard commercial ventures do not.

Examples include the intensity of the regulatory influence in the areas of patient care and financial stability. A specific example is having to provide patient care in spite of the patient's ability to pay. Tax-exempt institutions are by definition charitable institutions and mandated to provide such care. Care to be provided by the institution is not elective. Therefore this introduces a key and unavoidable financial risk experienced by those types of healthcare institutions. However, even though this is significant, it is only one small portion of the total risk picture that needs to be considered in the healthcare arena.

The healthcare business is all about delivering high-quality patient care in the most effective manner possible. The primary core processes of the healthcare business are admitting the patient, performing diagnostic routines, delivering a pattern of care, facilitating or increasing the quality of life for the patient, and being financially rewarded for those efforts. In order to risk-assess a healthcare system, it is essential to understand its primary functionality. Once we have defined that, then we can begin to risk assess the situation but not before.

## Determining the Core Business Processes

There are a number of core processes that constitute the delivery of quality healthcare. No one part of the system can deliver all of the requirements of the patients and therefore must work as part of a unified interrelated set of processes. It is the same for any business of any type. Any business or organization is nothing more than a set of interrelated processes that must work together to deliver a defined product or service.

If we look at the issue of risk assessment logically, there are strong arguments as to why we would want to use the organizational structure as the means of performing it. As a result, before risk assessment can be effectively performed, we need to understand the business structure. The best way is to perform a core structure analysis as follows.

Extending the logic to a healthcare model, it would be critical that a similar analysis be performed. This would then allow us to logically and systematically assess the risk to the organization. A similar, but limited in scope, hierarchy-based core business analysis of a healthcare organization might appear as shown in Figure 3.2.

## Understanding a Core Process: The Laboratory

We must bear in mind that depending upon how you are analyzing the business there can be many structures within structures. For example, within the laboratory there will be core processes that support its overall functionality. Each one of those core processes will have a set of subprocesses that support them. In this discussion we'll be treating the laboratory as a core process of a hospital. The hospital will be treated as a core business unit of a healthcare system.

This is the exact same logic that will be applied whenever we discuss risk as it relates to business. All healthcare systems, and of course hospitals, have a laboratory as the key focal point of their diagnostic capabilities. The lab may be captive, or it may be an independent. Whatever the situation, the intensity of the risk directly related to the lab activities and indirectly extended to the healthcare system should never be underestimated. It is imperative that when we talk about a core process, we realize that the business cannot function

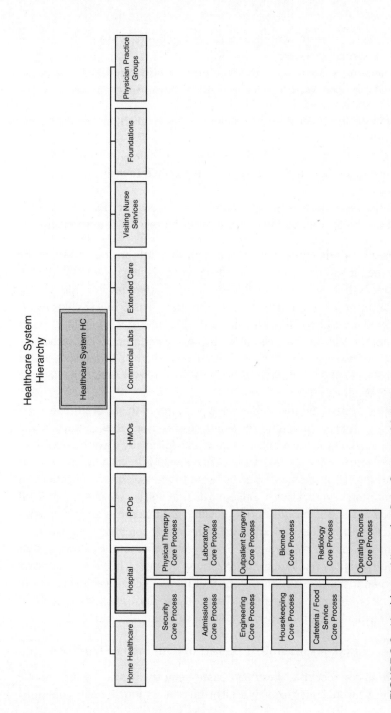

**FIGURE 3.2** Healthcare Hierarchy Core Structure Mapping

without it. Core processes are those parts of the business structure that are absolutely essential to its existence.

The laboratory, as is any other business, is also comprised of a set of interrelated core processes. The laboratory has four primary processes:

1. The physician's order must be obtained, which constitutes the authorization to test.
2. The gathering of the sample that is necessary for analysis and testing.
3. The testing of the sample is performed as required to arrive at the correct diagnosis.
4. The processing of a timely and accurate result is required for the physician to make the appropriate diagnosis in determining the pattern of care.

It could be argued at this point that there is a fifth process, which is the billing of the patient or the business office process as it is commonly known. This process is the one that normally gets the most attention even though it is not core to the primary functionality of the business. This is and should always be considered a peripheral functionality of the business, not a core function. It results from the fact that the laboratory exists and performs its core processes successfully and accurately. Lacking that, there would be no need for a billing and/or business office function. In Figure 3.3 the core processes of a reference laboratory are illustrated.

Once we understand the primary core processes of the laboratory, we can then develop an appreciation for the subprocesses, which directly support the core processes. If any of the primary subprocesses fail in any way, there will be a detrimental impact on the core process. Therefore, it is implicit in any analysis of risk that the risk assessment must be taken to the lowest level of activity in the organization being reviewed. Failing to do that will lead to unsubstantiated evaluations of the organization's risk profile. It is inherent in any risk assessment that the risk be able to be analyzed at the lowest potential point of failure.

When we analyze risk, we must bear in mind that minor failures and/or minuscule events can result in catastrophic consequences. Therefore, it is always inappropriate to perform a risk assessment at too high of a level and expect to achieve any type of meaningful result. To provide an illustration of this thought process we will now consider risk assessment in a multi-level analysis.

## Multi-level Risk Assessment Based on Business Structure

If we were to consider risk assessment based upon the business structure of a laboratory, we would have to analyze all of the primary functionality contained

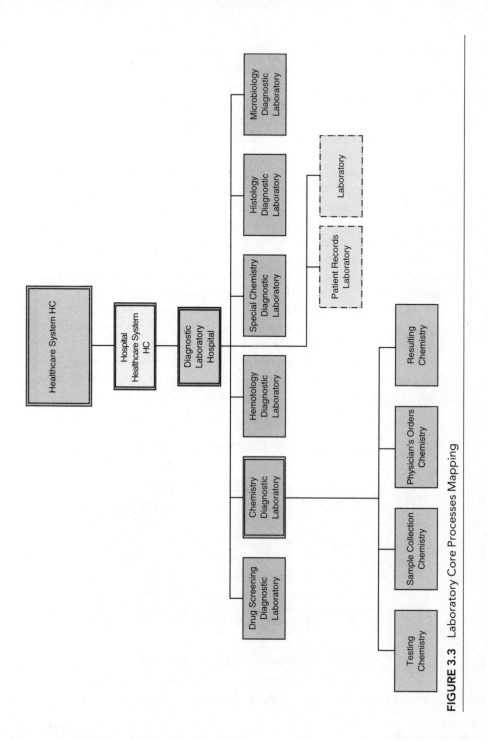

**FIGURE 3.3** Laboratory Core Processes Mapping

47

within the core processes. To illustrate the example, let us consider the ultimate risk in a laboratory setting. The ultimate risk is the delivery of an inaccurate result to a critical test that has been ordered.

For example, let us talk about a bad reading on a histology test, a pap smear, for instance, required to determine if the patient has cancer or is cancer free. Obviously, the basic risks that confront the laboratory are its reputation and its failure to execute its primary functionality. However, there is a much bigger risk in the offing. When a histology test of this nature is performed, in many cases the life of the patient is the ultimate risk.

The failure to recognize fundamental operating process failures and the risks of same are what eventually lead to the ultimate risk becoming a reality and transforming itself into an exposure. Let us now review a set of events that can result in the ultimate exposure. If the risks are clearly not eradicated at the point of occurrence and they continue to corrupt the business process, then ultimately the risk picture of the organization escalates rapidly.

To illustrate this situation let's look at a simple example that provides insight into how inadvertent actions translate into risks that eventually corrupt the fundamental business process. We will first present a limited diagram of a core structure analysis for a laboratory (see Figure 3.4). The diagram will not incorporate all of the critical steps that are necessary to completely illustrate the total functionality of the day-to-day operations. However, it will provide a

## Laboratory with Core Processes/Risks

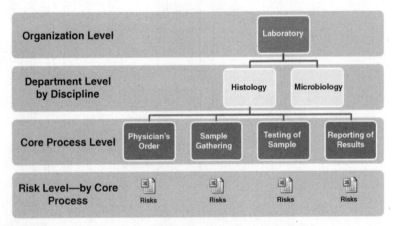

FIGURE 3.4 Laboratory Core Processes Mapping Related Risks

baseline to illustrate the upper progression of risk that takes place in an organization's environment when it is not mitigated on the front lines where it occurs.

A laboratory scenario will be presented, an event will be depicted, and the potential outcomes discussed. All of the outcomes will be expressed in terms of specific business risks that will be incurred as a result of the actions caused by the event. The central focal point of the discussion will be that risk normally evolves to a higher and higher degree of intensity the farther it goes up the organizational structure.

Take note that the precursor of risk, if not mitigated, gives rise to multiple interrelated risks (associated/allied risks) and ultimate exposures. The outcome of a singular event, if not mitigated, triggers a chain reaction of interrelated events, which accelerate the intensity of the exposure as they unfold.

Unfortunately, in most risk models a risk is thought of as a singular event with a related outcome. The reality is that in virtually all real-life business scenarios that is not true at all. Risks, if unmitigated, can lead to catastrophic outcomes (exposures) even if they have humble beginnings. As such risks must be dealt with effectively at their lowest potential level of occurrence. The sequence of events that follows describes a phenomenon I describe as risk chaining and demonstrates how the intensity of risk development triggered off of a set of specific actions taken.

**Event 1:** Due to the intense demands on the time of the physician, the physician does not take the required time to isolate exactly the test that needs to be performed on a sample taken from the patient. Instead the physician orders a complete panel of tests (multiple test formats) that will cover all the possibilities, but 80 percent of the tests are not necessary. These types of ordering patterns have become commonplace among the physicians practicing at the healthcare institution and are now an acceptable part of the daily routine. Why? The reason is to save time on hospital rounds and get back to the office to generate income by seeing patients with appointments.

■ **Direct risk 1.** The laboratory technicians, who are already understaffed, come under more intense pressure due to the excess demands put upon them by the unnecessary tests. In an effort to maintain an acceptable level of turnaround time, the lab technicians work faster, but unfortunately inaccuracy in the test readings starts to occur due to the shortened time frames.

The volume of tests continues to accelerate, the staffing levels do not keep pace due to fiscal constraints, and the degree of inaccuracies becomes more intense. Eventually, a critical call on a cancer test is missed.

- **Allied risk 1.** Employee dissatisfaction starts to build, and turnover rates increase rapidly. Loss of experienced personnel results in higher recruitment fees, increased inefficiency, and further degradation in turnaround time.
- **Direct risk 2.** The tests the physicians are ordering appear on the patient's bills and are being challenged by insurance companies or other payers. Therefore, the laboratory is not only overburdened, but the medical institution, or laboratory that bills the patient, is also penalized because they have incurred the cost and are then subsequently denied the revenue.
- **Allied risk 2.** Because of the ordering patterns of the physicians, the turnaround time is negatively impacted. As a result, the physicians begin to order all tests stat, or for immediate resulting, normally in a life or death situation. Confusion starts to dominate the environment because no one can sort out what is stat and what is not truly stat.
- **Allied risk 2a.** Because practicing physicians are now utilizing stat tests as a primary method of reducing turnaround time, confusion can result potentially jeopardizing the life of an ER patient in a trauma situation because no one can establish priorities on the lab technician's testing table.
- **Direct risk 3.** Because the test was misread and the patient was not diagnosed correctly, the patient suffers adverse circumstances and ultimately dies. This results in a cause of action for wrongful death and/or malpractice. Litigation expenses become excessive, the liquidated damages are oppressive, and the focus of the institution and laboratory are misdirected during that time frame.
- **Allied risk 3.** As a result of the multitude of stat tests and the inability of the lab personnel to determine what is truly priority, a patient in the ER who requires immediate results is delayed. The patient in the ER subsequently dies because of the physician's inability to determine required treatment. Another wrongful death action is imminent.
- **Direct risk 4.** The corporate image and reputation of the laboratory and the medical system are irreparably damaged.
- **Allied risk 4.** The reputation of the laboratory staffing and the management of the lab are irreparably damaged.

As shown in Figure 3.5, you can plot your risk across the enterprise by employing a technique called Multi-level Risk Ownership (MRO). In each and every one of the locations, determination of the risk at every level of that location can be determined by establishing ownership of risk by subprocess, process, and organization.

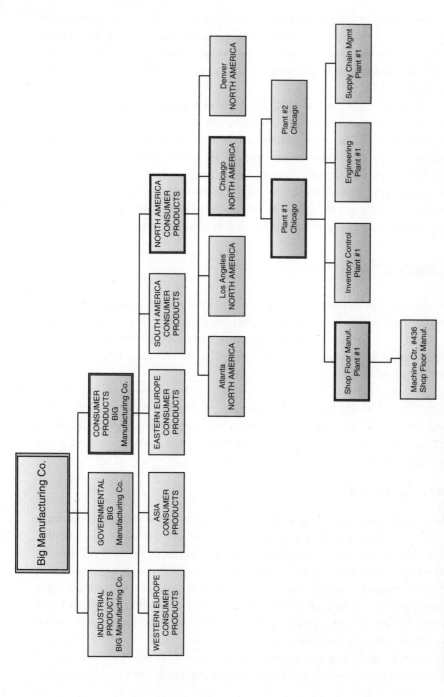

**FIGURE 3.5** Global Enterprise Mapping—Manufacturing

Once those are determined, they can be input to a database or spreadsheet to establish risk inventories, which can then be matched to associated metrics so they can be measured real time or near time. Those results can be available as fast as the data can be processed and reported, virtually instantaneously if required.

In Figure 3.5, I have used the example of a manufacturing organization with locations scattered across the globe. At each one of the locations, an inventory of risks is created; they are evaluated objectively and reported onward to the corporate headquarters. This model corresponds directly to the ERM environment that I advocate in this book. A model such as this allows an organization to validate its risk on a continuous basis across the entire enterprise. As we go through other discussions in this book this capability will be a continued point of reference, as well as this diagram.

 ## IMPACT ANALYSIS

Another critical factor in enterprise risk management is impact analysis. As discussed in Chapter 2, it is imperative to understand not only the probability of a risk but also its impact on the organization. Impact analysis becomes a critical part of determining what types of actions will be taken to mitigate or eliminate risk and at what cost.

As is discussed in Chapters 5 through 7 the presence of data will be essential in the determination of impact and eventually on what bearing it will have on the risks to be managed. Just as with probability, impact becomes a critical part of the whole risk management formula in making any kind of risk management plan realistic.

### TREC and MORE

The phenomena that result from situations such as the laboratory example presented earlier are the interrelationship of risks that must be evaluated anytime a risk assessment is performed. An area of risk analysis that is virtually always ignored in many types of ERM methodologies is the area of true impact analysis. Impact analysis must be an integral part of any professionally performed risk assessment. The interrelationship between risks, which begin as insignificant events, and their ultimate significant exposures is the basis for the discussion of risk impact analysis.

Once a risk manifests itself into an exposure, it spawns numerous sets of interrelated events, which must be measured and evaluated to understand the true exposure that a risk can present to the organization. The two primary aspects of impact analysis that must be understood are The Risk Evolution Chain (TREC) and the Multiplied Organizational Risk Effect (MORE), each having its own unique characteristics.

The concept of TREC is the realization that a set of related and interrelated risks will evolve from even insignificant events. A risk, which represents even a minimal exposure at a lower level of the organization, usually travels up the organizational structure, and with every new evolution its intensity and impact multiplies exponentially.

In other words, most risks are in no way simple isolated events. The fact is that they evolve in chains, which are logically and systematically related to the original source of the risk. If a risk is not mitigated at or close to its source and there is no method of containment to minimize the exposure, a higher level and usually more complex form of the risk tends to evolve with much greater exposure attached to it.

The necessity to recognize even minor risks at their point of origination therefore becomes imperative. Failing to do so simply allows the seriousness of the risk to increase exponentially as the fallout from it continues to unfold.

TREC is one of the most formidable outcomes resulting from ineffective risk mitigation. The impact of TREC can essentially be unlimited, in that, unchecked it could in fact consume the entire organization.

A blast from the past example of this type of occurrence is the John Mansville Corp., which was dependent upon asbestos-based building products for a large part of its revenue stream. When the risks attendant to asbestos were discovered, which should have been known much earlier by Mansville, the entire organization was essentially consumed in litigation and eventually had to declare bankruptcy. It later emerged, but as a shadow of its former self.

Of course, more modern-day examples would be Lehman Bros. and Enron. Their failure to address their relative risk positions in the areas of subprime loans, exotic investments, and energy trading eventually led to their total undoing. When these practices originated within these two organizations, they all started out very small relatively, but failing to manage the risk associated with these ideas became fatal.

MORE represents the realization that risks rarely if ever manifest themselves as singular events. They virtually always breed an extensive set of interrelated or allied risks that other parts of the organization may inherit and have to manage through no fault of their own. In other words, as a result of the original risk having manifested itself within the organization, a set of allied risks and exposures are created within related organizations and even unrelated operations or functions. Once the risk has been initiated by some event, the ripple effect of the allied risks and associated exposures generated cannot be escaped.

The risks simply build one upon the other, and the undesired outcomes proliferate to all parts of the organization. The risks and related exposures spread out in numerous directions from a central event impacting numerous areas of the organization, which appear to be, or actually are, unrelated operationally to the original source of the risk. These seemingly unrelated corporate or organizational functions are directly or indirectly impacted, therefore taking on a set of their own risks and/or related exposures.

It is imperative to understand this point if you are going to correctly assess the ultimate exposure that is associated with any risk that takes place in the organization; you must understand these multidimensional aspects of business risk.

To illustrate the concepts of TREC and MORE, let's use the example of a missed maintenance step on a piece of machinery in a mining/quarry operation and review the risk and subsequent ripple effect of this seemingly minor event.

The situation is as follows: the maintenance person at the facility is to check all components of the brake system on the large truck haulers that transport rock from the pit to the jaw crushers. The jaw crushers then reduce the rock to a usable and marketable product. To reach the jaw crushers, the truck must travel up a steep incline known as the wall.

During the maintenance process, the mechanic failed to review the brake line for damage. Since the last maintenance checkup the truck has encountered some loose rock on the roadway, which has damaged the line but has not as yet caused a leak. The damage is not detected in the current maintenance session, and the truck is released to operations. The truck hauls 100 tons of rock per load in a normal run. On the third load of the day, the truck is heading up the wall, but is forced to stop midway up because of traffic on the road. As the driver applies pressure to the brakes, the damaged brake line yields, and the brakes fail. The truck then begins to roll backwards down the wall and eventually falls over the edge killing the driver.

## TREC

The effect of TREC in this illustration would be as follows. The initial risk of failing to do the required maintenance steps on the brake line of the truck appears to be totally insignificant. Unfortunately, for the driver of the truck it ultimately becomes his most significant risk. The risk chain is then created as follows:

- The first link in the risk chain is a routine preventative maintenance risk. The mandated maintenance steps and safety review are not performed on the truck as required. The related exposure of failing to mitigate this risk at first is essentially not even considered or recognized.

▪ The second link in the risk chain is an operations risk—the ability of the equipment to be operated safely in performing its routine tasks. The related exposure of failing to mitigate this risk is unknown, but certainly more complex and much larger and much harder to contain.

▪ The third link in the risk chain is also an operations/regulatory compliance risk—that the operator of the vehicle will in fact be injured or killed as a result of the equipment not being in a safe, operable condition. The related exposure of the injury (or in this case death) of the operator when it occurs is extremely significant with the ultimate impact unknown at the time of occurrence.

▪ The fourth link in the risk chain is the legal liability risk. It is the wrongful death suit that will certainly be filed as soon as a lawyer can contact the family. At that point, the determining factor of how large the exposure becomes is simply a matter of the amount of money the organization has and the effectiveness of their legal counsel. However, it is almost certain that the impact will multiply the original cost to perform the mundane maintenance task by thousands or, in fact, millions of times.

At this point the normal rule that prevails is the bigger they are the harder they fall or translated more correctly, the more they pay in damages.

Let us assume for purposes of this example that the death benefit, which constitutes the exposure related to this risk, paid over and above the insured amount is $2 million.

## MORE

The MORE phenomenon is directly related to and is an extension of the TREC concept discussed earlier. The effect is essentially that a risk starts out in one part of the organization and spreads allied or interrelated risks and exposures to numerous other parts of the organization.

What then happens is the other parts of the organization incur significant expense and effort to deal with a situation that is totally unrelated to any actions initiated by them and that originally was totally out of their control. Unfortunately due to the MORE impact the outcomes are virtually inescapable. The only way to avoid this effect would have been to eradicate the risk at its source. The sequence of events detailed next is indicative of how a risk begins as a minimal event or failure to take appropriate care and evolves into a catastrophic occurrence with significant organizational impact.

- **Original source of the risk (risk bearer):** Engineering/Maintenance Department
  - **Risk:** Maintenance inspection of brake line not performed
  - Mitigation cost = cost of mitigating risk by inspecting properly: $1.00 (= 3 minutes inspection time @ $20/hour)
- **Allied risk No. 1:** Damage requiring repairs incurred by other vehicles when brakes fail on the rock hauler, very high-cost specialized equipment
  - Risk bearer: Production/Operations
  - Exposure = cost to repair specialized equipment: $50,000
- **Allied risk No. 2:** Downtime suffered by operations when accident occurs and operations cease
  - Risk bearer: Production/Operations
  - Exposure = idle time by other workers: $125,000
- **Allied risk No. 3:** Lost production
  - Risk bearer: Production/Operations
  - Exposure = lost shipments due to downtime: $250,000
- **Allied risk No. 4:** Termination and hiring activities for maintenance personnel
  - Risk bearer: Production/Operations
  - Exposure = cost to take all necessary steps: $15,000
- **Allied risk No. 5:** Recruiting and processing expenses to replace personnel in maintenance
  - Risk bearer: Human Resources
  - Exposure = cost to take all necessary steps: $15,000
- **Allied risk No. 6:** Equipment rental to replace equipment in for repair
  - Risk bearer: Production/Operations
  - Exposure = cost to take all necessary steps: $50,000
- **Allied risk No. 7:** Dealing with OSHA and MSHA regulators and on-site inspectors regarding additional reviews, fines, and penalties
  - Risk bearer: Risk Manager/Production/Operations
  - Exposure = cost to take all necessary steps: $75,000
- **Allied risk No. 8:** The necessity to perform additional safety training by the corporate safety officer with travel expenses
  - Risk bearer: Corporate Safety/Production/Operations
  - Exposure = cost to take all necessary steps: $30,000

- **Allied risk No. 9:** Preventing significant fallout and damage to the corporate image within the community with all expenses related to public relations
  - Risk bearer: Corporate Public Relations
  - Exposure = cost to take all necessary steps: $35,000
- **Allied risk No. 10:** Acquiring bids, selecting vendors, and purchasing new equipment to replace that destroyed in the accident after insurance payments adjusted for depreciation
  - Risk bearer: Corporate Purchasing/Operations
  - Exposure = cost to take all necessary steps: $120,000
- **Allied risk No. 11:** Increase in insurance premiums across the board for liability, workers compensation, and other umbrella policies as a result of negative impact on experience ratings
  - Risk bearer: Corporate Risk Management/Operations
  - Exposure = cost to take all necessary steps: $200,000
- **Allied risk No. 12:** Gather all the facts to prepare for litigation, engage outside counsel, offer settlements, meetings, filings, and so on
  - Risk bearer: General Counsel/Legal Counsel
  - Exposure = cost to take all necessary steps: $100,000

I will terminate the example here, as you can clearly see I could take the allied risks that result from this accident and continue the cost buildup for a very, very long time. This is just the tip of the iceberg, and the numbers are clearly presented for illustrative purposes only. Not even pricing the internal costs of TREC and adding in the $2 million wrongful death award, the costs here are in the $3 to $3.2 million range. Not really a fair exchange for $1 in maintenance effort, with parts added, maybe $50. Those are scary impacts for what may have been perceived as a minimal risk event.

Like every other risk that takes place in an organization, there are so many hidden and insidious costs associated with the manifestation of a risk into exposure that their intensity is rarely fully realized. That does not mean, however, that the costs are not incurred; they just are not recognized and related back to the original risk.

Even in this truncated example, with regard to the allied risks and their related exposures, if you do some fast mathematics, the exposure costs to this point represent a ratio of 3,000,000 to 1 relative to the original labor cost to mitigate the primary risk in the maintenance department. The impacts of the allied and interrelated risks and their attendant exposures should never be underestimated in estimating the potential outcome of any identified business risk.

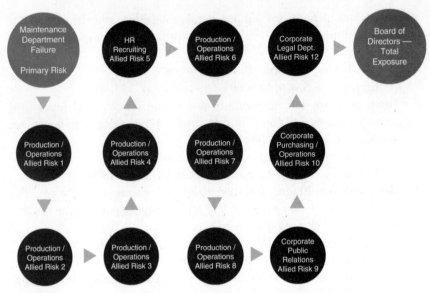

**FIGURE 3.6** Aligned Risk Impact Linkages—Quarry Operations

## Aligned Risk Impact Linkages

Shown in Figure 3.6 are the impact linkages that occur when a risk takes place. This is one of the critical reasons why ERMs must be top of game in their approach to managing risk. Without the most progressive approach being utilized to prevent risks from occurring, the organization is victimized not only by the original risk but the aligned risks, which in many cases may be far more serious and bring about a much larger impact.

Now that we should be comfortable with the concept of what the business is and risks as they relate to process, we will explore other subject matter. It is imperative that we explore a number of related issues such as business risk categorization, outcomes as a critical component of risk assessment, and other key concepts to be presented in Chapter 4.

CHAPTER FOUR

# 4

# Defining What True Business Risk Is

 **IT'S ABOUT THE OUTCOME, STUPID!**

An essential thing to understand about risk management, and also risk assessment, is that the practice must be anchored in the recognition of what is really critical to the organization. If you go into any organization today, both large and small, you'll find that things that are measured and supposedly managed are focused on entirely the wrong scenario. Virtually all processes are measured utilizing what are called KPIs. The problem emanates from the fact that virtually all KPIs are determined based on outputs, which are quite useless in the measurement of risks.

There are two critical attributes that can be measured as a result of any process. These two attributes are output and outcome. The difference between the words may seem inconsequential, but it is extremely important in the context of evaluating and managing risk. Outputs are simply an expression of a volume of activity that has taken place within a process. Outcome defines the success or failure of the process itself in accomplishing its key objective. In evaluating risk, the most significant question is whether the process is accomplishing its critical outcomes.

To illustrate the difference between output and outcome, here is a real-life scenario.

At the age of 56, I took on one of the biggest risks in my life, I became a dad. My wife and I adopted two children from Russia. Now let's say I took my two children to a private school and was sitting down interviewing the headmaster. I ask, "Why should I have the privilege of paying you $5,000 per child to put my two children in your institution of learning?"

Suppose the headmaster looks back at me and says, "Mr. Duckert, you should pay me $5,000 per child because we graduate 100 percent of our students." What should be my response?

Well, my response would be, "That is not my question, sir. My question to you is what will I get for my money, and what will my children get for their education? In other words, when they leave this institution, will they be prepared to do whatever they would like to make their life better and happier? Will they be able to go to college, for instance, engage in a field of study, be successful at it, and make themselves comfortable during their lifetime? Or perhaps, go to a technical college to learn how to be plumbers but be the best plumbers they can possibly be and be happy doing it. Or even, in fact, I do not care if they go to California and surf their brains out for the rest of their life but they must be good at it and be extremely happy doing it. The question to you, sir, is will you give them a well-rounded education, teach them how to be good people and respectful of others, and also to be good citizens and fulfill their civic responsibilities? I will instill these same values at home, but will you do the same here?" A well-educated, well-rounded, socially responsible person, of course, represents the desired *outcome*.

"Or as the alternative, will you simply shove the piece of paper in their hands and say, 'You have now graduated. Have a good life?'" This unfortunately represents the most common alternative, which is that children are shoved through a system, given a piece of paper, and left unequipped to deal with what life has to offer. But some school administrator somewhere shows it as a successful statistic in the graduation roles.

This clearly represents a situation where the education system is generating large amounts of *outputs* but *not* the same amount of *outcomes*. This is not the point and is a useless measure for the success of the education system. Education means education. If an education is not provided, the outcome has not been achieved, and the process has failed. In the context of this work, the process is risky.

Here are some other examples from the business world. Every business process can be reduced to a set of desired outcomes. If you look at something as commonplace, but very critical, like Payroll, it can be defined quite easily in the context of desired outcomes. The key outcomes of the Payroll process are:

- Pay the right person
- The right amount
- At the right time
- At the right place

Those are the key outcomes that will make payroll either highly successful or unsuccessful. If the payroll process fails to fulfill any of those requirements, or outcomes, it is risky. This is what defines it as a valued part of the Enterprise; therefore failing to do these primary things with a high degree of accuracy is simply unacceptable.

Another example would be Purchasing or supply chain management. The key outcomes would be defined as follows:

- They must purchase the right thing
- At the right time
- For the right place
- In the right quantity
- Of the right quality
- For the right price

Again the key here is that relevant parts of the organization do all of these things to the highest degree of their abilities and if they fail to do these things well, then by definition the process is at risk. Just as in the payroll example, all of these things can be measured to yield an objective-based or data-centric risk model. This will be discussed in greater detail in Chapters 6 and 7, but here is an example of the way in which these would be measured for the purposes of risk assessment and management.

Risk Metrics to evaluate the procurement process include:

- Purchasing the right thing:
  Risk Metrics: Rejects at inspection for failure to meet specs, and returns to vendor
- Right time:
  Risk Metrics: Shutdowns due to lack of material, 0 quantities in critical items
- Right place:

Risk Metrics: Out-of-stock conditions at required site, overstock at other sites, added transportation costs to relocate stock

- Right quantity:
Risk Metrics: Overstock, obsolete and slow moving inventory, out-of-stock conditions
- Right quality:
Risk Metrics: Rejected for quality issues at receiving; scrap out in production; failure in product use by customer
- Right price:
Risk Metrics: Purchase Price Variance; Average unit price

If you look at the impact of measuring outcome versus output in an organization, there is no better way to evaluate risk on a continuous basis. You can equate outcomes to business objectives if you prefer that as a terminology. The most important thing is to realize that by measuring the actual outcome of the process, you can determine risk quite easily. This will be explored more in Chapter 6.

 **RISK NEVER LIVES ALONE**

The concept that risk never lives alone is one of the things that everybody who deals with risk should understand but may not immediately realize. A risk event is like tossing a pebble into a pool of water and watching the ripples spread out from the center. The one fact that is inescapable is that when risks take place they simply trigger other risks in their wake.

When reviewing the enterprise risk management program of an organization, one of the key attributes must be that the risk management program take into account all related/aligned risks as part of the overall picture of risk evaluation and assessment. It is not sufficient to simply have a situation where risk is viewed in isolation and action is only taken on that particular risk event.

Let's take a simple example to illustrate the point. Human Resources does not perform an appropriate deep background check on Ivan Madeoffwithit. He was a person hired to fill a highly sensitive asset management position. They did not discover that this person is a convicted felon with numerous fraud charges in his background. The person is hired and given responsibility for a critical portfolio of a key customer in the organization. The person manages the portfolio fine for a period of time and then begins to pilfer the account and steal the customer's assets.

The customer detects the problem in his account and launches an inquiry with the State Attorney General. The Attorney General comes in, investigates, and determines that a significant fraud has taken place within the customer's account. What other related risks then develop as a result of HR's failure to perform an adequate background check on this individual? Let us list them:

- We now have a problem employee whom we must deal with. Even though this person may be convicted eventually of a felony, the victims are likely to sue us for some type of failure on our part to detect his background and protect the organization.
- The customer will remove his account from our organization and tell every one of his close associates of our failure to fulfill our fiduciary duties and protect his assets.
- The event will most likely make the newspapers and tarnish our corporate image as a safe place to invest people's money.
- This will lead to loss of customer base and confidence in us as an organization.
- The legal department will have to be involved to handle any subsequent litigation, which is certain to be forthcoming.
- Our insurer will be raising our rates as a result of our inability to control our employees in a suitable manner. The fraud event will certainly increase our experience rating and cost us more in premiums.
- We now have to go out and try to collect the headhunter's premium that we paid to recruit that employee in the first place, or engage in other litigation to determine who was at fault.
- We have to go through the recruitment process again to find another qualified candidate to fill the position.
- In the interim, we begin to overextend our other employees to take up the slack for the lost position, which potentially leads to higher rates of the error and/or employee dissatisfaction.

It is imperative that we stop all risks at their source. Therefore the necessity to map out the entire organization to the lowest level possible is absolutely essential to an effective enterprise risk management program. The failure to do this is going to leave a number of gaping holes in the entire risk management process. These holes will only undermine the structure of the organization and impede its effectiveness. This should never be our intent or the outcome.

## DEFINING BASELINE CATEGORIES OF BUSINESS RISK

Defining baseline categories of business risk is one of the most important exercises to be conducted when building a risk model. Everyone has his own version of risk categories and in many cases has developed them to coincide primarily with his line of business instead of being cognizant of a much broader base of risk. For example, the banking industry in virtually all cases uses the nine categories of risk as developed by the OCC:

1. Compliance
2. Credit
3. Foreign Exchange
4. Interest Rate
5. Liquidity
6. Price
7. Reputation
8. Strategy
9. Transaction

These nine categories of risk developed by the OCC are deemed appropriate for the banking industry as a whole. When you analyze the categories, however, you can see that there is an overriding financial influence on the categories. "Credit," "Foreign Exchange," "Interest Rate," "Liquidity," "Price," and "Transaction," are all financially related. The first category ("Compliance") will be financially influenced in that the primary compliance issues would be financial in nature relative to reporting and financial positioning of the organization. The only two remaining categories are "Strategic" and "Reputation."

"Strategic" in its broadest sense may incorporate such things as product development, mergers and acquisitions, and market positioning. Another category, "Reputation," could encompass a number of things and is actually one of the most critical of all the nine categories. However, when standing on its own amid all the overriding financially influenced categories, it seems to get lost and appears relatively insignificant.

What is interesting about these nine categories is that there is no specific referencing of common operational risks that normally will be the source of the majority of your exposure. In addition, there appears to be absolutely no mention of any type of information systems and/or information technology concerns. There are numerous areas of risk that can occur within these categories that can be seriously detrimental to the overall organization and its relationship with its customer base.

When you consider risk assessment categories it is imperative that you bear in mind that the risk assessment categories should be all-encompassing, covering virtually every facet of the business. The risk is not limited to the balance sheet in the accounting department as we discussed earlier, it occurs in each and every part of the business.

Therefore the categories used should facilitate these types of discussions. However, what you should not do is try to make so many categories that the exercise becomes one of futility. What is required is a general set of categories that embrace all of the risks that a business can experience, without over-burdening the thought process.

As a baseline for developing a meaningful set of categories for your own organization, the following are ten categories of business risk that I consider critical. These are categories of business risk I have used myself for evaluating potential areas of risk for a number of years now. This is not to say that these are the only categories of risk that can or should be used, but they do encompass virtually all types of business risk that can be experienced:

1. Financial
2. Legal liability
3. Regulatory compliance
4. Corporate image
5. Industry specific
6. Data integrity and reliability
7. Confidentiality of data
8. Safeguarding proprietary data
9. Disaster recovery/contingency planning
10. Operations

We are striving to make sure that every type of risk receives equal treatment and consideration. Within the categories key consideration is given to information systems and information technology concerns. This is part and parcel of a thought process that essentially says nothing that we do of importance today in businesses or any type of organization is done without a computer. Bearing this in mind, we must consider all types of risk relative to these environments in any type of evaluation process.

## Financial

The risk categories are not listed in the order of importance or prioritization. If they were, "Financial" would probably be last on the list of critical risks. The reason for this is that very few, if any, risks within an organization arise out of something that is purely financial. The fact is such things as a fraud both management and employee initiated, such as the Enron debacle, is a type of risk that would be financial in nature. It arises from a personal decision that is made by someone in a position of authority to perpetrate a fraud of significant proportion.

It is a situation where the persons empowered take advantage of an opportunity to circumvent what is known to be an acceptable business practice. A similar situation of financial risk, so-called smoothing of the financial statements, is another situation where a personal decision is made and actions taken. In both of these occurrences it is done for personal profit or gain.

But if you think about what constitutes a purely financial risk, you will quickly arrive at the same conclusion that I did, which is that few, if any, risks really arise within the financial area. There are some risks that are very financial in nature which in many cases are out of the control of the organization. These would be such things as adverse economic conditions, and others such as significant shifts in interest rates and foreign exchange fluctuation. However, these types of risk must be mitigated and/or eliminated by operational strategic initiatives within the organization itself.

The remaining things that appear within the financial realm of risk are not really risks but are the exposures resulting from other types of business risk. It is interesting that for years, if not decades, auditors of all types have focused very, very intently on the financial area in regard to what controls were in place and how well they were being executed. That is certainly a valid concern and justified. However, the financial area is not where the majority of the risk resides in most organizations, and as such "Financial" would be last on the list of key risk areas to be visited.

## Legal Liability

"Legal Liability" is a category that constitutes a very large part of the risk picture for companies and organizations as a whole. This is especially true in the United States where litigation is a national pastime when it comes to any high-profile corporation or organization. Legal liability includes virtually anything that you can be sued for. This, of course, means product liability, regulatory violations, contract noncompliance, and so on. Corporations and/or organizations can be sued by their vendors, their customers, their employees, and regulators as well as many other subsets of the same.

Any known or unknown deficiency within the organization is going to force a corporate decision to either fight or to pay. Neither of these outcomes is desirable, in that it drains corporate assets and energy and distracts the organization from its primary focal point of doing business. In many cases, management simply resigns itself to the lesser of two evils. Anything that can shelter the organization from litigation in any form is an extremely valuable exercise in risk mitigation.

## Regulatory Compliance

"Regulatory Compliance" is another area of risk that can become a bottomless pit of wasted time, energy, and money. As Microsoft experienced in its go-around with the regulators, even if you win you lose. You lose time, talent, energy, momentum, money, and face. What is tragic about the situation is once you go around with the regulators in the United States, then the European regulators jump on board riding the same train. It is a never-ending seesaw of ups and downs. There are so many exposure points in the area of regulatory compliance that risk in this category is rampant. We are seeing numerous instances over recent history of situations where regulatory compliance can bring very large corporations and organizations to their knees.

The public exposure can be humbling, and the negative reflection on the corporate management and board of directors is nothing short of horrendous. When you look at the spectrum of risk that can occur within the area of regulatory compliance, you can travel the gamut from environmental protection to child labor laws. Employees and the regulatory issues surrounding the employment base constitute a large majority of the risk to the organization. Discriminatory practices, harassment, wage and hour, contract labor, benefits law—the list goes on and on.

I think in this category it becomes increasingly clear that you cannot manage risk from the boardroom on all fronts. The risk must be managed at the front lines of the organization each and every day that you open the doors for business. Failure to manage these risks is an invitation to a regulatory action and without question subsequent litigation of a significant nature.

## Corporate Image

"Corporate Image" as a risk category that embraces a number of topics. One of the biggest risks in this category is not having a plan to deal with undesirable events when they occur. The inability to manage such occurrences shows an extremely vulnerable side of the corporation or organization, and therefore a weak point that can be exploited. Corporate image risk is probably one of the most expensive ones from which the organization has to recover.

Any type of long-term damage to the corporation's reputation puts the organization as a whole in jeopardy. It may significantly weaken the company's position in the marketplace or undermine any type of strategic initiatives, such as mergers and acquisitions or other types of major undertakings. What is interesting about corporate image risk is that depending upon the industry in which the company or organization operates, corporate image can be compromised easily, and the results can be catastrophic. The reason for this is that there are numerous suitable substitutes to which the marketplace can migrate if the reputation of a particular organization becomes tarnished.

A good example of this would be the banking industry. Within the banking industry, it is hard to build customer loyalty and to retain a constant customer base. Yet it is extremely easy to drive customers away from the organization through nothing more serious than lack of good and consistent customer service in their primary product lines. Some examples of corporate image risks would be consistent downtime on their ATMs or other electronic banking facilities; poor customer service at the teller line or other personal contact areas such as telephone call centers; and slow turnaround time on loan or mortgage commitments, where in many cases time is of the essence to avoid interest rate shifts or to insure exact property availability.

The fact is that there is another bank at the end of the block that can take away the customer at a moment's notice. In addition, there are numerous financial institutions that are now offering services via the Internet. If a certain banking institution does a poor job of designing their Internet site or reacting slowly to any major business shift, then the customer will simply surf a little farther down the Net.

These are basic examples of risks that occur every day that the bank opens its doors and at every second when their Internet site is alive—or dead. These are quite indicative of the types of risks that occur; however, they can cost a banking institution millions of dollars or more in business a year. There are certainly catastrophic occurrences that wreaked far more havoc and are much more widely known such as the *Exxon Valdez* oil spill, the Union Carbide poisonous gas incident, and the giant Arthur Andersen exodus, to mention only a few of hundreds of examples that still rank high on the scale of things you would not want your corporation known for.

## Industry-Specific

"Industry-Specific" is any type of risk that can be incurred by an organization that relates specifically to their ability to compete and to manage their market share effectively. In addition, it deals with any particular risks that are inherent in the industry itself. Examples of these types of risk would be the following: obsolescence in the high-tech industry, liability for smoking-related deaths in the tobacco industry, liability for personal injury and death benefits for crashes in the airline industry, and malpractice claims within the healthcare industry.

By the nature of business that is conducted in these industries the risk is inescapable. Industry-specific is an all-encompassing category that deals with the many hazards of doing business in a specific sector of the economy. Some of the competitive pressures that are brought to bear on companies or organizations can be some of the most intense risks that the organization can experience in this category. There are many facets to the risks that are included here, and as such organizations must be very cognizant of the exposures that they are subject to. Each company must decide which risks it is going to manage and which they are going to mitigate to arrive at a workable plan within this category.

## Data Integrity and Reliability

"Data Integrity and Reliability" is a category of risk that has far-reaching implications within any organization. It impacts information services and technology, everyday decision making within the business, the investing public's confidence in its financial reporting, and numerous other aspects of the organization. It is imperative that data integrity and reliability be above reproach to build confidence in organizations. Data integrity enters into virtually everything that is done within the organization. The importance of this cannot be stressed enough because organizations are totally dependent upon the computer systems and the data that they generate. If the data does not have integrity or lacks reliability, then every business decision that is made is suspect. In certain instances, lack of data integrity can have catastrophic or extremely expensive consequences.

One such example would be the failed NASA attempt to land a $125 million explorer on the planet Mars. The "rocket scientists" involved in the operation failed to verify units of measure for critical operations that were created at separate locations. The "scientists" were unclear as to whether the instruction set called for meters or feet and made the wrong uneducated guess. The result, we littered the surface of Mars with $125 million of taxpayer's money instead of exploring it and expanding our knowledge base.

## Confidentiality of Data

"Confidentiality of Data" has become the cause of the day—finally after many embarrassing mishaps and disclosures that have taken place in the distant and recent past. This risk is one of the most liquid and volatile of all of the risks that are in play. The risk and related exposures multiply exponentially for many reasons:

- The amount of data being created and gathered on a minute-by-minute basis is staggering.
- The proliferation of computers and computing power being extended to virtually everyone with the money to acquire one have made the ability to access and manipulate data second nature.
- The expansion of data storage capability and devices that make vast quantities of data highly transportable has accelerated the exposure curve.
- The advent of the Internet and its related environs has made available limitless information on every subject, every person, and every event.
- There is an increasing desire and need for personal privacy in all aspects of daily life, and when a violation occurs, there is requisite and costly litigation.
- The continuing evolution, slow as it may be, of legislation in this area is increasing the accountability of all organizations. The HIPAA regulations in the healthcare industry aimed at maintaining the confidentiality of electronic medical records are a good example. The issue that I am struggling with is that I thought they were always supposed to be confidential. Why are medical institutions scrambling now to put this security in place when it should have been there all along?
- The still mystifying lack of urgency to use computer systems' access and security measures, even though they are readily available undermines any efforts at confidentiality.
- The reluctance on the part of large organizations to make the necessary expenditures in some instances to maximize the effectiveness of access security when new systems that are installed openly expose the data.
- Even in the light of the legislation mentioned, there are frighteningly contradictory situations in existence. For example, the Medical Information Bureau is an organization that maintains or accesses volumes of confidential information on people, which is then made available to its membership for review. The key is to have someone's social security number, and the information can be obtained. This is one-stop shopping for a person's medical records, driving records, criminal records, and credit records. It was established as an underwriting resource for a number of large insurers and has mushroomed from there. Yes, it is correct that your medical records along with everything else are readily available. Frightening prospect isn't it, when you consider that the systems are maintained

with the same diligence as the credit bureaus? See data integrity risk previously discussed.

One of the other significant sources of information disclosure is the sale or trade in of laptops and desktop computers without correctly scrubbing the hard drives by degaussing, overwriting with zeroes, total reformatting, and taking other effective means—or smashing them with a hammer. The amount of confidential information that has the potential to fall into outside hands is mind blowing.

If you ever want to get some idea of how prolific this problem of confidential information disclosure is, just search the Internet for confidential data breaches and you will see a laundry list of who's who that have disclosed everything from confidential personal and financial information to detailed medical records. I am sure that none of us would want our medical records no matter how mundane or uninteresting in the public domain. The amount of damage that could be done to certain unfortunate individuals challenges the imagination. As can be logically deduced these types of disclosures have the ability to create life-altering events, most of them negative in nature.

## Safeguarding Proprietary Data

"Safeguarding Proprietary Data" covers the protection from disclosure of such things as formulas, designs, patent secrets, merger and acquisition information, strategic initiatives, customer lists, product cost structure, research and development, military tactics and maneuvers, and so on. Clearly this information governs the current and future success of the organization in all of its significant initiatives. All organizations of every type have some version of proprietary information. Where this information resides, how this information is protected, and how widely distributed the information may be are good estimators of the degree of risk that is in the offering.

A very good, but different, example of the types of risk that can be incurred would be in the area of new systems development. New systems are developed and/or acquired by many different means. One of the more obscure ways is where the system is actually developed by an employee and introduced into the organization, eventually becoming a critical part of its operations. However, here are the facts and circumstances regarding the system.

The system is not covered by any type of formal agreement, which defines ownership of the intellectual property. The employee develops the system on her own initiative and creates the majority of the system on her own time and machine. As a service to the employer, she makes it part of a key process that is critical to the overall functionality of the organization to the extent that the organization literally cannot run without the system. The system as designed would also be commercially marketable and extremely useful to your competitors. It becomes necessary to reduce operating expenses, and the employee who created the system is laid off.

The following potential risks will now become exposures:

- There will be no backup for the system or any ability to run it in the absence of the employee.
- The employee will remove all versions of the code from the premises including any backups.
- The organization's operations will come to a screeching halt until the gap created by the system can be filled.
- This will negatively impact your ability to deliver product to your customers and cause them to seek other alternatives.
- The employee will transport the system to a competitor or make it commercially available thus undercutting your prior advantages.
- A circumstance like this occurred when an engineer in a smaller organization did this very thing, and then was retired early by the organization to make way for younger, less-expensive workers. The company literally shut down for 15 months until a new system could be created and installed, narrowly escaping failing entirely. The consequences of not knowing which systems constituted nonowned proprietary information were devastating.

## Disaster Recovery/Contingency Planning

"Disaster Recovery/Contingency Planning" takes into account any type of occurrence in which the organization as a whole cannot function. For instance, a September 11th situation, a critical part of the organization is taken offline, some external force like a power outage precludes operations, or something as straightforward as "the system going down."

The incident or catastrophe can be temporary or permanent in nature. It can occur incrementally or totally stop operations immediately. This risk category has to be recognized as a major exposure point for most organizations today. The unfortunate reality of the world today is that we must be prepared to deal with any and all undesirable circumstances. This includes, but is certainly not limited to, any type of business interruption and/or other type of catastrophic occurrence.

Strategies for mitigating this type of risk take numerous forms and range from a manual fallback position to totally redundant data centers for IS/IT concerns. This has always been one of the most ignored areas of risk. It has always been the position of many corporate executives that "it will never happen here." That position, of course, is no longer valid and as a result cannot be the answer when a discussion of this type of risk is brought to the table. Hopefully, corporate America, the government, educational institutions, and all other major organizations have learned a lesson from the events of the past, especially the recent past. The importance of this category of risk cannot be underestimated nor ignored. Anyone who makes that type of uninformed decision is seriously undermining his credibility as a leader or is simply ignoring his fiduciary responsibilities and reality.

## Operations

"Operations" risk is most easily defined as any risk that prevents a business or organization from delivering high quality products and services to its customers in a timely and cost-efficient manner. There are numerous types of operations risk that take place on a daily basis within any organization.

A major risk that takes place in this category, however, is one that in many cases is the least recognizable. The reason for this is that such risks tend to be the small costs or excess expenses that accumulate day after day and build up over time. These are the small process changes that are introduced to the business model daily by design or inadvertently just from the way that people do their jobs. The overall costs that are associated with these types of problems can be massive over time. In addition, they can lead to significant declines in productivity and customer service. In effect, these types of risks impact all of the major areas of operations and ability to service clients.

There are also numerous significant risks that are categorized within the area of operations. An example would be worker safety, which also has a related component in the area of regulatory compliance. Other types of operational risk include equipment downtime, out of stock conditions in inventory, unavailability of a skilled labor force, and so on.

Operations risk in virtually all instances is one of the major categories of concern when it comes to overall risk evaluation. Lacking the ability to be able to deliver our product and/or services to clients literally cuts off the ability to generate revenue or to sustain cash flow. In addition, any time that we have a material or serious impact on any members of our workforce, the outcome has the potential for being catastrophic.

There are not many organizations of any type that can sustain a long-term withdrawal from their customer or client relationship. It is essential for any type of organization to be deemed a going concern that is able to produce and sell a product to the satisfaction of their customers on a continuous basis. Any organization that fails to manage and/or mitigate significantly deep-rooted operational risks is in peril; there should be no mistake made about that. Enron proved this point very eloquently and succeeded in taking a once powerful and influential organization and literally gutting it due to their inability to manage their operational problems. The answer they believed lay in the magic of the pen relative to their accounting records, but you can only mask so much in the art of accounting.

It is important to bear in mind that no matter which types of risk categories you may use, it always comes back to one fundamental thing. The key to success lies in the ability to recognize the risks for what they are and to not fail to take the necessary actions to mitigate the risks or manage them effectively. You may classify the risks in any way that you may feel is appropriate, but the real issue is what you are doing about them!

## EVALUATING ALL OF THE POSSIBILITIES: THE RISK UNIVERSE

Every organization has to define its own risk universe. This is not an exercise that can be done generically across a number of organizations. Every organization has a unique and distinct business model under which it functions. The uniqueness of the business model is what necessitates the custom nature of the risk assessment that is performed. Without a custom-based approach to the risk assessment exercise, any accuracy relative to the risk assessment will be suspect. When we talk about the risk universe of any organization, we are discussing all of the logical business subsets that could and do encounter risk. In addition, defining the risk universe means that we must take an inventory of all of the potential risks each of these logical business subsets can encounter.

When doing this, a great degree of caution must be exercised. It is easy to theorize that the number of risks a logical business subset could be subjected to is limitless. In other words, you could adopt the Chicken Little theory that the sky is falling and utter catastrophe is imminent. However, this quickly becomes a meaningless exercise, since 90 percent or more of all of the catastrophic things that could happen have absolutely no chance of occurring. There is no benefit in analyzing or evaluating risks that will never occur. The key to risk assessment is to focus on the business risks that are most likely to impact the business under consideration.

There is no merit in identifying the risks, evaluating their probabilities, spending other valuable resources predicting their outcome if it is impossible for them to occur within the normal course of events. Therefore, the exercise of evaluating the audit universe for an organization would include in the risk inventory only the most relevant risks. It is imperative that we understand the business that we are trying to risk-assess to preclude the possibility of introducing irrelevancy into the analysis.

One of the best ways to analyze an organization and divide it into its logical business subsets is to follow the corporate or organizational structure or primary functionality. The reason for this is to ensure that there is a clear understanding of what the business or organization is composed of in order to determine the best way to evaluate the risk picture in its entirety.

There are a number of ways to do this. You can divide it up into geographic regions, legal entities, product lines, key responsibilities, or on a process basis. The important thing is to use a methodology that most clearly reflects the underlying way in which the business or the organization performs its primary tasks and accomplishes its primary goals. In virtually all instances it will be easily recognized that the most effective way to subdivide the organization for risk purposes and to ensure consistency in the analysis is to use a process-based approach. The reason is that every business or organization is nothing more than a set of interrelated or mutually dependent processes. Process-based analysis lends itself to an organized structural approach, and easily facilitates the analysis of risks throughout the business at any desired level.

The key reason to employ process-based analysis is to ensure that there are neither gaps in the logic nor omissions of significant parts of the risk assessment. Once the processes and logical business subsets are determined, an inventory of the relevant risks can be arrived at in the means of evaluating their probability and impact decided upon.

What should always be maintained within any risk analysis is a logical approach and thought process. In this way, you can mitigate any type of confusion and/or misunderstanding. In addition, the method of arriving at the risk assessment will always be easily explained and defended. There is no merit in creating a risk-based analysis that you cannot explain or defend. The inability to defend the risk analysis immediately goes to the heart of its credibility. Espousing a risk analysis that lacks credibility is a very risky venture in and of itself. It is much more prudent to develop a sound basis for assessing the risk that can be defended no matter how it may be challenged and that it is easily communicated and explained.

In the next section I will discuss an example of driving the risk off of the business structure. The structure as presented will be simple and understandable. However, it is representative of virtually every type of organizational hierarchy, which means that in virtually all cases it can be universally applied. The importance of this is that it can be easily adjusted to meet any and all criteria for risk analysis.

 ## USING THE BUSINESS STRUCTURE TO DRIVE THE RISKS

When approached logically, it is obvious that the best way to structure any risk assessment is to follow the same pathway in which the risks are generated. That pathway is the logical business structure that is used to operate the organization on a daily basis. The reason for this is that the risk is generated in all parts of the business. This is why the business structure is the most logical method for evaluating risk.

When you look at where risks are generated, it becomes pretty clear that even though all parts of the organization create risks, the majority of them are generated at the front-line operations. No matter what business you are in, the place where your product or service is created or delivered to the customer is the focal point of utmost risk.

There are certain risks that are limited to specific parts of the business, such as strategic decision making. Those would normally be limited to the executive offices or the boardroom and would be very large but isolated in nature. The most common risks originate from the day-to-day operations of the organization, are numerous in nature, and vary significantly in size. By utilizing the business structure to determine the risk assessment, you can literally trace the risk to its very source of creation. In addition, you can follow the pathway that is created when it branches out into other risk conditions.

By looking at the business structure, you can see how the risks travel well-defined pathways; this also quite conveniently provides two very powerful tools for risk assessment. The first tool is data analysis, which can be utilized to isolate the risk and the related exposure as well as the probability of occurrence.

The second tool is root cause analysis, which allows the organization to determine the primary cause of the risk and mitigate it or eliminate it. The structure of the business facilitates following the data pathway to the risk, and then provides the ability to mitigate or eliminate the risk through root cause analysis. By looking at the abbreviated corporate structure and the risk example provided in Figure 4.1, you can see clearly how beneficial this type of analysis can be.

The logical data pathway (LDP) in Figure 4.1 illustrates the risk that is occurring in the organization as the result of lost-time injuries. It demonstrates that by following the logical data pathway you can literally follow the risk back to its source, or root cause. The importance is to ensure that a resolution of the risk root cause is brought about to eliminate it as a cause of concern in the future.

It is also a critical exercise in the determination of data integrity. If the data terminates or cannot be logically pursued down the LDP, then there is clearly a question in regard to its integrity and accuracy, which raises a number of governance risks and concerns.

## DISTRIBUTED RISK ASSESSMENT AND MANAGEMENT (DRAM)

Another advantage of following the business structure in performing a risk assessment is to facilitate what I call Distributed Risk Assessment and Management (DRAM). The logic behind this is to distribute responsibility for being aware of and managing the risk to the level of the organization where the risk most commonly occurs. By doing so the organization has a much better chance of managing and controlling its risk because responsibility has been disseminated. This goes back to the point made in the preface that complying with Sarbanes-Oxley can only really be accomplished on an ongoing basis by distributing the responsibility for risks and controls across the organization.

Each and every executive, departmental manager, and their subordinates must be responsible for the risks that normally occur within their respective areas of responsibility. It is impossible for an executive sitting at the top of a very large organization to really have the pulse of that organization on an ongoing basis—daily. Without disseminating the responsibility for risk management and assessment across the organization, there is absolutely no way that an executive can attest to the fact that the organization is in control and risk-free.

By making everyone in the organization responsible for their own individual risk areas, it is possible that an ongoing basis risk could be detected early and mitigated immediately. As you can imagine, however, this cannot be done

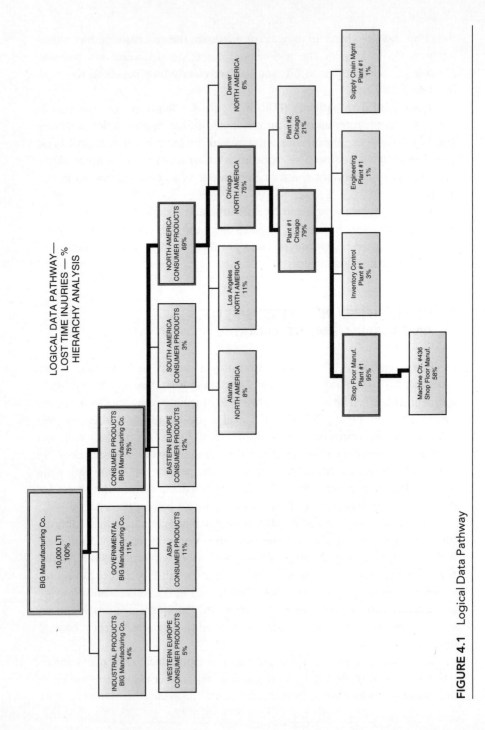

LOGICAL DATA PATHWAY—
LOST TIME INJURIES — %
HIERARCHY ANALYSIS

**FIGURE 4.1** Logical Data Pathway

manually: this creates the obvious need for the task to become data-centric. This implies by definition that systems must be created with great care and with the primary focus being on risk and the mitigation of risk.

When such systems are properly implemented, there is virtually no risk that cannot be timely detected and dealt with immediately. Implementing such a methodology obviously lessens any type of negative impact to a very significant degree, clearly leading to a stronger financial and operational position for the organization. The natural result of this is a better-run organization, a more cost-effective organization, and then by definition, a more market-competitive organization. All of these things will eventually lead to market dominance for any organization practicing these principles on an ongoing basis.

The various risks that can be experienced by an organization are numerous, but the key to the success of ERM is determining a highly effective way of evaluating and managing risk. The discussion of utilizing data and analytics as the baseline for ERM will be undertaken in Chapter 5.

# CHAPTER FIVE

# Objectively Defining Risk

 **DEFINING RISK IN THE CONTEXT OF THE BUSINESS**

When we talk about defining risk in the context of the business, we mean that risk must somehow be systematically related to how the business runs. Universally, every organization is measured financially and operationally, utilizing data. It stands to reason then that if you are going to measure risk in the context of the organization you must use business terms and conditions to express that risk—because every organization is a business because they all take in money and they all disperse money. So it does not really matter whether the organization is a governmental body, or a nontaxable or taxable corporation. Each of these is a business and prepares measurements of their success or failure just like any other business.

The best vehicle to accomplish the measurement of risk would then be to use the data that the organization generates. Data is the universal language of management and of business. It provides a common vehicle of understanding, so that virtually anybody who understands the numbers or measures can easily interpret the results in relation to risk. Armed with some limited knowledge of the business and some factual measures of the organization, the determination of risk within a specific business segment can be systematically evaluated. Once determined, the behavior pattern of the data quickly paints a picture of risk, or no risk, in virtually every situation where it is correctly targeted.

It is also very important to note that only then can the risk be recognized—and its impact estimated and its probability calculated. Data is critical to all of these primary functionalities, and without the data any kind of risk assessment, if it could be called that, is pure speculation. The business generates data on an ongoing basis, which allows for dynamic data collection and as such the ability to evaluate risk continuously.

## USING THE BUSINESS-DEFINED DATA STRUCTURE

If we are going to successfully evaluate risk in any business situation, we are going to have to use the parameters that are most closely associated with the subject matter. It is no secret that every business and organizational structure is unique in their own special ways. Therefore the data that is used to measure the risk will vary by organization, process, and functionality. In essentially every situation, when measuring risk the best point of reference is measuring yourself against yourself. One of the great mistakes made in decision making is to benchmark against what can be the unknown.

It is unwise to employ benchmarking unless you have definitive knowledge about the methods used to gather the benchmarking information, the integrity of the gathering process, and the one-to-one correlation to your specific situation. As with people, it would be a virtual impossibility that two organizations would be exactly the same in all aspects or even significantly similar. Therefore, it would stand to reason that the chances you would end up matching at least a section of an orange with the core of an apple is a very high probability.

The issues that complicate benchmarking businesses are the following:

- No two businesses have the same management structure.
- No two businesses have the same systems.
- No two businesses have the same business model.
- No two businesses have the exact same geographic location.
- No two businesses have the exact same infrastructure.
- No two businesses have the exact same customer base.

## WHY USE DATA TO DEFINE RISK? THE THREE ATTRIBUTES

It is important to realize that risk assessment has three critical attributes that must be satisfied. When utilizing traditional "risk assessment" that is performed using subjective-based judgment, it is important to note that risk assessment cannot truly be accomplished. As mentioned in Chapter 2, to truly perform risk assessment you must employ the following three attributes:

1. Identify the risk
2. Calculate the probability of occurrence
3. Determine the impact/exposure

Identifying the risk event is one of the most critical disciplines of the entire exercise. It is amazing in many cases how people cannot distinguish between risk events and exposures, which are often confused with one another. Exposures or impacts are the aftermath or result of a risk event taking place.

For example, you walk across the street with a blindfold on without taking any precautions. Being hit by a car or other vehicle is the potential risk event that could take place. The probability of being hit and injured by a vehicle is directly related to the time of day and volume of traffic on the street, as well as the attentiveness of the drivers. You could safely make it to the other side, or be struck by a vehicle, risk event occurs, sustaining minor or major injuries or in fact you could die. These are your potential exposures.

Risk events are those things that could occur that would have an adverse impact on the organization and/or person and in most cases would be highly undesirable. Identifying risk events is an extremely important exercise in that there are numerous risk events that take place on a daily basis. The critical discipline that must be employed is the identification of those risks that are really significant to the business.

This should not be an exercise in trying to list as many things as possible that can go wrong in any given time period just for the sake of building a massive risk register. Building a risk register for an enterprise risk management environment should not be an exercise in quantity but an exercise in quality. The most critical aspect of this is to make sure that each and every person understands that when risk is identified it is a key risk to the organization that must be addressed with some type of appropriate risk response.

There should be well-disciplined roles put into place for people to follow, and they should not be disregarded. If we have a lack of discipline in the process, it will simply lead to an accumulation of risk events that may be important in some aspects, but are not critical to the organization as a whole. For that reason, before embarking on any exercise of building a risk register for an organization, there must be very explicit procedures and methodologies set out, and they must be followed on a consistent basis.

The calculation of the probability of occurrence must employ the use of data as a critical part of the methodology. The probability of occurrence is one of the two critical aspects that determines whether a risk is worthy of management, or control, or not. An example of how probability' should not be used would be the following. I once saw a risk assessment that was created at a very high cost by a large consulting firm that had as one of the risks in the risk register the possibility of a direct meteor strike on the corporate headquarters. I immediately laughed out loud at the idiocy of this type of observation. What is the point of making this type of risk part of the enterprise risk management schema?

First of all, it would not take a direct strike on the corporate headquarters to bring about impending disaster. Second, what exactly will you do about it as a risk response: build a large protective bubble over corporate headquarters for the purpose of deflecting the meteor as it speeds toward earth? But the most important question to ask is, "What is the probability of occurrence?" It is clearly very small, or virtually nonexistent. Therefore by definition this type of risk and its related probability should be taken off of the radar screen of risks to be considered in any realistic enterprise risk management scenario.

What we want to see is the realistic determination of probability for those risks that are likely to impact the business in some unfavorable fashion. We do not want to go off the deep end to consider all possibilities, even those with clearly no relationship to probability. For every key risk that is identified to the organization, there must be a corresponding accurate probability that is determined by the enterprise risk management personnel.

This probability must be determined based upon some type of relevant factual information, however. In subjective-based models, people try and score the probability of risk events and the fact that they may occur, based on their predetermined views of the world. But what is the relevance and what is the accuracy of such practices? The one key thing that will always undermine this type of practice is lack of consistency. As we all know, every person that sits down to perform any task will always do it differently from another person tasked with the exact same exercise. In addition, it is also true that the very same person will perform the same exercise differently given a different time and different space scenario. You know as well as I do you will not do the exact same thing in a given situation from one day to the next.

For example, you will not write a report exactly the same on Friday as you would write it on Monday. The reason is the version on Friday will tend to be much more optimistic based on the upcoming weekend and your intent to go out and have a good time. The one on Monday will be much more, shall we say downbeat, due to the fact that the good times are now over. Also any subjective parts of the report will in fact be influenced by space and time and your attitude at that very moment.

The one thing, however, that will remain unchanged is the data in the report because the data will always be the data as it existed at the point at which it was gathered. Therefore if probability is based on data and the data is accepted as accurate and reliable, the estimate of probability will be a much truer reflection of the situation. Virtually all things can be measured in the world with the high degree of technology and competence we have today, and so why would we guess at probability when it can be calculated or evaluated using facts? As an oversimplified example, if you are trying to determine the risk of getting wet and whether you should take an umbrella, wouldn't it make more sense to look out of a window, instead of sitting in a closed room and guessing?

Consider Figure 5.1. The graph represents a summarization of five key business risks calculated using mean dispersion analysis, or distance from the mean as a criteria. The bars on the graph are the summarization of the key operational risks that occurred at each one of the locations relative to their key *outcomes*. The key operational outcomes were defined as follows:

1. Maximization of extraction of materials by tons
2. Maximization of materials at the lowest cost per ton
3. Maximization of the selling price per ton
4. Maintaining a safe work environment
5. Maximizing the up time on the equipment utilized for extraction

The key risks then are the inverse of these outcomes and are measured by the relevant metrics associated with each of these outcomes. When the outcomes are not achieved, measured by the most relevant key risk indicators (KRIs), the process and, by association, the business are at risk.

Each of these KRIs was extracted from information that is already readily reported to the organization as a whole. The cost factors can be extracted from the Enterprise Resource Planning (ERP) system, the production amounts can be extracted from operational statistics, the safety data was extracted from the safety database, and the maintenance information was extracted from the maintenance database.

By looking at the graphical depiction, it becomes clear which locations are incurring the maximum risks. These business risks were utilized because they are the key business risks of these types of operations. Based on the information

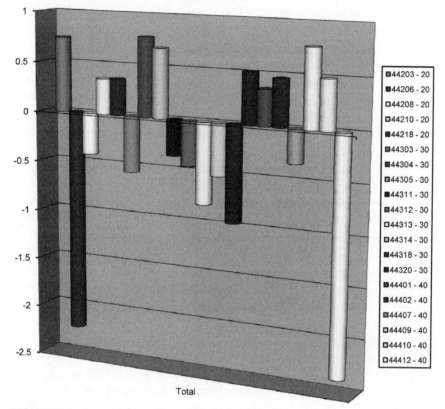

**FIGURE 5.1**  Mining Key Outcomes—Risk Indicators

presented if you are an operations manager in charge of these areas, and/or an auditor who was responsible for reviewing the riskiest parts of the enterprise, which locations would you choose to devote your valuable resources toward in addressing these risks?

I would hope that nobody would want to debate as to whether it's clear or not clear in this scenario. If the same exercise was conducted subjectively, you would get many various opinions relative to where the risk was, how important it was, and whether it should be addressed. The facts make it perfectly clear as to where the risks exist, whether the probability of occurrence is high, and where precisely the risk is centered. Now, some people may argue that in these cases the risk has already occurred, which could or could not be true, in that the events may be still in the offing as a result of the data measured and the timing. The key lessons to be learned in this scenario are that in a data-based model of risk assessment the first versions of the models will be reactive by nature.

It goes back to the old adage that you must look backward to look forward. In other words, you must know your baseline in history to predict the future. Therein lies the key as to why data-based analysis of risk is so valuable. The first models are reactive by nature, but once the pattern has been established and you have drawn the line in the sand, all future models become predictive from that point forward.

In regard to impact analysis, there is absolutely no way to calculate impact of any accuracy without using data and facts. Every risk must have a calculation or evaluation of the impact that it may have on the organization. As discussed in the previous section, impact analysis is critical to understanding the true importance to be placed on the risk in the enterprise risk management (ERM) environment. You not only have to consider the impact of the immediate risk event, but also the impact of the aligned risks that have occurred as a result of the original risk event taking place. Knowing this helps enterprise risk management to start to place increased emphasis on those risk events that have the potential to bring about large-scale detrimental impacts both primary and aligned to the organization.

It is clear that conditions 2 and 3 cannot be satisfied without the utilization of data. There is absolutely no possibility of calculating probability or determining real impact without using data. That is why all traditional "risk assessment" methodology that is subjectively based is not truly risk assessment. It is simply a listing of risks with someone's best guess applied to it. That raises another very interesting question. If you went to a medical laboratory for a test to determine whether you were fatally ill with cancer, what would you want the lab technicians to do? Simply guess, or would you like them to use the factual information derived from the sample and the testing process to determine your condition?

If we live in a world where all information is delivered virtually immediately by some kind of factual representation of the events, why would we want to resort to archaic methods of evaluating risk when real information is readily available? These issues are critical to the effectiveness of risk management for each and every organization. I do not think that you would want to trust such a valuable endeavor to guesswork. It is imperative that all risk assessment be objective/fact-based to ensure that an accurate risk assessment is performed.

## DATA-CENTRIC ERM (DCERM)

Data-centric ERM (DCERM) is a concept that is finally getting some much-needed attention. It is becoming eminently clear that data-centric risk assessment is the preferable method of establishing a real-world view of the risks of an organization. All one has to do is look around business as we know it today to determine the importance of data in its everyday operation. We spend hundreds of billions of dollars a year implementing new systems in organizations around the world. Why is this done? Clearly, the obvious conclusion is for the generation and creation of data to better run the organization. To put it in perspective I asked myself three questions many, many years ago to try and get focused on where my energies as an auditor should be concentrated:

1.  What of any importance takes place on a daily basis in any organization that does not touch a computer?
2.  What is the most valuable asset an organization has that does not appear in its financial statements?
3.  How long would an organization last if it lost all of its critical data?

The answer to the first question, of course, is virtually nothing. In most organizations to effect good perimeter security, you cannot even walk into the building without going through the badge-in process. What does that mean? It means that immediately upon entry you have created a data footprint that says you are entitled to be on the premises or you are not. Utilizing that data, the organization can immediately evaluate the risk of an interloper on the premises if, for instance, you must be signed onto an information system to be performing your job. A simple comparison of the persons who have badged-in with the persons who are signed on can yield instantaneously an increased risk on the premises of someone who does not belong there.

The answer to the second question is data. Some people may respond with the answer that it is people; however, if you were to place a value on all of the data of the organization it would have to be equal to the net value of the organization. It is virtually impossible today to run any size organization whatsoever without its critical data. The ultimate risk to most organizations today would be a loss of and/or the inability to utilize their critical data.

The answer to the third question is perhaps days, hours, minutes, and in some instances, seconds. It wasn't that many years ago when an organization could in fact revert back to manual procedures to run their business successfully. Today this is a virtual impossibility.

So having answered the three questions, what is the significance of what we have determined? The determination is that data is the only common element that welds an organization together. It is also the only universal element that everybody in the world understands. In other words, when I travel around the world to discuss risk I do not have to speak each and every language of every location when addressing that subject matter. If I present an example discussing risk that contains data and I show a trend analysis or data pattern, everybody sees the same thing I do. They see the risk manifesting itself in the objective data and factual information; it does not need to be explained and in many instances does not even need to be addressed in minute detail. The risk is clear, and everybody understands it.

The COSO/ERM Model with its extensive emphasis on risk assessment was a very significant step forward. If you look at the individual components of the framework in detail, you will find numerous references to the use of data as it relates to the practice of risk assessment. You'll see references to key process indicators, or KPIs (a concept that will be discussed in the next section), threshold triggers, and other key measures that can be utilized for the objective assessment of risk. This is a significant step forward in that it comes from one of the most significant influences on today's business environment, namely the Committee of Sponsoring Organizations (COSO). The model finally issued in October 2004 presents a framework for how all organizations should assess risk.

Even though it advocates data to only a limited extent, it still presents the concept, and that is an extremely important step forward in getting people to understand that data is a critical part of an ERM environment that will be effective and efficient.

 ## MULTI-DIMENSIONAL RISK ASSESSMENT

Multi-Dimensional Risk Assessment can be thought of in a number of different ways. It can be the evaluation of the intensity of risks that occur at various levels of the organization when allied or associated risks are triggered by a singular risk event, the Multiplied Organizational Risk Effect (MORE) and The Risk Evolution Chain (TREC) concepts discussed in Chapter 3. It can also be the process of evaluating a number of different risks using a singular risk indicator or set of indicators. The key objective in evaluating risk using data is to try to minimize the data and maximize the risk assessment. In other words, you want to evaluate as many risks and/or risk events as possible using the exact same data elements.

For instance, evaluating risk across an enterprise can be accomplished many times by using the exact same indicators for similar operations, processes, systems, and so on. It should never be the objective to maximize the number of key risk indicators; this is usually a situation in which more is not necessarily better. To accomplish this, you could use universal risk indicators that have the ability to evaluate more than one risk and also to evaluate the same risk across similar situations.

The best way to accomplish this is to set up what are known as universal risk profiles. Universal risk profiles can be employed to look at risk across many different aspects of the enterprise for the purpose of consistency, efficiency, and effectiveness in the enterprise risk management methodology. To illustrate, let us use a couple of examples: one IT example and a soft skill management example.

The IT example is the most straightforward way to evaluate the risk of failure and processing accuracy within application systems. In developing metrics for evaluating the stability of an application system my BADSYS, or bad system profile, could be employed:

- Downtime
- Help desk incidents volume
- User change request volume
- Abends (abnormal termination of job stream)/with emergency fix procedures-volume
- Suspense file volume
- Maintenance expenses volume
- Number of significant recovery events

An example in banking environments of a universal risk indicator that could be applied across the bank would be the following. Every bank experiences the situation of having abandoned property where the client has died or lost track of the property itself. This abandoned property must be maintained for a period of time within the control of the bank by law, and then it is escheated to the appropriate state authority at the end of that time frame. Obviously, it poses a significant risk if the property is lost, stolen, or otherwise compromised while in the possession of the bank. A universal indicator that could be utilized throughout the banking system to evaluate these types of risk would be the number of accesses granted to dormant accounts, and/or the number of attempted accesses to the dormant accounts.

The management soft skills example is interesting in that most people would maintain that you cannot evaluate the risk of soft skills. This is totally untrue as you can evaluate the risk of soft skills with hard facts and data. For example, if you are trying to isolate a bad manager you could use my BADMAN, or bad manager profile, as follows:

- Employee turnover statistics
- Number of requests for transfer
- Complaints to human resources
- Maximizing the use of vacation days
- Maximizing the use of sick days
- Maximizing the use of personal time off
- Refusal to work overtime
- High number of unexcused absences

If you apply these indicators to a population of employees all under the control of the single manager and found that the statistics were universally moving in a negative direction it would be extremely clear that a bad manager is in evidence. The following are some of the potential risks associated with this situation:

- Highly talented employees could be driven out of the organization by a person like this.
- Turnover expenses will be extremely high as well as new recruitment efforts/costs.
- The entire organization's image as a place to work could be negatively impacted.
- Productivity will be minimal.
- The chances of being litigated as a result of this person's activities are extremely high.

The whole idea is to maximize the ability to evaluate risk objectively while minimizing the amount of input and/or data or information that would be required. Developing a set of universal risk indicators that can be employed across the enterprise will allow you to dynamically assess risk on a continuous basis with minimal effort once the system is established. By developing a set of universal risk indicators, you will minimize maintenance and maximize outcome.

If an enterprise risk management environment is going to function successfully, it must be based upon a good foundation. The best and most solid foundation for enterprise risk management is the utilization of a well-defined, well-organized set of risk events supported by an effective set of risk indicators. The KRIs can then be used to calculate probability and also to estimate impact if properly designed.

Building an effective ERM environment should never be viewed as a short-term business objective, but rather a strategic initiative for the long-term well-being of the organization.

Now that we have introduced the concept of supporting risk assessment and management with metrics and data, we will now expand the conversation to analytics and specialized types of risk indicators. This will set the basis for the conversation about how a data-centric ERM environment can and should be built.

CHAPTER SIX

# Building a Fluid/ Dynamic Risk Model

## THE MODEL AND WHY IT IS NECESSARY

It will require discipline and patience to build a fluid/dynamic ERM environment; however, the rewards of doing it will yield a highly effective universal governance model that will be unsurpassed by anybody in your industry. Building a risk model of this nature is a strategic initiative that every CEO and board of directors should have an active interest in pursuing. Again invoking the mantra of how we live in this day and age, valuing the immediacy of information, why would you not want a data-centric ERM environment evaluating your organization? Organizations today are extremely complex, and they are overwhelming to oversee physically. However, with the appropriately designed ERM environment logical oversight would become the mode of operation.

It has now become impossible in most instances to oversee any of these organizations physically with a high degree of effectiveness. All Boards of Directors and key executives should be mandating the building of a model like this. Providing the ability to oversee things logically is the only way in which effective governance can be achieved. We have long passed the time where we can rely on reactionary measures, or simply not knowing, if we want to be leaders in our particular industries.

The assumption that these organizations could be leaders of their industries is premised on the fact that when these models are built people will pay attention to them. Why would I say this? It seems almost impossible for me to believe that sophisticated organizations like Lehman Brothers, Merrill Lynch, and so on did not have risk models screaming at them that they were overcommitted to dangerous investments in subprime mortgages. I wouldn't think for a moment that big red flags were not waving in front of the key executives of these organizations on a regular basis. If they weren't, then I stand corrected.

However, this would imply by definition that they did not have advanced data-driven risk models to be utilized in running these organizations. That would simply enforce my position that it is absolutely essential that these models be built and utilized on a day-to-day basis to manage our large-scale enterprises effectively.

These models can be as simple or as complicated as you would like to make them. Using a commonsense approach, I would opt for as simple as can be tolerated. When more sophistication is required, however, it should certainly be built into the model, as that will yield the maximum benefit to the organization.

Every organization is unique; that is why all risk assessment must be custom built to the organization itself. There is no such thing as a one-size-fits-all risk assessment and management model. The model must be built with an eye toward the present and the future, and should never be shortsighted in how it is designed, or it will cease to be effective as you move forward, and you will suffer for it as an organization.

We will now discuss some of the key attributes of a fluid/dynamic risk model that need to be taken into account should you undertake this journey.

 ## MOVING FROM REACTIVE TO PROACTIVE RISK MANAGEMENT

As mentioned previously any time you set about trying to evaluate risk assessment using data, you must establish a realistic link with the past. What that means is that you must become grounded in history in order to predict the future in most instances. By the very nature of how all these models are built, you will be utilizing data in a historical context to determine the most effective way to evaluate risk in the future.

As a result, the first few models will be reactive by definition. However, once you establish the baseline in data to be able to evaluate risk looking forward, you'll be accomplishing the entire purpose of risk assessment in the first place. That is what must be accomplished eventually, namely the ability to predict, with a high degree of accuracy, the risk before it occurs. That is the one key advantage that a data-driven risk model can yield that a subjective-based model can never accomplish, predicting the future with a certain degree of accuracy.

To reduce this to a very simple illustration, a risk model that is capable of predicting risk is like driving an automobile looking through the windshield and being able to see someone in the road before you run over him. Doing the risk assessment subjectively and reacting to risks that were not in fact predicted will always make you reactive. This is the equivalent of driving an automobile down the road looking only in the rearview mirror and never out of the windshield. The long-term result of driving an automobile that way is quite predictable, eventually you will crash and burn and kill numerous other innocent bystanders along the way.

It is essential that every model that is to be effectively employed in managing risk today has the required features necessary to predict risk tomorrow, next week, next year, in the next decade, and eventually in the next century.

 ## OUTCOME/RAW (OR) DATA AND WHY IT IS CRITICAL

When building an objectively based risk model, you cannot simply use any type of data. The data must have specific qualities. Some data lends itself to doing risk analysis; other data does not. That may sound unusual; however, when we review the key aspects of data that is effective for risk assessment, you will understand the difference.

There are two key qualities that data should have to be used most effectively in building an objectively based risk model. If data possesses both of these key qualities it is called OR (Outcome/Raw) data. The first quality of data is that it is *outcome*-focused data. As discussed in Chapter 5, it is imperative that when you perform risk assessment you concentrate on what are the critical outcomes of the business. These can be designated as business objectives, goals, or outcomes.

Why is this important? It is important because every key business subset (a process, an operation, a program, etc.) should have a set of desired outcomes that are to be achieved by that logical business subset. In performing risk management, one of the easiest ways to think about it is to simply take what are the key outcomes of the business, and then determine the risk, which by logical deduction is the inverse of the outcome. In other words, if the outcome has not been achieved then the process, operation, or whatever is at risk.

Therefore, if we have already identified the key outcomes of the business, by definition anytime the outcome has not been achieved that part of the business is at risk. The key thing that we want to identify once we know the outcome is the measure that will in fact correctly reflect whether the outcome has been achieved or that the outcome has failed to be achieved. When we can isolate that particular measure, then we can successfully evaluate risk on a total logical basis using automation and systems. In later sections of this chapter, we will give examples of the types of data that you would utilize to evaluate outcomes. In Chapter 5 we referred to the BADMAN and BADSYS profiles as indicators of the failure to achieve the desired outcomes. The desired outcomes in these situations were effective management and a stable system environment.

The second quality of data that is highly effective in determining risk is *raw* data. Raw data is necessary to effectively evaluate risk throughout the organization. What is raw data? Raw data is any data element that stands on its own and has meaning on its own. In other words, when you see the raw data element or raw data elements trending in a particular direction, you can decipher quite easily what the risks are and whether your risk position is increasing or decreasing.

There are two basic types of data, raw and blended. Blended data is the combination of one or more raw data elements to form a new data element. However, the problem with blended data is that in many cases it is not clear what it means. When it changes it is not known by just looking at it what is causing it to change. It could be one of the underlying values, subsets of data, or components that is causing it to change, but the question is which one. Therefore by logical extension, blended data is virtually useless in the analysis of risk and should never be used as a Key Risk Indicator (KRI).

An excellent example to illustrate the difference in the usefulness of raw data and blended data for decision making and risk analysis is a stoplight. When you see a red light, nothing else needs to be known; you must stop. The red light is the raw data element, and it conveys a message that is crystal clear for everybody to understand. The same can be said for the green light: when you see the green light, it indicates you can go. You do not need to know anything else at that point, except of course if some crazy idiot is running a red light. But that is all part of risk assessment.

The thing that gets confusing on a stoplight is yellow. Yellow could be used to illustrate the concept of a blended data element. The problem when you encounter a blended data element is that you do not know exactly what the data element is telling you. Therefore, you may react in a number of different ways, or you may interpret the data element incorrectly. For instance, on a yellow light some people may take that as a cue to go faster and get through the light, while others would take that as a cue to slow down and stop because the red light is coming.

The problem is you never quite know what a person is going to do because they have a decision to make, because their options are not clear. A good example of this type of data and one that is commonly used in financial circles is called revenue. Revenue is frequently used to discuss the success or failure of an organization; however, as an indicator of risk it is actually quite useless. The problem with revenue is that it is clearly a blended data element. As discussed previously, a blended data element is of little or no value whatsoever in the evaluation of risk. The burning question that will be raised by the following example is why do people utilize revenue at all in the determination of risk, yet it is done all the time?

Figure 6.1 is a graphic depiction of revenue and its two base-state data elements. Revenue can be any number of combinations of things, depending upon how it is represented in a set of financial statements. However, in its base state of existence it is the combination of two raw data elements: volume and price. As can be seen in Figure 6.1, the revenue curve appears to be fine, does not indicate risk, and would not cause alarm. In other words, it is not risky.

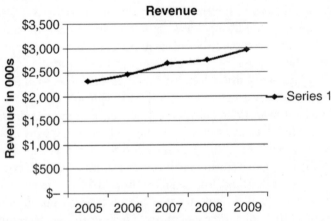

**FIGURE 6.1**   Revenue Curve—Blended Data

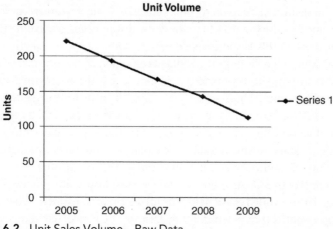

**FIGURE 6.2**  Unit Sales Volume—Raw Data

Now before we discuss the second two graphs, let us defray some of the economics arguments. In this example it is assumed that this is a highly competitive industry where price elasticity dominates. Therefore by definition this is a marketplace where the customer will always exit for best price. These products here are not Porsches or Ferraris.

When you look at Figures 6.2 and 6.3, volume first and then price, it becomes painfully obvious that the organization that is represented by these graphs is in very bad shape. By looking at the volumes it is clear that its products are in the maturity and decline stage of their life cycles. This would

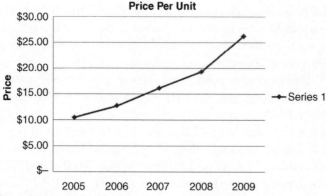

**FIGURE 6.3**  Pricing Trend—Raw Data

indicate by definition that there had better be some extremely well-focused research and development (R&D) going on in the organization, or the long-term prognosis of this situation is extremely bad.

In addition, by definition the rapid acceleration of the price curve is not a sustainable strategy in this marketplace/industry. If the company is to sustain any type of volumes whatsoever, it is going to have to reverse this pricing tendency and take a much more conservative pricing approach. If there are not viable products coming out of R&D and in fact the prices do decline, then you are going to start seeing a rapid turndown in the revenue curve of this organization. This of course will spell doom in the long term.

The point of this illustration is to indicate just how badly you can interpret a situation if the wrong type of data is utilized for risk assessment. Therefore it is absolutely essential that when utilizing data for any type of risk assessment you must employ a very fundamental philosophy. All data must be *outcome*-focused and *raw* (OR) data by definition. The worst mistake you can make in performing any type of risk assessment objectively is to select the wrong type of data elements and therefore interpret the risk incorrectly. However, if you employ a very simple commonsense approach and stick to these fundamental types of data, you should be quite successful in evaluating your risk logically.

 ## KRIs NOT KPIs

Distinguishing between key risk indicators (KRIs) and key process indicators (KPIs) is quite straightforward. Key risk indicators have the characteristics that we just discussed in the previous sections. In other words, those data elements that would be KRIs would be outcome-focused and raw data elements.

Quite honestly, what is wrong with most corporations and organizations is that they measure KPIs that are output-focused. The reason for this, unfortunately, is that KPIs are easy to manipulate since they are, in fact, output-focused. The measurement of outputs, however, does virtually nothing for you in the context of recognizing risk that may be present or potentially going to impact the organization negatively.

For instance, what makes the most sense to measure in the following scenario? Is it more important that General Motors measure that they built 10,000 automobiles in a day or that the cars can be started and driven to the appropriate shipping points at the end of the assembly line? If they manufacture 10,000 cars in a day but 9,000 of them cannot be driven away from the end of the assembly line in a condition of high quality, then what was really accomplished? Obviously very little, or nothing has actually been accomplished at all. With a 90 percent failure rate from a quality perspective, then the risk that a good sound automobile cannot be built on that assembly line is extremely high and certainly unacceptably high.

Therefore, one of the first steps that should be undertaken to move in the direction of a logically based, objectively driven risk model is to redefine the way we measure success or failure in our organizations. Any executive and/or Board of Directors that is truly intent on managing risk in an organization must clearly control the way that things are measured if effective governance is to be achieved.

Building an effective set of KRIs requires a certain degree of talent and expertise. One of the reasons you do not see inventories of KRIs is that people have not really undertaken the challenge of building effective risk indicators that are objectively based. This results from the fact that virtually all risk models built up until this point in time, with the exception of certain models in the banking industry, have always been subjective in nature.

I believe that this is going to be a science that people are going to become actively engaged in. I would envision that this practice will become a highly sought-after profession. By definition those that are proficient at it will become valued members, if not the leaders, of most enterprise risk management groups in the future.

KRIs provide the basis and foundation for a sound, objectively based risk management environment. It is worth taking the time to ensure that we do it right and that KRIs that are derived are accurate and reliable. All of this rests on the premise that the data in the organization has integrity. Therefore, by definition, we must be sure that our systems are yielding accurate and reliable information on a consistent basis and that we are not being deluged with inaccurate information.

As discussed in Chapter 1, we can have data, data everywhere, and still not have any information. One thing to be cautious of, if we use data from a data warehouse and/or data farm, whichever terminology you prefer, we must be absolutely positively sure that the data has integrity back to its sourcing system. If the data integrity in the data warehouse has not been proven back to the source system, it should never be used for evaluating risk in any context, let alone reporting key results.

I will present numerous examples of KRIs throughout various parts of the administrative and operational sections of the organization in Chapter 7. These can serve as examples of the types of indicators that should be sought out in building a logically based model for risk management. It is imperative to build a highly effective yet limited set of risk indicators so that they are manageable in the context of day-to-day operations of the risk management environment. Again, remember the exercise here is not quantity but quality. Quality should be the dominant factor in all efforts to build a logic-based risk environment.

## OPTIONS ON HOW TO DRIVE THE MODEL

There are many ways in which a logic-based risk model can be driven. You can start with a very simple and direct method of building a model to serve as a foundation, and expand the model as your level of sophistication and ability to automate grows in the future. Detailed in the following sections are various options that could be pursued based upon your particular business model, mode of operation, and degree of sophistication.

### Cost Concentration

One of the most basic types of objective-based models can be set up around the whole concept of cost concentration. In the past years of corporate evolution, it has clearly become a point of vital concern to control costs. As regional markets have given way to national markets and national markets have given way to world markets, it has become increasingly obvious that the only way to be successful in the world market today is to be cost-effective. Therefore, if the best source of information you have is only your cost of operation, you can still build an objective-based risk model that can be focused on one of the most critical aspects of your organization's survival. You can take any number of cost factors as your primary point of risk emphasis. For example, some of the following may be in order.

On a macro costs level these types of things could be thought about:

- Research and development costs directly related to product development tracked by product. These development costs should then be tracked directly to the performance of the product in the marketplace. Where the development costs are very high when compared to the performance of the product in the marketplace, this may be indicative of poor and/or ineffective research and development efforts within the organization.
- Another example would be the cost of an advertising campaign to launch a new product. The cost of the campaign should be tracked and matched against the profits realized from subsequent sales. If the profits realized and subsequent sales are not a very high multiple of the cost of the campaign, some very serious risk may be in play within the advertising area such as

the focus groups used to determine the market for the products were inaccurate or the medium used to reach the target market was inappropriate: for example, utilizing newspapers to reach a 20- and 30-something marketplace, where clearly the Internet with its numerous social networking environments offers much better options.

On a micro cost level these types of things could be considered:

- Material cost per unit sold—if the material cost for units sold is rising at a rather escalated pace, it may be indicative of ineffective purchasing. It can also be indicative of highly competitive conditions in the marketplace, which means perhaps an alternative material should be employed in the design of your product.
- Labor cost per unit sold—if the labor cost per unit sold is extremely high, for example, in a retail operation, it may be indicative of overstaffing and/or perhaps not matching the level of staffing to the customer flow or traffic pattern at any point in time. However, you must be mindful of the fact that minimal staffing must be maintained to facilitate customer service should the demand rapidly appear.

These are simple examples of the types of things that could be looked at. However, if you desire, you can look at cost concentration on a much broader scale to do a very straightforward type of risk assessment. For instance, if you are evaluating the movie industry, you could look at the cost concentration in the movie industry, which is predominantly front-end loaded. In other words, if you are trying to minimize risk and maximize reward in shooting the movie, you must keep your production costs in line.

Unless there is unlimited potential in the marketplace for the ability to generate profits from ticket sales, a movie company must be cognizant of the front-end cost factors of bringing the movie to the marketplace itself. If the acceptability of the movie in the marketplace has been miscalculated, or the costs are not within some degree of control, the risk of having an extremely unsuccessful movie, or a flop, is very high.

## Process-Based Analysis

Process-based analysis is probably the most straightforward of any type of enterprise risk management modeling. The reason is that all organizations, no matter what types of operations they have, are nothing more than a set of interrelated processes. The key question to concentrate on is this: What are the processes that make this organization run, and how do we effectively evaluate them from a risk perspective?

If you take a fundamental financial process such as accounts receivable, it is all based on some very straightforward concepts. The key outcomes of the processes related to accounts receivable are as follows:

- Invoice timely
- Invoice accurately
- Send the invoice to the right customer at the right location
- Collect the cash
- Accurately post all transaction activity

There is nothing mysterious about this in evaluating risk within this process. One of the ways in which this can be done is to employ simple ratio analysis. When the *days in accounts receivable are rising* this is indicative of some fundamental risks, which could be any one of or more than one of the following:

- Bad economic times are strapping our customers' cash flow.
- We have overextended customers by giving them too high credit limits which they cannot now pay off.
- Customers are dissatisfied with something that we have done and not resolved, and are refusing to pay. Therefore it may be a service or product quality issue.
- It is a fraud situation, and there really is no customer at the other end of the transaction.
- We have invoiced customers inaccurately, and they are not going to pay until the invoice is properly presented.

Another aspect of process-based analysis of risk is that in some processes the risk is built-in and has become part of the process, or how the game is played so to speak. Let's look at something as fundamental as the budget process. The budget process should be a critical process that is highly disciplined and highly effective when operating within the context of any organization.

One of the most disappointing parts of most budget processes is that they are more gamesmanship than fact. The reason for this is because the games have become part of the process, and therefore by definition the risk is built into the process and has become virtually inescapable. Let's discuss a couple of examples to illustrate the point being made.

Take the revenue budget, for example. One of the key strategies of the sales and marketing area is to soft sell the revenue line. In other words, they understate what they know they can sell to ensure that they will be able to make their sales targets and thereby earn their bonuses as has been the tradition for a number of years.

That may be all well and good, but the problem that it creates is the following. When, in fact, the revenue targets are understated in a normal budget process, the capital budget (the money that is going to be used to build the infrastructure of the organization) is tied to the revenue budget. What then happens is clearly predictable and is a risk of great significance to the organization as a whole.

The revenue number is oversold by the sales people, thus achieving their goals and earning their bonuses, which looks fine on the surface. But let's say that they do this for five years in a row, and the amount that they oversell the revenue line is 20 percent on average every year. What is the impact? It looks great on paper, but they have created a very significant capacity risk for the organization by utilizing this practice.

As was mentioned, the capital budget is normally tied to the revenue budget, but as the revenue budget is consistently oversold what happens is that the infrastructure and the capital required to support the sales are constrained artificially by the budget process. Eventually, a capacity problem develops, and the customer's needs can no longer be met utilizing the existing capabilities. Therefore what eventually will happen is the inability to supply the customer with the product and/or services, resulting in a loss of sales and customer base.

What is the data indicator that would reveal this problem? It would be a highly favorable variance on the revenue line of the organization. The future shortfall in capacity can be predicted by the excess on the revenue line and the corresponding shortfall of capacity to support it.

Another favorite budget game is padding the expense lines by 50 percent to make sure that when the budget is sent upstairs for the ceremonial 30 percent chopping by the executives, there will still be a 20 percent cushion within the expense areas. The same rules apply everywhere; just tell me what the game is, and let's play.

What is the data indicator here, and what is the risk? The data indicator is favorable variances on all of the expense lines, which some people could interpret as stellar performance and conservatism on the part of the individual budgeted departments. This, of course, is totally untrue. What has really happened is that they have artificially captured working capital within these respective areas. The unfortunate consequence is that this gamesmanship has deprived other areas of the organization of much-needed working capital, which in this day and age may be hard to come by.

The resulting impact is that gamesmanship has constrained the growth possibilities and perhaps forgone a needed critical expansion of the customer base for the future of the organization.

We could go through numerous examples of these situations, but suffice it to say that budgeting is one of the most troublesome of all processes in the context of the rest of the organization. It is meant to be a primary control mechanism of the organization but ceases to do that in the common context of how it is used.

As mentioned previously, the key is to concentrate on what the outcomes of the defined processes are that we are attempting to risk assess. Since all organizations are made up of a number of interrelated processes, what we try to determine is what the key outcome of each and every process is and how we can then use that to evaluate the risk of the process.

One of the key reference points for this exercise should be the process owner who, by definition, should be the most knowledgeable, and would be the point person on trying to determine what the key outcomes of the process are. It would be extremely frightening if we were to consult with the process owner and he or she was unaware of what the key outcomes are. As an enterprise risk management organization, we would not want to see that the process owners are unfamiliar with their key outcomes and then are only able to discuss outputs semi-intelligently.

When we look at the organization as a whole, we can take the corporate or organizational mapping, which we discussed earlier and will visit in more detail later, and then dissect the corporation or organizational structure process by process. Every core part of the business, every critical support unit and peripheral functionality of the organization are made up of key processes that must function successfully every day.

The secret to determining effective enterprise risk management is to decipher what these key processes do every day for a living and how we would then evaluate that in the context of risk. Once we can determine what the key risks of each and every process are, then the next logical step and logical leap would be to figure out how we can measure them objectively and turn those types of measurements into an objective-based risk model.

So in the context of how we would approach this, it would be a step-by-step progression of looking at the business logically and then applying a logical data-based methodology in evaluating the risk of the enterprise.

Every process should be evaluated in the context of its daily functionality; for instance, the primary outcomes of the tax department are to make sure to pay any and all taxes that are due to the appropriate government authorities on a timely basis—but also not to overpay taxes. So the key objective here would be determined if this is being done and if not, why not. We can measure a number of things that would indicate whether this is being accomplished in a satisfactory manner.

For instance, we can look at filing dates and determine how many days prior to or subsequent to the filing date the appropriate forms are filed. If the timeliness of filing is delinquent on a continuous basis, it is pretty clear that the tax department is not fulfilling one of its primary obligations to the organization. In addition, we could look at a number of other things such as Private Letter Rulings from the IRS. If the taxing authorities take exception to most of the positions that our tax department have taken, we may want to evaluate the risk of how aggressively we are being in our positioning.

In addition, we can review the organization's expense accounts for fines and penalties, and determine the amount of fines and penalties that taxing authorities have been levying against the organization. This may indicate that our tax department has been lax in its execution of its responsibilities. However, if we do not see any type of Private Letter Rulings or we do not see any type of aggressive tax positioning being undertaken by the tax department, it may also indicate that we have a risk that they are not exploring important opportunities.

Another example of areas of risk within the tax department would be the payment of real estate and personal property taxes. One of the things that should be in evidence is that real estate assessed valuations that have been assigned to our properties are fair. If we were to see a significant increase in our real estate tax base and ultimate payment of taxes as a data indicator, then the question should be raised as to whether this represents fair valuations of our properties. We would expect that the tax department is aggressively pursuing these types of questions with the tax assessor and ensuring that we are getting a fair valuation of our properties and therefore our tax liabilities.

Another key data indicator would be a constant upward progression in the payments made on personal property taxes in relation to our fixed asset base. If the fixed asset base is shrinking and moreover our capital position has been restrained in recent history, we would not expect to see significant increases in personal property taxes. In addition, if we have had a significant number of transfers and/or asset sales, we would also expect that the basis of the personal property taxes would be reduced in those particular taxable jurisdictions where the reductions in basis have taken place.

These are just some examples of the types of things that could be explored on a process basis within the administration areas. We will discuss many more of these types of situations as we get further into the process mapping of the organization scenario.

## Process Chaining

Process chaining is another method in which you can do both macro-level and micro-level analysis of risk. Take, for example, the following situation in which the macro-level analysis of a major risk indicator is then coupled with micro-level analysis via process chaining. For example, I will take a high-level risk indicator, or a macro-level indicator, for an organization in the manufacturing industry. The scenario would be as follows.

Inventory turnover (ITO) is decreasing within the organization as a whole. This is a rather significant risk to the organization in that it ties up excessive amounts of capital and is indicative of poor management on a number of fronts. The most logical way in which this could then be analyzed from a risk perspective would be to first utilize the logical data pathway, or LDP, created by the data. As it is reported upward from the process level to the corporate enterprise level, you can pursue all those locations where the inventory turnover has slowed the most. This is a concept that will be explored in more detail in the mapping discussion.

Once the organizational units that are showing the greatest slowdown in inventory turnover have been isolated, then the microanalysis of risk can take over to determine where the root cause of the problem lies. The process would be conducted as follows.

First, the process chain would be identified that would be utilized as the key for pursuing the root cause of the inventory turnover problem.

The process chain to be used would be:

1. Sales forecasting
2. Order entry
3. Engineering
4. Production planning and control
5. Purchasing
6. Inventory control
7. Manufacturing
8. Pick, pack, and stage
9. Shipping

Once we have determined this process chain, then we can begin to analyze logically where the root cause of the risk actually exists. This would be done by logically going through each link in this process chain and determining objectively where the risk is resident and if that is a weak link in the chain. In other words, the analysis is clearly a methodology of identifying the weak links that are indicative of potential root causes of the problem. As can also be seen, this is a very logical stepwise progression to analyze a situation. This will be indicative of each and every tool that is utilized in this book.

The analysis would be pursued as follows, for each and every link in the chain there would be an identified set of individual risk indicators that would be utilized for the purposes of isolating potential root causal events. For the links in the chain identified in this example, the following would be the key indicators that would be pursued.

### Sales Forecasting

For sales forecasting, the key data element to evaluate risk would be the difference between the actual shipments and the sales forecast by product line. If the sales forecast is actually the weak link in the chain, what you would expect to see is a significant gap between these two figures. What that implies then by definition is that the sales forecast is driving the other functionalities further down the chain to either build inventory that is not required and worse additionally to have to build inventory that is selling, but not forecast.

Therefore, by definition, a very risky position is to have a sales forecast that is radically different or even significantly different from the actual sales being experienced. In that case, the sales forecasting process would have to have an extensive review to determine where the error conditions are creeping in. Is it the result of outside events in the marketplace that were unusual and unanticipated, and if so, why was this development not foreseen? Or is it the result of an internal failure of the process itself?

### Order Entry

Regarding order entry, if orders are received via the telephone, and/or are input via the Internet, a number of undesirable risks can take place. For instance, if the person taking the order via the telephone does not verify with a customer the exact quantity that is being ordered, the person keying in the order could input the quantity 10,000 by hitting one extra zero, or an additional keystroke, when the customer in fact only desired 1,000. Without reverification of the quantity the risk becomes obvious. The same situation could occur on the Internet if the customer goes to a screen and inputs the quantity for their order. If there are no edit checks that force a customer to reverify the input quantity, he too could input 10,000 by mistake when in fact he intended to order only 1,000. In both situations, the impact is as follows: 9,000 more units of the product are shipped than are required by the customer.

The aligned risks that start to take place are as follows. We ship out an excess of 9,000 units to one customer at the same time that other customers are demanding those units; we then build and/or buy more of the units to meet that demand. We are, of course, unaware at that time that there are 9,000 units that are pending return. What happens then is that we start to build excess inventories when the 9,000 units return, which were unintended shipments. The data indicator that can be utilized to isolate this type of problem would be credit memoranda for units returned. When credit memoranda for units returned are in evidence, they can only be the result of three other areas of the identified process chain: order entry; pick, pack, and stage; and/or shipping, if not the result of order entry. If these are in evidence, start to look in order entry and work your way down.

### Engineering

In the area of engineering, there are a number of things that can occur that will lead to a significant uptick in the inventory levels. The most common occurrence would be a change in the bill of materials (BOM). When engineering makes changes to the bills of material in isolation, they may discontinue the use of particular parts or subassemblies. The problem occurs when they do this without consulting with inventory control to determine the number of the items that are in physical inventory; with a keystroke they can deactivate hundreds of thousands of units of inventory. This leads to inventory builds and unacceptably high levels of inventories in such items.

The data indicators that would be indicative of this type of problem would be obsolete and/or slow-moving inventories. Whenever this problem is in evidence, a critical review of the process of making changes to the bills of material must be undertaken.

### Production Planning and Control

Production planning and control is another key player in the area of potential inventory builds. How may they cause this problem, you might ask? It may be traceable back to their compensation scheme. If by design they are compensated for getting the productivity up in the facility, they may manufacture a number of items that are called "bunnies" or "easy builds." They do this to get their productivity ratios higher. This creates an excess of nonsalable merchandise, which then must be inventoried. Once this occurs, your inventories start to build, and inventory turnovers slow down as evidenced by the decrease in the inventory turnover ratio.

The easiest way to isolate the risk in this area is as follows. If the sales forecast is equal to or near equal to the actual shipments, its accuracy has been proven. Therefore, production planning and control should be issuing a production plan that is equal to the forecast of the organization. If this is not being done, here lies part of the problem with inventory turnover management.

### Purchasing

Purchasing is the next in line. Just like production planning and control, purchasing should be intricately linked to the sales forecast. In other words, if the sales forecast is accurate, and the production plan is linked to the forecast, then the next logical conclusion can only be that purchasing should be linked to the production plan. If the data indicates that purchasing is buying in quantities that are varying from the production plan, then purchasing is part of the problem. Why would they do this? In the end, it may revert back to their compensation scheme. They may be compensated to reduce the unit cost of every item they purchase to the lowest possible level. The problem is that this works against the best interests of the organization.

What will happen is the following. They will buy in large quantities to maximize the quantity discounts from their vendors. The quantities will be far in excess of what is required by the organization to meet its demands in the production plan. What will eventually happen is that we will start to build inventories that will be excessive and slow moving. We will write off more in lost inventories or unusable inventory than we would have ever gained by the savings in the original volume discounts. Therefore, one of the key data indicators is excess and slow-moving inventories within our critical product lines, but also you should take a good look at the compensation scheme of the purchasing personnel.

### Inventory Control

What in the world could inventory control possibly do to build inventories? Also, why would they do that if it is not in their best interest? Not so fast. Key activities that inventory control undertakes on a regular basis are called "cycle counts." These are done to compare the physical existence of the inventories to the inventory stock status reports.

What may occur is that they will do a cycle count and detect a physical overage of items relative to the stock status. However, there is a great disincentive to having any type of inventory shortfall during the annual year-end physical count. This again may go back to their compensation scheme. As a result, they are unlikely to book the overages unless required or mandated to do so.

Why, you might ask? Because they will then have a cushion going into their year-end count and as a result are much more likely to have a physical inventory gain as opposed to an undesirable shrink in inventories. The key data indicators that could be reviewed in this situation to see if this risk is present is to look at the recorded adjustments to the stock status after cycle counts have been conducted.

If only negative adjustments are in evidence, that may indicate that positive adjustments are not being made. This also raises the specter of another undesirable risk: that is, that the stock status is significantly in error on an ongoing basis and as a result cannot be trusted regarding physical presence of the items in inventories.

## Manufacturing

Manufacturing may also have an incentive that requires them to keep up efficiency on the shop floor as part of their compensation scheme. As a result they may also have a tendency to manufacture items that are not required within the context of the forecast simply to get their efficiency ratings up on the shop floor.

One of the key things that can be looked at to determine if this problem is present is to look for a departure from those items required on the production plan. If items that are not called for on the plan are being manufactured on the shop floor and added to inventories, part of the problem may lie here. Therefore, one of the key data indicators of risk is to investigate any orders on the shop floor for items that are being produced and are not included in the production plan. Another thought is to check items that are not part of the production plan but are being added to the inventory balances on a daily basis.

## Pick, Pack, and Stage

Pick, pack, and stage is an area where inventoried buildup problems become fairly obvious. The key issue here is the incorrect assembling of the orders and the overshipment of items to the customer. This error creates the exact same type of problem that was indicated in the order entry section. The customer ends up with more items than needed and will return those items to the organization. If these items are unknown, then the organization will produce and/or acquire the goods to meet current demand, not knowing that the other items will be returned in the future. This also gives rise to a number of other problems as you may imagine.

One of the key aligned risks in this situation is the cost of freight. In every situation where additional items that are not required by the customer are sent, or wrong items are shipped, our freight expense doubles, or triples, or worse. It is absolutely critical that these types of events not occur on a regular basis; otherwise, freight expenses can be extremely high, and with the cost of fuel these days freight expenses will become a bigger part of expense problems. Marked increases in freight expenses is also a key risk indicator in these situations.

### Shipping

As you would anticipate, the problems in shipping that would arise would be exactly the same as in pick, pack, and stage. When they ship the wrong items or overship items, both inventory problems and freight expense occur. These are unacceptable in a well-organized business.

 ## DASHBOARD INDICATORS

Dashboard indicators are concepts that have been around for a period of time now. They are extremely useful and should be employed on a continuous basis by the key executives of all organizations. Dashboard indicators should, however, be tied to the key risks of the organization, these being the failures to accomplish critical business outcomes. What this means is that these must be very strategically determined, and they must be specifically aligned with the risks of the organization.

For dashboard indicators to be of any use, they must give a constant read on how the key risks of the organization are faring on a daily, if not continuous basis. In other words, these should be more than simple high-level financial indicators of what is going on but rather all-encompassing indicators of risks that can be used to govern the enterprise as a whole more effectively. They must be structured appropriately for the visionaries at the high levels of the corporation to be able to grasp their meaning and take necessary action virtually instantaneously.

Therefore, by definition, the indicators must be extremely well targeted to the risk, they must be aligned with very significant risks, and they must be able to be visually consumed. That means that any type of dashboard indicator must be presented with maximum emphasis on presentation. That means everything visible, with little or no audio noise, a.k.a. excessive wordiness.

It is a well known fact that people that reside at the top of the organization and also on the Board of Directors of most companies or organizations are visionaries; they are not audiophiles. To present any type of dashboard risk-based environments, you must have an extremely good grasp of how to summarize key risks of the organization in some type of visual format. This constitutes one of the great challenges but also one of the great opportunities for the enterprise risk management group. The key obligations of the enterprise risk management environment are to timely and logically present their concerns to those at the highest levels of the organization.

By building a data-based risk management environment that is highly automated, and is visually oriented in its presentation, they can demonstrate a prowess in the area of risk management that will be un-equaled. Therefore all types of dashboard indicator environments should be limited to the most critical risks of the organization and be effectively presented on a continuous basis.

The dashboard indicator environment should be the central location of all critical risks that must be monitored on an ongoing basis. This should present at a glance the complete key risk picture of the enterprise in all aspects, ranging from strategic to critical operational, to regulatory, to financial, and beyond.

The dashboard should be logically structured and compartmentalized so that it can be viewed by the key executives as well as the Board of Directors in some kind of selective fashion. One way in which they could be compartmentalized would be to follow the FORT (financial, operational, regulatory, and technological) criteria.

In each one of these areas, there could be subsets of logical as well as physical risk. In addition to these compartments of risk, there could also be an area dedicated solely to strategic risks in and of themselves. Such an area of strategic risk would include:

- Key outsourcing arrangements
- Critical acquisitions
- Major divestitures
- Major organizational realignments such as decentralization
- Major information systems restructuring

In each of these areas, key risk indicators should have been developed and should be monitored on an ongoing basis to determine how successfully or how poorly each of these environments is performing on a day-to-day basis. These risk indicators should have been determined at the outset of the events in concert with the key corporate sponsor of that strategic initiative. These could then be entered into the dashboard and be a subject of review for all senior executives who have a vested interest in the success and/or great concerns about the failure of these key strategic areas. These could also be reported regularly to the Board of Directors so that they can monitor ongoing success or failure in key strategic areas.

In general, dashboard indicators are going to vary significantly from organization to organization. The reason for this is that no two organizations are exactly the same and as a result are interested in monitoring much different items on a day-to-day basis to achieve ideal corporate governance. It is like anything else in risk assessment and management; dashboard indicators as well as enterprise risk management must be customized precisely to the organization to which they pertain. One-size-fits-all dashboard indicators would be no more be valid than one-size-fits-all enterprise risk management.

Dashboard indicators should constitute a critical part of the enterprise risk management environment. Therefore, they should be extremely well done with virtually no room for misinterpretation of the facts. Examples of metrics that could be used for dashboard indicators will be presented in the following sections, but they should be selected on a customized basis for your particular organization. Figure 6.4 illustrates conceptually how dashboard indicators could be presented for the oversight of the organization.

 ## KEY EARLY WARNING INDICATORS

Key early warning indicators (KEWIs) can be a subset of dashboard indicators or can stand on their own as major indications of the necessity for immediacy of action. These types of indicators should be specifically related to major areas of risk concern where they can be seen well in advance of a risk event taking place. This makes it possible to take appropriate actions as necessary. Obviously, this could encompass a number of items within a very large corporation and/or organization; however, you want to be selective with those that are employed specifically as KEWIs.

These types of indicators should be built to recognize patterns that predict an unacceptable risk that may take place in the future. Some examples would

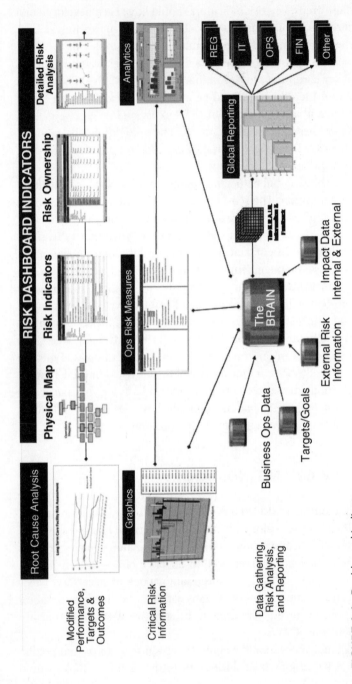

**FIGURE 6.4** Dashboard Indicators

be building employee turnover rates in the area of research and development, significant downturns in unit sales with a key distributor of our products in China, or extremely high turnover in critical software design engineers working on one of our proprietary information systems projects in Mumbai. Each and every one of these is a major precursor to a loss of significant intellectual property and would certainly mandate quick intervention to protect our vital interests.

There are numerous types of KEWIs that can be employed in an organization. These should be focused on the critical risk areas of the organization that would suffer significant adverse impacts should the risks manifest themselves as significant exposures. KEWIs should be reserved for those areas of the organization that are essential to our organizational mission or survival from an enterprise perspective.

Selectivity and sense of purpose are the key criteria for establishing these types of warning indicators. When integrated with the dashboard indicators, they can be a powerful tool in the overall governance structure of the organization. If the establishment of these key early warning indicators is not undertaken, critical risks of the organization can remain below the radar screen until eventually they undermine the organization, piece by piece, slowly but surely, day in and day out.

In recent history we have seen ample evidence of these types of occurrences, and we have discussed some in this book. Key early warning indicators, just like dashboard indicators and enterprise risk management, are also customized to the organization. Those indicators that fit the bank across the street are not the indicators you should use in your bank. Those indicators that work in a hospital down the road are not the ones that you should use in your hospital. Risk assessment is very institution-specific and must be treated accordingly. This does not mean that there will not be common indicators, but they may be measured differently and evaluated differently even if they are the exact same indicators from organization to organization.

 ## DETERMINING THE KEY RISK INDICATORS

As you would expect, KRIs must be determined differently from organization to organization, from process to process, from system to system, from business subset to business subset. KRIs and their determination should be the primary responsibility of each of the individual risk owners throughout the organization. Therefore, the engineers should have their own set of KRIs as should the accountants, lawyers, inventory control specialists, security analysts, bond traders, and so on. The KRIs should be very specific to each and every aspect of the organization across the enterprise. No one should be more knowledgeable about what KRIs should be in place than the process owners themselves.

However, as we mentioned earlier, unfortunately many process owners view themselves in the context of outputs instead of outcomes. As was illustrated in the areas of purchasing and payroll, there are many KRIs that should be established throughout the enterprise. Each and every critical process should have a set of KRIs, and those should be evaluated on a continuous basis by the risk owners. Let's present another scenario of the types of KRIs that should be developed. This time we will consider investment management within an organization.

Those that are responsible for managing the investments of the organization should have KRIs that are properly aligned with their desired outcomes. The desired outcomes of investment managers would normally be:

- Maximization of return
- Minimization of risk
- Investing within the guidelines as required

Therefore, by definition, the key risk indicators that would be aligned with each of these objectives would be as follows:

- **Maximization of return.** The KRI is normal return in the marketplace given portfolio concentration guidelines. If the returns being earned are far above normal, then the risk clearly indicated is that the portfolio is way too risky or the returns being stated are actually fraudulent. If returns are way below normal, it may indicate too conservative of positioning on behalf of the investment management group, and as a result their prowess as investment gurus should be in question.
- **Minimization of risk.** The KRI here is the same as stated in maximization of return. If the returns are too high, the chances are excellent that the portfolio undertaken as investments is far too risky. Therefore, intervention to correct the situation should be undertaken to ensure that excessive losses will not be incurred, as soon as this trend is detected.
- **Investing within the guidelines as required.** Prescribed guidelines should be mandatory. These guidelines could be those issued by the Board of Directors regarding investments. By definition, investment managers should be operating within those guidelines. The KRIs in this situation

would be an inventory of the active investment portfolio. In other words, you can evaluate their investments by categorization and compare it to the approved investment guidelines of the Board. The percentage of the portfolio to be devoted to fixed income could be compared to the fixed income investments under management, and so on.

KRIs are a critical part of the overall enterprise risk management process. The key risk indicators must be developed with vision and foresight. The best skills should be involved in determining what the right KRIs are for all the various parts of the enterprise. To put it another way, this should not be an exercise taken on in a haphazard fashion by people with no knowledge of how that business or logical business subset actually operates. We will identify a number of KRIs that can be employed in the following section, but they will only serve as points of reference. The actual KRIs that you must develop for your own organizations, as we all know by now, must be customized.

 ## UNIVERSAL RISK INDICATORS

In some of the previous sections, you may have been scratching your head and wondering, *Oh my goodness, will I have to develop risk indicators for each and every part of the enterprise?* It depends on how extensively you want to deploy risk management, but it also depends upon the amount of automation and sophistication your organization is capable of. It is important that you make some very key decisions in developing KRIs to ensure that what you create can be managed on some kind of palatable basis.

Therefore, only employ what you are capable of managing effectively. Do not overextend yourself by trying to develop the world's largest inventory of risk indicators. If you pursue too large a population, you may subvert the notion of *key*, which is the important operative word in this scenario.

In developing an inventory of key risk indicators, due consideration should be given to the possibility of employing universal risk indicators whenever possible. Universal risk indicators are those that can be employed across numerous locations and business subsets of the enterprise with the intent of minimizing the number of indicators that must be managed on a day-to-day basis. These types of universal indicators will result from similarity of operations and also from similarity of purpose in these related business units.

These business subsets do not have to be the exact same size, because when you employ universal risk indicators you would normally use some type of ratio analysis, which would common-size and/or equalize the units under consideration. For example, in a mining operation in which the enterprise is a collection of six different types of businesses, you may want to employ universal risk indicators in those parts of the business that are similar. Such a scenario would be as follows.

One of the business subsets of the mining organization is an operation known as an open pit limestone quarry. In its most simple terms, this operation digs limestone out of the earth, crushes it to various sizes and/or specifications, and then sells it in the open marketplace or on contract.

If you want to establish a scheme of risk indicators for this type of operation, you would have to concentrate on what are the most critical outcomes that this type of a business should accomplish on a daily basis. These are:

- Maximizing the tonnage of limestone produced
- Minimizing the cost per ton of limestone produced
- Maximizing the sales value per ton of limestone sold
- Keeping people safe
- Keeping the machinery maintained; maximizing up time

Even if you don't know anything about mining I think all would agree that these are the critical outcomes of this type of an operation. In trying to establish a set of universal indicators for risk, always begin the exercise by identifying what are the critical outcomes of the business.

Once you know the critical outcomes of the business, many times they start to dictate what the critical risk indicators or KRIs are that should be utilized. For instance, in accordance with the previous key outcomes, these would be the risk indicators that would be measured for this type of operation.

- Average tons produced by quarry over a specific timeframe
- Average cost per ton produced over a specific time
- Sale price per ton over a specific time
- Lost-time injuries and workers' compensation claims per 100 hours worked
- Machinery downtime, preventive maintenance cost, unanticipated replacement or repair costs

These types of measurements could be applied to each and every one of the numerous limestone quarries across this enterprise. Once these metrics have been established, then they can be compared by quarry, within district, within region, within division, and across the enterprise as desired. These would then be considered universal risk indicators for this type of business.

When establishing universal indicators, the most important thing to remember is that you must tie it to the direct functionality of the business. You can make universal risk indicators as high-level or low-level as you like; it all depends on what the objective of the exercise is.

An example of a universal risk indicator in a manufacturing setting for instance would be stock outs. Stock outs would be the result of the following risks and would result in the following impacts.

## Risks that could give rise to the problem

- Inaccurate sales forecasting
- Poor production planning
- Ineffective purchasing function
- Poor material management and inventory control
- Shipping errors (over-ships)

## Impacts that may result from the issue

- Lost sales
- Customer dissatisfaction
- Disruption in production planning

These are only a few of the risks and a few of the impacts that could occur. But, it would obviously be in the best interests of the organization to discover the root cause of the stock-out problem as soon as possible to ensure that it does not have undesirable impacts.

One of the most simple and pattern-sensitive of all universal risk indicators are credit memos issued to correct deficiencies in performance by the organization. If you ever want to know what is going wrong in operations, do an analysis of credit memos. If properly coded and classified, they are extremely good clues and insights into the many key risks that you have in play.

The operative word here is *if* they are properly coded and classified. One of the greatest risks that most organizations run is that the data they collect is crap. One of the key indicators of this is doing stratification analysis of the codes for credit memos issued. If you see that 70 percent plus of the codes are "miscellaneous and other," you have big-time problems. It goes back to the old adage: You can't solve a problem you don't know you have; you don't know you have it if you don't measure it; if you don't measure it, you can't solve it. Nothing is a bigger risk in an organization than the gathering of bad data.

In the case of reason codes for credit memos, performing simple stratification analysis on well-coded data can point out quite quickly the undesirable patterns of operations risk that are taking place. Being an auditor by trade, I was always confused by a lot of things that were and are still done in the auditing profession. For instance, auditors will come in, select a sample of credit memos, tick tie, and foot them to make sure they are accurate. They will then trace them to Accounts Receivable to see that they are properly applied and then check the signature to make sure they are properly approved.

The question I have always asked is why are the credit memos there in the first place? Those are key indicators of operational failure; they should not be there. Unless we are running a charitable organization, why should we be giving our money away? The causal events of the credit memos should be actively investigated by operations and done away with by fixing the root cause.

## FINANCIAL, OPERATIONAL, REGULATORY, AND TECHNOLOGICAL KRIs

FORT (financial, operational, regulatory, and technological) is an acronym for the key areas where risk indicators are normally determined for most organizations. They tend to represent the most common areas of risks throughout the enterprise and as a result can be utilized to evaluate risk objectively in a highly efficient and effective manner.

Chapter 7 will present an inventory of various types of key risk indicators in the format of the risk event and the key risk indicator. The indicators that can be utilized can be kept at a very high level or can be taken down to the lowest level of the operational area. In Chapter 7 there will be numerous examples of how you can take these indicators to very low levels. If you are capable of measuring the data at these levels, you can get a tremendously good idea of your risk picture, utilizing nothing but metrics. Following that illustration will be a set of high-level risk indicators for each category within the FORT classification.

You can go on endlessly with indicators of risk. That is why whenever you are initiating a Data-Centric ERM you must be very conscious of the fact that there may be limitations on the amount of data that can be utilized. This may be the result of available automation capabilities. Even though this could possibly be a constraint at the beginning of creating an ERM that is objectively based, it should never be a long-term problem condition. Any organization that is intent upon being highly successful in the area of enterprise risk management is going to have to come to terms with the fact that their future lies in automation.

Chapter 8 discusses more about the issue of automation within the ERM environment. It is definitely something that should be considered strategically from day one. In building an objective-based risk environment, tomorrow is not soon enough to start planning for automation. It is imperative that every organization think seriously about these requirements and plan accordingly.

The future lies in the ability to maximize the utilization of data for managing the enterprise from a risk perspective.

# CHAPTER SEVEN

# Top-Down Risk Assessment: Evolving the Fluid ERM Environment—A Step-by-Step Approach

 **BUILDING ERM ONE STEP AT A TIME**

To effectively implement an enterprise risk management environment it would be very helpful in all instances to have some type of specific guidance on how one of these models could be evolved. In this chapter, how to build one of these models in step-by-step sequence is discussed. The very first thing that must be remembered is that when you are going to build one of these models you must have a strategic objective in mind. Therefore, you must sit down and logically think out what would you like to accomplish with the model and how you are going to go about doing that. The sequence that we are going to follow for discussion in this particular chapter is set out next.

The key subject matter that is discussed in the subsequent sections will be as follows:

- An example will be presented of how to lay out the physical structure of your organization and create a physical map of same.
- How to determine key business risks based on critical outcomes of those subsets of the organization.
- How to build a risk register and what should be in it.
- How risk registers and other valuable risk information can be embedded in the physical mapping created for the enterprise risk management environment.
- A discussion of utilizing logical data pathways (LDPs) to understand how risk can be analyzed at all levels of the organization starting from the top and moving to the bottom will be undertaken. In other words, a classic top-down, risk-based approach.

## MAPPING THE PHYSICAL STRUCTURE OF THE ENTERPRISE

The only way to take an inventory of the entire enterprise is to physically map it out by location, groups of similar subsets of the organization, or some other methodology that best presents a complete picture of the organization. It is best if you can geographically map it in those instances where the following factors would be of significance in how risk would be evaluated. Examples of these types of risk considerations would be: geography, culture, cost of operation of being physically dispersed, or where geopolitical considerations play a large role in the risk evaluation and management landscape.

### Mapping the Physical Structure of the Administrative Areas

An effective way of building an enterprise risk management structure that is clearly delineated and easily understandable is to separate those types of centralized functions from normal operations. The reason is that when creating a physical map of the organization it will become way too confusing if you try and incorporate centralized functions and how they relate to each one of the operating units. So the very first thing I will do is talk about how to build a physical map of your administrative or centralized areas.

Figure 7.1 is an illustration of a physical mapping of an administrative scheme that represents a fairly normal situation for most organizations or corporations. The critical administrative processes are as follows:

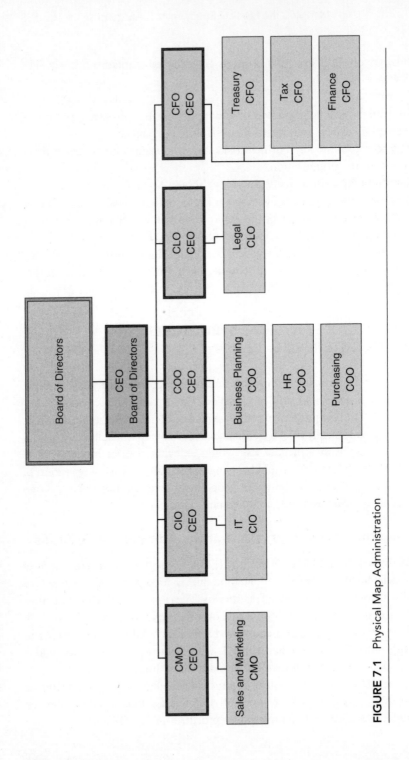

**FIGURE 7.1** Physical Map Administration

- Finance
- Accounting
- Treasury
- Tax
- Legal
- Human Resources (HR)
- IT
- Business Planning
- Purchasing
- Sales and Marketing

These functionalities are illustrated as subsets of the organization itself. The top of the organization is assumed to be the executive officers and those types of administrative functions. The critical outcomes and corresponding risk metrics (KRIs) for each will be presented. As a prelude to that discussion we will discuss a special area of risk relative to IT.

## IT

The key functionality of IT is to provide accurate and timely information and safeguard the critical information for the organization. They are also responsible for deploying the latest and best technology to serve the needs of the organization as required. Later in this chapter we will discuss the risk indicators to measure the primary outcomes of IT. However, another category of risk that must be taken into account is that of physical risks. This is why mapping the physical structure of the Enterprise is just as critical, if not more so, in the area of IT.

It is a common misconception that the most critical risks in IT are logical in nature. In reality, some of the primary risks that take place are physical. Let's explore some of these and determinate whether this is true. I will present two different scenarios in which I believe the risks of losing information in IT are much more significant physically than logically.

Scenario number one would be the following. If I wanted to steal your information physically from you and you were a publicly listed corporation, I would invoke the following strategy. I would buy one share of your stock and then contact your shareholder relations department. I would ask them to forward to me a copy of your annual report for my review. In that report will be all the smiling faces and all the glossy pictures of the officers and the Board of Directors. I would then select the person of that group who would most likely possess all the corporate critical information that I would like to steal.

Once that had been determined, I would then take up a position somewhere within observation distance of the corporate headquarters and commence to follow her when she emerges carrying her laptop. The chances are excellent that she will have all of that critical information on the laptop, and the chances are even better it is not properly protected or encrypted. At that point it is simply a matter of following her until she makes the inevitable mistake: to set the case containing the laptop down at some opportune time or place, and then turn her back.

Scenario two is somewhat more complex but may well be worth the effort. This would involve the "let's get inside" strategy. That strategy would start with my forming a number of small companies each performing a necessary function for your organization. The six companies that I would start would be the following:

1. Janitorial
2. Security guards
3. Maintenance and installation all types
4. Paper recycling
5. PC recycling
6. Courier service for backups to hot site

Let's explore the possibilities that establishing these "businesses" would present for me to accomplish my underlying hidden agenda of usurping your data. In each of these scenarios, I would present pricing and special incentives to your purchasing people that would be virtually irresistible to them. Better yet, I would play right into the easiest of all avenues, the unabated thirst to outsource everything in sight, for the sake of the short-term vision of "cost savings." As a result I would secure all of the contracts in these areas either at your facility or those of your outsourcers.

## Janitorial

The key here is that these people have more or less free roaming capabilities on the premises with little or no oversight. If I were to hire a highly skilled group of software engineers, hackers, or someone of similar capabilities, present them as janitors and introduce them to your premises, how would you really know? These highly talented individuals would then have open season on your systems and "secure" environments with little or no risk of detection, unless these environments are monitored constantly.

However, sad but true, we know they are not, in fact. In most instances, the security logs are deactivated—why, too much overhead on the IT environment? Oh please, tell me we are not still buying that old smoke and mirrors story.

No names will be mentioned, but what organization was it that had this exact circumstance in play? As a result it was victimized by a denial of service attack on all of their Internet connection points, which kept their customers from accessing them for a period of 24 hours.

## Security Guards

This is one of my favorite of all strategies. Make the protectors the worst enemy you can possibly have on the premises. In most instances, the security service is actually mandated to enter all of the areas of the premises to ensure that they are secure. What sweet irony that would be to find out that the security people who are supposed to preserve security are actually undermining it. It brings to mind an instance that a colleague of mine brought to my attention. This occurred outside of the United States in an organization that was part of the national government structure.

A security outsourcer had been retained to bring personnel onto the grounds of the organization that was storing some very critical and expensive technology components. There had been some minor theft, and they were concerned that this might escalate. It was not long after the new security organization took control that the frequency and quantity of thefts actually increased significantly. This went on for a period of time with numerous explanations of why it was not being prevented coming from the outsourcer. It was not until the governmental body actually hired another contractor to do surveillance that they detected it was the security company stealing the components.

Again the strategy remains the same: put highly talented technicians on the premises to masquerade as security and then steal the data. Nothing complicated—but it will work, that is for sure.

## Maintenance and Installation

Every organization has maintenance needs, whether they own the property or do not. Equipment and property of all types need repair. Cables need to be run, physical configurations of work space need to take place, and many other tasks have to be completed. The key is to not interfere with the workday, however, as you may negatively impact productivity. Therefore, my maintenance service would guarantee that we would perform all maintenance tasks after business hours with minimal impact on productivity. We are always looking out for your best interest, and we are all about excellent customer service. Same old, same old—highly skilled technicians make excellent maintenance persons for my kind of company. Give excellent service and rock bottom prices, who would complain?

## Paper Recycling

I have nothing against going green. In fact I think it is a critical strategy for the future of the environment. But in business risk terms, this presents a golden opportunity for information to be compromised, by design and by sheer happenstance. In my case, I cannot wait to get my hands on all of that information residing in those recycling bins. There is so much valuable information contained there, both for the organization itself and its clients. If this information remains in its native state until I pick it up, it is as good as gone. Thank you very much. One of the ways in which we cut costs to give you the lowest prices possible is not to have any expensive paper pulverization equipment on our trucks. But don't you worry, we will tend to that back at the recycling center.

Hug a tree, give away your secrets, Oh! by all means please do. Clearly, a better strategy is to not have so much paper and not print out all of these things in the first place and save the added cost. That way, it is easier for my hackers in these scenarios to steal it and transport it in digitized form; paper is way too bulky and bothersome to reconvert.

## PC Recycling

One of the great things that does help me out here in stealing your information is the fact that PCs (both desktop and laptop) are becoming so cheap they are basically throwaways at this point. That is excellent. If I come in and offer you exceptional trade-in prices on your existing machines, when you buy new ones from my PC distributor, the trap is nicely set. What is even more beautiful is that the hard drives and the amount of data on them are massive.

Another of the areas of data security, which is sorely overlooked, is how data is dealt with that resides on all those large-capacity hard drives in those machines. Back not too many years ago, we used to have to be concerned with kilobytes of data, but now we have gigs of data on these drives, which provides much more information to folks like me. Organizations are hopefully becoming more sophisticated in how they are dealing with data removal on old technology, but in many cases not so.

There are of course a number of options that can be employed to solve this problem. Overwrite the drives with 0s, reformat the drives a number of times, smash them with a hammer, shred them with newer devices designed for that purpose, and use wiping software—to name a few. Even those, however, may not be adequate to the task. Also, I may have to severely downgrade your trade-in value if the drives are destroyed or rendered inoperable in any way. You do understand, of course? A wealth of information is available in the recycling business if you apply yourself.

I believe that we have all heard the horror stories of information lost in this manner. Let's see what government agency was it that traded away super-confidential information because they failed to properly remove the information and used the *.* delete command instead? (We will omit the agency and the event in this book.)

### Courier Service for Backups to Hot Site

To obtain data on a larger scale, it is a much nicer setup that I just come every day and pick it up in total in the form of backups. Since I will have everything in one convenient grouping, it will save me a lot of unnecessary running around. The ability to obtain the information in bulk will facilitate the speed with which I can evaluate it and disseminate it for my purposes.

Oh heck, let's just make this easier. Why don't I just set up an electronic archival company located somewhere in a cave. That should provide better security for your critical data, shouldn't it? Then you can just transmit it to me electronically, and that way I don't have the bother or the expense of coming to get it. Yes, in fact, that will work better for me; let's do it that way.

Each and every one of these services has the potential of stealing massive amounts of information from your organization at any time. The key thing here is the ability to gain physical access, which then provides the ability to compromise the information with the appropriate skill sets in some instances and in others with little or no special skills. In fact, another physical risk factor working in my favor in many of these instances is this. Some security folks in their zeal to heighten security in their organizations actually accomplish the opposite.

For example, one of the "brilliant" ways to supposedly enhance security is to make the passwords that people use for access more complex in format. You have probably seen these in your own organizations. They would be in a form that utilizes combinations of capital and small letters as well as digits, and they are lengthy to add to the complexity.

For example: **ThIS26CHArACterPWdOeS0GOod**

The problem is that no one can remember a complex conglomeration such as this, so they write it down. They then put it in convenient places for my hackers to find, like in their desk, taped to the terminal, or under their chair. Thank you, thank you, and thank you, O great security gurus, for this concept.

Regarding risk metrics on the activities described in these scenarios, Table 7.1 shows some that could be considered for review and/or trending.

Other types of physical risks also come into play in the context of things that should be monitored in IT. Table 7.2 shows some examples of risks that the organization may want to take a look at.

These are just a few examples of the types of issues that highly effective oversight in the context of evaluating and managing physical risks would certainly take into account.

**TABLE 7.1**  Physical Risks with Metrics—IT

| Key Risk | Risk Metric |
|---|---|
| Unauthorized access after hours | Monitoring of accesses to critical data sets for abnormalities |
| Unknown persons on the premises | Mandatory deep background checks on all persons with unsupervised after-hours/critical data access versus access |
| Loss of data on portable devices | Number of devices without mandatory encryption/secure wireless links as percentage of all devices |
| Loss of confidential data | Number of servers/repositories of confidential data in the organization |

**TABLE 7.2**  Additional Physical Risks with Metrics—IT

| Key Risk | Risk Metric |
|---|---|
| Unsupervised access by employees | Entrance and exit times of employees if badge entry |
| Failure of UPS devices | Periodic testing or self-testing and monitoring failures |
| Vandalism, fire, physical threats | Incident monitoring, frequency of police/fire calls |
| Outside unintentional threats | Number of inspections of proximity to rail lines/airports/pipelines and results/number of incidents that have taken place |

## Mapping the Physical Structure of the Operational Areas

The exact same exercise can be completed for the operational side of the house. In Figure 7.2 the mapping exercise illustrated takes into account all of the key operational areas of a manufacturing concern.

As an introduction to operations, we will have a discussion of the receiving area and how an insignificant area with what appear to be nonrisky activities can actually spawn massive organizational risks when proper care is not taken to do things right.

## Receiving

From an operations perspective, this function is the gatekeeper that can either minimize your costs of operation or expand them greatly. Among the many critical functions they perform are the receipt of goods on a daily basis, verification that the goods are as ordered and meet the specifications required, that quantities are correct, and that the goods are not damaged in any way. The number and variety of risks that can be introduced into the Enterprise as the result of an ineffective receiving department can range from minimal to catastrophic. The reason is that they are the first line of defense to stop problems from entering the premises. If they fail to detect problems, the undesirable attributes are then introduced into the inventories and eventually into the products themselves. Let me see, time for another example to illustrate the point I am trying to develop.

Close your eyes and imagine yourself standing in a tropical forest in Southeast Asia outside of a small manufacturing plant. The company that owns this plant performs contract manufacturing for large organizations around the world. See anything risky yet?

You are observing the loading dock where goods and materials are received, which are to be used in manufacturing. You see a truck pull up to the dock; a forklift comes out and unloads a pallet of materials off of the truck bed and onto the dock. See anything risky yet?

You continue to observe as the person from the receiving department comes out with a clipboard and starts to verify the receipt of goods against a purchase order, and you can see that the materials are large metal drums of paint. See anything risky yet?

At that point, the truck leaves, and the forklift driver takes the pallet of paint inside the building as you follow along. You then see the forklift driver deliver the paint to the inventory control area that takes possession of it, and checks it in, and adds it to the inventory stock status on the system. See anything risky yet?

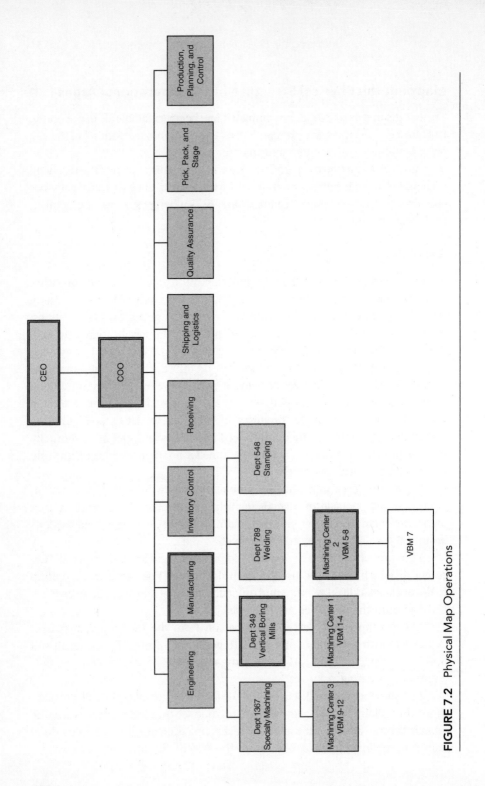

**FIGURE 7.2** Physical Map Operations

A few moments later a person from production comes to the inventory control area, requests a drum of the paint just received, and has a fork lift driver move it the manufacturing line and properly mount it in the appropriate spot to be attached to the painting system. See anything risky yet?

The drum is then properly attached and the paint starts flowing into the appropriate application tools, and the run of products to be painted are started down the production line. See anything risky yet?

As the dolls start making their way down the line, the beautifully colored lead-based paint is meticulously applied to each and every doll with great care and diligence. See anything risky yet?

When they reach the end of the line, the dolls are carefully placed in the brightly colored boxes with the name and logo of one of the world's best-known toy companies boldly emblazoned on the outside. The dolls are then boxed and loaded into shipping containers. They now begin their long trip to stores in the United States and other key markets around the world. See anything risky yet?

Right about now, the C-suite of that toy manufacturer can see that risk from half a world away, and in not too many days the same C-suite members are going to be seeing that risk splashed all over the evening news. Then the C-suite as well as the members of the Board of Directors will be seeing red from the boardroom to the bottom line as the individuals responsible for governance and oversight realize that they will have to spend millions on damage control. Do you see the pattern of aligned risks that are starting to fan out across the enterprise? Do you see anything risky now?

This rather extended example is indicative of one of the key challenges that the enterprise risk management group is confronted with every day: the ability to truly know, predict, and manage your risks across the globe both within your own organization and in outsourced situations as well.

## DEFINING THE BUSINESS RISKS OF THE ENTERPRISE: UTILIZING KEY OUTCOMES

Throughout the previous sections of this book, I have interspersed examples of this concept of centering ERM on the key outcomes defined by process or subset of the organization. The primary purpose for utilizing this philosophy is to utilize risk indicators that are key to the organization as well as keep the number of metrics reasonable.

The KRIs utilized to evaluate key outcomes should be thought of as high-level or global indicators of risk within the respective business subsets. In Chapter 6, I introduced risk metrics that can be employed on a much more detailed basis when a high degree of automation and data sophistication are gained. Utilizing a defined set of key outcomes, usually ranging from five to seven items, and the associated key risk indicators (KRIs), we can keep the analysis meaningful and manageable with limited automation and data sophistication.

Each of the following areas will have the key outcomes identified for each of the enterprise subsets identified. You may identify these slightly differently for your own organization, but I think you will find that they are quite representative of what should be looked at and monitored. We will look first at the administrative areas and how they might be risk evaluated.

## Administration

The Administration area of the organization, even though it does not directly generate revenue and consumes more cash than it provides, is the glue that normally binds everything together and has its own set of unique risks.

### Finance

As noted in the previous section, Finance, even though it is a peripheral function of the organization, is extremely important in sustaining it on a daily basis. The key is the accuracy and integrity of the information provided. Nothing will undermine the organization faster than financial statement manipulation, because the inevitable result is eventually to not know what is going on in the real business at all. Too much gaming of the numbers will distort reality to the point of losing the ability to run the business and the ability to determine who is on first and what is on second.

Numerous large organizations have succumbed to the sirens of "pleasing the analysts" at whatever cost, only to end up as another carcass of a once great ocean liner shipwrecked on the shore of reality. Every time that I watch the quarterly or annual financial reports on CNBC or other financial outlets, I cannot help but wonder when I hear the following phrases: "They just beat the analyst's expectations by a penny" or "They met the analyst's expectations exactly." Are those grey things breaking the surface rocks ahead? Or even more troubling than that is this question: Do the people running these companies have rocks in their heads?

## Accounting

The critical outcomes of Accounting are timely generation and accuracy of the financial statements. The accounting function is what in many ways and in particular with many people creates the "public face" of the enterprise. The key or critical outcomes of accounting are the following:

- Timeliness of financial information
- Accuracy of financial information
- Accurate costing of products
- Accurate filings and reporting of information

## Treasury

The following are some of the key outcomes of Treasury, clearly emphasizing their key functionality of keeping the enterprise solvent and in possession of adequate low-cost working capital:

- Manage cash effectively
- Maximize return on cash
- Minimize cash management costs
- Minimize banking and relationship fees
- Minimize cost of borrowing

## Tax

Tax must be sure to attain their key outcomes to minimize significant adverse impacts on the organization. The importance of monitoring the areas of risk in Tax is that many of the areas of risk in taxation are quite subtle in nature and nearly impossible to decipher for most people. Therefore, a lot of risk can go undetected and then, by definition, unmanaged. Key outcomes in Tax include the following:

- Minimize income tax impact
- Minimize personal property taxes
- Aggressively pursue tax positions
- Successfully defend tax positions
- Minimize real estate taxes

## Legal

The legal eagles of the organization have an intricate knowledge of the subject matter of risk. They literally manage nothing but risk on a daily basis. In addition, if there were one major collection point for aligned risks, it would be the office of in-house counsel. They are the repository of all things done wrong by the other parts of the enterprise. The key in this area from an ERM perspective is to make sure that the linkages are preserved between the source of the problem and the litigation issue. In other words, great diligence should be applied to cross-referencing the source of the risk to the eventual outcome of the litigation. Why? From an ERM perspective it is to key in on the patterning that is taking place, if any, with the causal events of the litigation.

For instance, an extremely large retailer was experiencing a horrendous influx of personal injury litigation for people falling and injuring themselves in the retailer's stores. The original position was to treat them essentially as a nuisance situation and pay the claims off with a ceremonious amount to make the issue go away. When the volumes finally became so large (key risk indicator of unchallenged legal initiatives), they began to contest the claims in court.

When they began researching the patterns, they were extremely alarmed to see that a number of the claimants were the same individuals in different parts of the country. Upon further research, they were able to conclude that there appeared to be bands of people making a living by traveling around the country, faking their injuries and filing an action anticipating the easy settlement. Using the data patterning clearly indicating the risk, they then formulated the strategy to fight the claims. In a relatively short period of time, the claims volumes dropped dramatically. Some key outcomes that should be achieved by legal are the following:

- Minimize legal expense
- Discourage litigation
- Effectively manage costs-litigating
- Minimize legal losses
- Demonstrate litigation prowess
- Highly effective selection of outside counsel
- Highly effective management of outside counsel

## HR

Nothing against the fine people of HR—but this area is a landmine of risk. First, they are the gatekeepers of one of our key assets—the employees. The need to hire highly qualified individuals at a cost-effective rate in a highly mobile society is no small challenge. A recent survey just released within the last couple of days cited that 45 percent of all employees were dissatisfied with their current positions. This should not be unexpected, in that the employee/ employer relationship has changed dramatically in the years that have passed since I exited the campus life.

For instance, when I graduated it was not unusual that if you went to work for a prestigious employer like say, IBM, you would stay there for life. In fact, my cousin's husband has worked for that fine organization for his entire career. He has been with them since he graduated in the late 1960s with an Electrical Engineering degree from Wisconsin. That is not only commendable; it is something to truly be admired. The problem is that those days are long gone and far away. Today, there is little, if any, loyalty between an employer and its employee—and vice versa. This gives rise to a tremendous amount of risk when you are running a revolving door employment policy. The following are some of the risks/impacts that are brought about by this type of operating condition:

- **Risk:** Instability in the workforce is the rule of operation. This leads to ever-decreasing productivity as skill sets are never really fully developed and training is a constant state of operation.
- **Impact:** Costs of operations rise at an exponential rate.
- **Risk:** It will be inevitable that there will be a significant loss of intellectual property and knowledge base.
- **Impact:** Excessive costs will be incurred during the process of re-creating same as well as the competitive exposure that is brought to bear on the organization.
- **Risk:** Inability to establish a meaningful and highly functional succession plan, where definitive replacements for key individuals have been identified and groomed to take over.
- **Impact:** This will result in a loss of expertise and leadership that may result in the necessity to outsource the functionality for lack of knowledgeable resources. The other alternative is to bring in outsiders and then try to bring them up to speed. Higher operational costs are incurred.

These are just a few examples and actually just touch the tip of the iceberg of the risks that could be explored, but hopefully they cast some light on how serious the talent bleed is in the context of risk. If you were to analyze HR from a key risk standpoint the following key outcomes could be utilized:

- Minimize loss of talent
- Provide good work environment

- Adhere to all key regulations
- Perform effective recruiting
- Perform background checks
- Effective compensation program
- Provide good benefits
- Provide cost-effective benefits

## IT

The key functionality of IT is to provide accurate and timely information, and safeguard the critical information for the organization. IT is also responsible for deploying the latest and best technology to serve the needs of the organization as required. Later we will show the risk indicators to measure the primary outcomes of IT. If you were to analyze IT from a key risk standpoint, the following key outcomes could be utilized:

- Delivering timely information
- Providing accurate information
- Safeguarding of data
- Effectively deploying technology
- Effectively utilizing technology
- Ensuring processing completeness
- Ensuring processing integrity
- Deploying new technology to maximize efficiency

## Business Planning

The key functionality of Business Planning is to provide the strategic course going forward for the organization. They are also responsible for analyzing all future actions with a high degree of accuracy and presenting their best recommendations to the senior executives and the Board of Directors. If you were to analyze business planning from a key risk standpoint, the following key outcomes would be some of the most critical to bear in mind:

- Identify potential acquisitions
- Identify synergies to be gained
- Evaluate success of acquisition
- Maximize return on investment
- Ensure due diligence is proper
- Proper valuation of acquisitions

- Proper valuation of dispositions
- ID highly successful organizations

## Purchasing

The key functionality of Purchasing is to ensure that whatever is required to run the enterprise on a daily basis is properly acquired within the appropriate time and value constraints. If you were to analyze purchasing from a key outcome standpoint, the following are the key outcomes they must accomplish every day that they operate to be successful:

- Acquire the right item
- Within the right time frame
- To the correct location
- With the right quality
- Acquire the right quantity
- Pay the right price
- Right specifications

## Sales and Marketing

Sales and Marketing are charged with key functionality of establishing our position within the given marketplace. It is no small task to gain brand recognition when there are so many competing environments and a worldwide market. If you were to evaluate sales and marketing from a key risk standpoint, the following key outcomes should be high on the list of things to be considered:

- Provide exceptional customer service
- Sell products at the right price
- Maintain customer base and expand it
- Preserve company's rights
- Accurately reporting sales performance for bonus purposes
- Maximize advertising money
- Establish products as brands

## Operations

We will now turn our attention to the operational areas of our example. As mentioned previously, it is the operations that drive the success or failure of virtually any organization. It makes no difference if it is a publicly listed corporation or a renowned institution of higher education: it is all about the operations. For instance, colleges that are held in high regard and are known worldwide have achieved that status as the result of their operating units, not in most cases as the result of the administration areas, no disrespect intended.

In other words, it is the research departments and the quality of their research that determines the flow of grant money to the institution. This also identifies them as institutions of a high degree of accomplishment in the area of research and thereby raises the prestige of the institution. The same can be said of the investment officers who manage the endowments. Their expertise contributes greatly to the reputation of the institution. But of most importance is the faculty; without a highly regarded faculty to deliver a high-caliber education there would be no students walking the hallowed halls of the institution. Thus, it does not make any difference what type of organization it is; operations is the driver, a characteristic often overlooked in the grand scheme of things.

The operational areas of a manufacturing concern and the key outcomes that can be considered are described in the following sections.

### Production Planning and Control (PP&C)

The process to be used here is the same logically as has been employed thus far. We should think always in the context of functionality and definitive purpose to find our points of maximum risk. In PP&C it is all about timing and coordination, and so we could use the following as key outcomes for the purpose of evaluating risk:

- Maximize production capabilities
- Complete production on schedule
- Maximize efficiency in scheduling
- Maximize coordination of schedule
- Release jobs to the shop floor timely
- Accommodate schedule changes

### Engineering

Many of the base functionalities of any manufacturing concern owe their existence to the engineers. However, one of the risks that creeps into organizations and severely undermines their ability to operate efficiently and effectively is the "don't approach the throne" syndrome. This occurs when the engineers begin to elevate themselves above the peasants of the shop floor, the ones who really know what to do and how to build it. In these situations you can get a lack of communication, which literally results in the shop floor building things the way they believe they should be done, and leaving the engineers out of it. There are a number of risks and impacts that are brought about as the result of this situation:

- **Risk:** The engineered BOM (bill of materials) is in error, as the shop floor is using different components to manufacture the goods.
- **Impact:** Whenever the BOM is released to the shop floor, the wrong components will be called out of inventory, will have to be returned and others obtained. This practice drives up handling and inventory costs dramatically depending upon frequency.
- **Impact:** In most Enterprise Resource Planning (ERP) environments today costing is "back flushed" (unpleasant visual isn't it?) based on the BOM. Costing of that product for those components is by definition incorrect. Pricing is wrong by definition because prices are based on costs, margins may be in jeopardy, or at a minimum misstated.
- **Impact:** Inventory stock status will be incorrect, and shortages will most likely result causing downtime and disruption in the production schedule. Costs head higher.

One relatively small risk was previously illustrated, and hundreds of others could be cited. But the ripple effect of risks and related impacts that start to take place throughout the organization are easily seen. Start multiplying those by all of the aligned risks; well, again you get the picture. Key outcomes for the engineering area to be considered include:

- Determine accurate BOMs
- Designs cost effective to build
- R&D designs meet market demand
- Designs to appropriate use criteria
- Design things timely
- Designs to appropriate specs

## Receiving

Receiving is one of the key areas in which excess costs to the organization can be eliminated. It can do this by stopping bad materials from being introduced into the production process, ensuring there are no damaged goods being introduced into inventory, and making sure that we get what we paid for. Receiving are the gatekeepers for materials entering the facility. If they fail to perform this key responsibility, the consequences can be dire. Some key outcomes include the following:

- Ensure backorders are created
- Ensure right quantities are received
- Ensure right items are received
- Ensure that quality items are received
- Ensure no damaged items are received
- Ensure that items received timely

## Inventory Control (IC)

You cannot build what you don't have, and you can't sell what you don't build. IC must ensure that what appears on the stock status is accurate and that the inventory levels are always verified to the physical inventory as required. It is critical that there be a high degree of accuracy maintained in the stock status as it impacts production planning and control, engineering, manufacturing, shipping, and everything in between and beyond. There are numerous risks that can take place here, but the key outcomes and points of maximum concern are the following:

- Maintain accurate inventory records
- Ensure adequate inventory levels
- Match the inventory to demand
- Not tie up excess capital
- Inventory is available as required

## Quality Assurance

QA has been playing a key role in the success of manufacturing concerns for decades. They constitute the hands-on reality check that is required on a daily basis. They should be evaluated on their effectiveness and efficiency based on their performance, as you would expect. These outcomes are those that determine its success or failure as a process on a daily basis. Some of the critical outcomes that could be considered for this function are the following:

- Ensure quality of raw materials
- Ensure quality of work in process
- Ensure quality of finished goods
- Apply consistent QA standards
- Enhance the product quality

## Manufacturing Departments

The product that determines the success or failure of the organization is squarely in the hands of these areas, the production departments. Their activities and the diligence with which they perform them are the keys to bigger and better things or the slow self-destruction of what was once a great thing.

Ford, as a high-profile manufacturing company, has done a tremendous job of improving its designs, quality, and overall desirability of the products while maintaining an intact and loyal dealership network.

In all situations the key outcomes that should be in evidence and utilized to evaluate these departments would be as follows:

- Produce high-quality product
- Produce product on time
- Produce the right quantity
- Produce at lowest cost
- Control production/report accurately
- Maintain a safe working area

## Pick, Pack, and Stage

Getting things organized is critical to ensure that efficient and timely shipping practices can be employed. There are a number of adverse impacts that will occur if customer orders are not properly staged and shipped as required. The goods to be shipped must be picked from inventory accurately, they must be packed properly to withstand the rigors of shipment, and they must be assembled with all other items that are part of the same order. Key outcomes that must be achieved in this area to determine success are as follows:

- Ensure all items are accurate in order
- Ensure order is properly packed
- Ensure that all items in order ship
- Ensure staging of items is proper
- Ensure orders are staged timely

## Shipping and Logistics

The shipping department is now tasked with the final critical task, which is to ensure that the products are finally transported in proper condition to the customer that ordered them. This constitutes another very risky part of the process. A number of undesirable things can happen when you have a lot of activity and equipment all competing for the same space as well as having outsiders present in the area. Key outcomes of these areas are presented as suggested things to be considered. Again, opinions may differ, but it is an excellent starting point for an extremely well-focused risk analysis if nothing else.

Key outcomes include:

- Ensure all items loaded as staged
- Ensure entire order is properly loaded and secured
- Ensure that all items in order ship at once
- Operate a safe working area
- Schedule shipping vehicles timely
- Utilize most efficient shipping method
- Utilize most effective shipping method
- Ship all items on schedule

Key outcomes for any area of the enterprise set the stage for assessing risk. The reason for this conclusion should be obvious. It is resident in the fact that the failure to achieve the key outcomes of any enterprise subset indicates a risky state of operation by default. In other words, any time you fail to achieve the desired outcome, that subset of the organization, program, or whatever is risky by definition.

For instance, an organization is responsible for a program such as "World Food Program." But here is what occurs. The food is shipped to the dictator's country and on to their warehouse. They then sell it on to their buddies so they can buy a bigger personal jet to leave the country faster when things get hot. Subsequent to all of the food being shipped to the country, the children still don't have rice in their bowls, the people are still malnourished, and the deaths from starvation still escalate. Does anyone see anything wrong with this picture?

*It's all about the outcome—nothing more, nothing less!*

## DEVELOPING KRIs FOR ASSESSING RISK FOR THE ENTIRE ENTERPRISE

KRIs can be developed for evaluating risk in a number of ways. In this section we will discuss and present extensive examples of the use of KRIs for these purposes. We will consider them in a couple of different contexts. We will discuss first the utilization of KRIs as they relate to identified critical outcomes of the enterprise. These KRIs may be used at all levels of the organization from enterprise, global or high-level risk analysis, to process or task-level risk analysis.

The second context in which KRIs will be presented is in the more detailed levels of risk analysis where they can be created for any and all types of risk that can and will occur throughout the organization. These can be employed in large numbers when the systemization of the ERM takes place and a very high level of sophistication of data-centric ERM has been achieved.

## KRIs Related to Key Outcomes

Utilizing the key outcomes from the previous section we will now present the related KRIs that could be employed to determine whether the outcome is being achieved or not.

### Accounting

In evaluating accounting, the KRIs in Table 7.3 could be utilized to determine their success or failure as a process.

### Treasury

Some of the key KRIs that could be utilized in an analysis of Treasury from a key risk standpoint are shown in Table 7.4.

**TABLE 7.3**  Financial Statement Accuracy Defined Outcomes/KRIs—Finance

| Key Outcomes | KRI |
| --- | --- |
| Timeliness of financial information | Days to close |
| Timeliness of financial information | Completed financials by due date |
| Accuracy of financial information | Number of adjusting journal entries |
| Accuracy of financial information | Dollar amounts of adjusting journal entries |
| Accuracy of financial information | Unreconciled balances |
| Accurate costing of products | Significant variances being recorded for labor, material, and overhead |
| Accurate costing of products | Margin compression in the product lines |

**TABLE 7.4** Treasury-Defined Outcomes/KRIs—Treasury

| Key Outcomes | KRI |
| --- | --- |
| Manage cash effectively | Minimization of interest expense |
| Maximize return on cash | Percent of interest earned |
| Minimize cash management costs | Bank fees, charges |
| Manage cash effectively | Idle cash balances |
| Minimize cost of borrowing | Effective interest rate on debt |

## Tax

Evaluating the Tax area without making it too taxing would perhaps be accomplished by utilizing the related KRIs in Table 7.5.

## Legal

The legal area should not abstain from the utilization of KRIs to evaluate its key outcomes and therefore due consideration should be given to Table 7.6.

**TABLE 7.5** Tax-Defined Outcomes/KRIs—Tax

| Key Outcomes | KRI |
| --- | --- |
| Minimize income tax impact | Taxes as a percent of net income |
| Minimize personal property taxes | Personal property tax rate as a percent of asset base |
| Aggressively pursue tax positions | Reserves related to tax events |
| Successfully defending tax positions | Reversal of reserves related to tax events |
| Minimizing real estate taxes | Number of challenges, reductions in assessments |

**TABLE 7.6** Legal-Defined Outcomes/KRIs—Law

| Key Outcomes | KRI |
| --- | --- |
| Minimize legal expense | Trends in legal expense |
| Discourage litigation | Number of litigation actions brought—trend |
| Effectively manage costs—litigating | Cost per litigated action—average |
| Minimize legal losses | Average settlements/verdict lost |
| Demonstrate litigation prowess | The victories as percent of total cases tried |
| Demonstrate litigation prowess | Number of cases referred to outside versus handled internally |
| Effectiveness of selecting counsel | Outside counsel cost per case |
| Effectiveness of selecting counsel | Victories in tried cases by outside counsel as percent |

## HR

Utilizing KRIs to analyze HR from a key risk standpoint can help to predict where the landmines of risk exist and can hopefully prevent us from stepping on them or on as few of them as possible (see Table 7.7).

## IT

IT is all about the data; data is what they do for a living. Doesn't seem logical that they should be evaluated from a risk standpoint by the very data they help to create. Utilizing that as an accepted premise, the following KRIs could be utilized in looking at the related key outcomes (see Table 7.8).

### Business Planning

In the world of business planning the future is the timeframe in which they operate. That is also true of a mature risk assessment environment; it is all

**TABLE 7.7** HR-Defined Outcomes/KRIs—HR

| Key Outcomes | KRI |
| --- | --- |
| Minimize loss of talent | ETO (Employee Turn Over) |
| Provide good work environment | ETO |
| Adhere to all key regulations | Fines, penalties, regulatory interventions |
| Perform effective recruiting | Average employee retention time |
| Perform background checks | Dismissal for cause statistics |
| Effective compensation program | ETO, market compensation rates |
| Provide good benefits | Benefits complaints from employees/ETO |
| Provide cost effective benefits | Benefits cost per employee |

**TABLE 7.8** IT-Defined Outcomes/KRIs—IT

| Key Outcomes | KRI |
| --- | --- |
| Delivering timely information | Downtime, deadlines missed |
| Provide accurate information | Errors detected in outputs, change requests volumes |
| Safeguarding of data | Incidents of unauthorized disclosure |
| Effectively deploying technology | Network downtime |
| Effectively utilizing technology | No/poor Internet presence |
| Ensuring processing completeness | Suspense file volumes |
| Ensuring processing integrity | Downtime, Hot Site test failures |
| Deploying new technology | Time elapsed since major upgrade of ERP |

**TABLE 7.9** Business Planning–Defined Outcomes/KRIs—BP

| Key Outcomes | KRI |
|---|---|
| Identify potential acquisitions | Number of candidates identified and analyzed versus selected for further investigation |
| Identify synergies to be gained | Actual efficiencies gained post-acquisition |
| Effectiveness of business planning | Number of acquisitions that met all original criteria |
| Maximize return on investment | Actual return on investment post-acquisition |
| Ensure due diligence is proper | Unanticipated poor results post-acquisition |
| Ensure due diligence is proper | Number of pre-acquisition adjustments made |
| Proper valuation of dispositions | Volume of negative price adjustments by an acquirer |
| ID highly successful organizations | Percentage of acquisitions exceeding expectations |

about the future. Therefore, developing a refined set of KRIs to evaluate business planning seems most appropriate. The risk metrics related to the key outcomes as defined are shown in Table 7.9.

## Purchasing

The primary outcomes of purchasing are very well defined, and its key functionalities are clear. The KRIs in keeping with those functionalities should be readily available in the financial and operational areas. If not, start to worry now (see Table 7.10).

## Sales and Marketing

The future potential of the organization is resting on its ability to effectively establish itself in the marketplace. Failure to do so is not a viable option for any organization anticipating a future. If you were to evaluate sales and marketing

**TABLE 7.10** Purchasing-Defined Outcomes/KRIs—SCM

| Key Outcomes | KRI |
|---|---|
| Acquire the right item | Quantity of returned items |
| Within the right time frame | Out of stocks, downtime |
| To the correct location | Inventory shortages/inventory overages |
| Right quality | Quality rejection rates |
| Acquire the right quantity | Excess and slow-moving inventories |
| Pay the right price | Unfavorable PPV, increasing average unit price |
| Right specifications | Rejections for failure to meet tolerances/requirements |

**TABLE 7.11** Sales and Marketing–Defined Outcomes/KRIs—Marketing

| Key Outcomes | KRI |
|---|---|
| Provide customer service | Customer complaints/lost volumes |
| Sell products at the right price | Average selling price/volumes of product sold |
| Maintain customer base and expand | Customer retention time/loss rates/unit volumes |
| Preserve company's rights | Number and amount of unauthorized deductions taken by customers |
| Accurately report performance for bonus purposes | Credit/promos/discount patterns after year end |
| Maximize advertising money | Patterns in results tied to promotion campaigns |
| Establish products as brands | Ability to command higher prices than competition |

from a key risk standpoint, the key outcomes above and related KRIs would be the appropriate starting point (see Table 7.11).

## Operations

We will now turn our attention to the operational areas of our discussion. The operational areas that were mentioned earlier could be evaluated utilizing the following key outcomes and related KRIs. These are suggestions and brain teasers, if you can identify better ones, by all means please do.

### Production Planning and Control

Planning implies looking ahead and not in the rearview mirror. Therefore the use of metrics for a forward look at things should resonate well here. The identified key outcomes and key risk indicators (KRIs) are set out here (see Table 7.12).

**TABLE 7.12** Production Planning and Control–Defined Outcomes/KRIs—PP&C

| Key Outcomes | KRI |
|---|---|
| Maximize production capabilities | Percent of idle capacity/zero activity cells/zero activity depts. |
| Complete production on schedule | Percent of missed ship dates/freight expense outbound |
| Maximize efficiency in scheduling | Length of cycle time from scheduled to completion |
| Maximize coordination of schedule | Delay times in subsets of customers' orders/late ships |
| Release jobs to the shop floor timely | Idle departments/downtime/indirect labor hours-standby |
| Accommodate schedule changes | Cycle time to introduce scrap/rework items |

## Engineering

The impacts of engineering as demonstrated in the prior discussion are far-reaching; therefore, the ability to mitigate or eliminate risk in this area should be of critical importance. Key outcomes and the related KRIs that might be considered for the engineering area are shown in Table 7.13.

## Receiving

Receiving has a number of points of measurement that can be utilized in the context of assessing risk. Some of the KRIs that could be well received are defined in Table 7.14.

**TABLE 7.13** Engineering-Defined Outcomes with KRIs—Engineering

| Key Outcomes | KRI |
| --- | --- |
| Determine accurate BOMs | Material substitution variances/unanticipated out of stock |
| Designs cost effective to build | Total cost per unit/labor or technology hours per unit |
| R&D designs meet market demand | Unit sales of new products introduced |
| Designs to appropriate use criteria | Warranty claims/average useful life/customer complaints |
| Design things timely | Delays in shipment to customer/idle departments |
| Designs to appropriate specs | Rejection rates customers/customer change orders |

**TABLE 7.14** Receiving-Defined Outcomes/KRIs—Receiving

| Key Outcomes | KRI |
| --- | --- |
| Ensure backorders are created | Backorders every time quantity less than PO |
| Ensure right quantities are received | Unanticipated stockouts in raw materials/shortages |
| Ensure right items are received | Items rejected on shop floor—not to spec/wrong item |
| Ensure that quality items are received | Scrap-out in production/rejected by QA in production |
| Ensure no damaged items received | Scrap-out in production/rejected by QA in production Ensure that items received timely |
| Expedited items are received timely | Expedited items cycle time/stock status update time |

## Inventory Control

Building an inventory of KRIs for inventory control should not be an overwhelming task. What we want to do, of course, is to keep them relevant to the key outcomes of the area. The KRIs that may be most relevant in this type of operation are shown in Table 7.15.

## Quality Assurance

When you undertake the task of developing KRIs for this area, you want to ensure that they are high quality, or they might not pass inspection. Based on the following critical outcomes, some of the KRIs that would yield a high-quality result are shown in Table 7.16.

## Manufacturing Departments

Developing a set of KRIs that are highly effective and useful is what we want to achieve in these enterprise subsets due to their critical nature. We don't want to just manufacture anything, hope it meets expectations, and hope it sells. We want to produce those sleek, highly functional products that will be

**TABLE 7.15**  Inventory Control–Defined Outcomes with KRIs—IC

| Key Outcomes | KRI |
| --- | --- |
| Maintain accurate inventory records | Volume of cycle count adjustments |
| Ensure adequate inventory levels | MRP inadequate stock levels incidents |
| Match the inventory to demand | Obsolete and slow-moving/stockouts |
| Do not tie up excess capital | Obsolete and slow-moving |
| Inventory available as required | Stockouts/indirect labor hours—material shortages |

**TABLE 7.16**  Quality Assurance–Defined Outcomes/KRIs—QA

| Key Outcomes | KRI |
| --- | --- |
| Ensure quality of raw materials | Rejection rates at receiving/scrapout rates in production |
| Ensure quality of work in process | Rejection rates in Work in Process (WIP) versus rejection rates in finished goods |
| Ensure quality of finished goods | Rejection rates in Finished Goods (FG)/returned product-quality issues |
| Apply consistent QA standards | Rejection rates trends/actual negative quality events |
| Enhance the product quality | Larger market share/branding/higher price |

**TABLE 7.17** Manufacturing-Defined Outcomes/KRIs—Manufacturing

| Key Outcomes | KRI |
| --- | --- |
| Produce high-quality product | Rejection rates in production cycle/finished goods |
| Produce product on time | Cycle time on the shop floor/missed production schedules |
| Produce the right quantity | Net quantity produced versus shop order requirements |
| Produce at lowest cost | Labor/material cost per unit/unfavorable variances |
| Control production/report accurately | Items reported—quantity versus added to inventory/shortages |
| Maintain a safe working area | Lost time injuries/workman's compensation claims |

extremely efficient and effective in the hands of the customer. Some relevant KRIs that could be utilized to evaluate these departments are shown in Table 7.17.

### Pick, Pack, and Stage

Highly insightful and meaningful KRIs are not just picked out of the air. They are carefully packaged and staged to yield the maximum result in evaluating risk in key areas such as this. Key outcomes in this area could be defined utilizing the KRIs presented in Table 7.18.

### Shipping and Logistics

Logistically your KRIs should be timely and focused, and lead you to the right destination. In this area with a well-defined set of related KRIs, your ship will sail smoothly across the seas of commerce. KRIs to keep in mind are shown in Table 7.19.

**TABLE 7.18** Pick, Pack, and Stage–Defined Outcomes/KRIs—PPS

| Key Outcomes | KRI |
| --- | --- |
| Ensure all items are accurate in order | Credit memos for wrong items/shipping expense $3\times+$ |
| Ensure order is properly packed | Credit memos for damaged goods—nontransport |
| Ensure that all items in order ship | Credit memo for items short/shipping expense $2\times+$ |
| Ensure staging of items together | Credit memo for items short/shipping expense $2\times+$ |
| Ensure orders staged timely | Demurrage charges/shipping expense $2\times+$ |

**TABLE 7.19** Shipping and Logistics–Defined Outcomes/KRIs—S&L

| Key Outcomes | KRI |
| --- | --- |
| Ensure all items loaded as staged | Credit memos for wrong items/shipping expense 3×+ |
| Ensure order is properly loaded | Credit memos for damaged goods in transit |
| Ensure that all items in order ship | Credit memo for items short/shipping expense 2×+ |
| Operate a safe working area | Lost time accidents/WC claims/litigation for injuries |
| Schedule shipping vehicles timely | Demurrage charges/shipping expense 2×+ |
| Most efficient shipping method | Freight/forwarding expense |
| Most effective shipping method | Customer claims/complaints |
| Ship all items on schedule | Missed shipping dates/delivery dates |

The ability to identify key outcomes and then to define KRIs that clearly measure whether the outcomes are being achieved or not is a science unto itself. I do not proclaim to be the only person that can do this by a long shot. However, I would not be reticent to state that I would have little difficulty in defining key outcomes for any organization of any type.

Then by association, I would have no reluctance in taking on the task of identifying the KRIs that should be utilized in any and all situations to objectively evaluate said outcomes. I sincerely believe that somehow, someway all outcomes and therefore by extension all risks can be measured with only rare exceptions. But to do this requires imagination, business knowledge, and desire.

## DETAILED INVENTORIES OF KRIs: WHEN GREATER AUTOMATION/SOPHISTICATION IS ACHIEVED

In an attempt to demonstrate that the closing paragraph of the preceding section is true, I will present a series of pairings of related risk events and KRIs. The pairings will be presented in various areas of the enterprise.

### Financial

Table 7.20 shows some lower-level and more specific KRIs that can be utilized to monitor or evaluate risk events in the financial area.

Some others of importance that could be considered might be those shown in Table 7.21.

**TABLE 7.20** Risk Events/KRIs—Financial

| Risk Event | KRI |
|---|---|
| Bond covenants violated | Notification of violation of covenants |
| Delays in financial reporting | Reporting deadlines missed |
| Financials inaccuracy | Significant deviation period to period |
| Failure to recognize expenses timely | Smoothing of financial results—expenses |
| Inventory valuation—misstated | Inventory adjustments—valuation |
| Management fraud—misrepresentation of financial statements | Inconsistency in financials versus market/economy |
| Misstatement of financials | Inconsistency with industry/competition |
| Net income manipulation | Cost/unit of volume inconsistent |
| Not funding/underfunding pension plan | Actuarial studies—investments versus liability |
| Repair accrual inadequate | Actual repairs > accrued balances |
| Unrecognized contingency/Off the B/S liabilities | Restoration requirements versus accruals |
| Director and officer liability for misstatement/inaccurate financials | Utilization of D&O liability insurance |
| Shareholder action versus organization | Shareholder action/initiatives proxy |
| The Enron Syndrome | Minimal deviation from budget/targets |
| IRS–FICA/withholding nonpayment | IRS interest penalties |
| IRS—income tax payments not made | IRS interest penalties |
| Failure to capture revenue/untimely capture | Average unit sales price declining |
| Improper revenue recognition | Average unit sales price increasing |
| Not capturing revenue accurately | Inconsistency in revenue/sales volumes |
| Payroll—duplicate payments | Inability to reconcile payroll |
| Payroll—overtime payments inaccurate | Employee complaints to payroll |
| Payroll—overpayment | Average labor cost per unit increasing |
| Payroll—ghost employees | Unclaimed W2s |
| Payroll—underpayments | Manual/reissued checks |
| A/P—Paying too much for goods/services | Missed cash discounts |
| A/P—Risk of restricted terms such as COD | Days in A/P increasing |
| Future liability—cash discounts taken not earned | Unearned cash discounts taken |

**TABLE 7.20** (*Continued*)

| Risk Event | KRI |
|---|---|
| Multiple accounts payable—locations vendors not paid timely | Vendors' interest charges |
| Improper aging of A/R | Significant favorable improvement in age buckets |
| Untimely/inaccurate invoicing | Customer complaints/credit memos issued |
| Credit risk/A/R buildup/fictitious sales | Days in A/R increasing |
| Customer insolvency | Receivables write-offs |
| Customer credit—overextended | Days in A/R increasing |
| Fixed assets value—misstated | Depreciation/amortization understated |
| Assets not transitioned correctly in system changeover | Variation of subledgers to new system balances |
| Construction in Progress (CIP) not moved to fixed assets timely | Completion versus capitalization date delay |

**TABLE 7.21** Risk Events/KRIs—Global Financial

| Risk Event | KRI |
|---|---|
| Significant Sarbanes-Oxley violation—financials | Days to close extending |
| Significant Sarbanes-Oxley violation—financials | Number of adjusting entries |
| Significant Sarbanes-Oxley violation—financials | Dollar volume of adjusting entries |
| Cash shortage | Accelerating accounts receivable |
| Cash shortage | Increasing accounts payable |
| Financial statement manipulation | Always matching expectations |
| Capital shortage | Aging asset base |
| Significant operational problems | High volumes of credit memos |
| Lack of pricing power | Downward trend in prices |

Examples of high-level global types of key risk indicators that could be utilized within the financial area are as follows:

- Cash position
- Increasing days in Accounts Receivable
- Increasing days in Accounts Payable
- Declining operating margins

- Declining fixed asset base
- Shrinking current ratio
- Declining sales volumes
- Increasing inventory balances
- Significant unfavorable purchase price variances
- Inverted loan portfolio curve
- Increasing inventory of nonperforming loans
- Increase the debt-to-equity ratio increasing interest expense
- Decreasing interest earnings
- Increase in interest expenses
- Increase in bad debt reserves
- Increase in inventories obsolescence reserves
- Volume of write-offs and obsolete and slow-moving inventories

## Operational

As in finance there are plenty of examples that can be offered up as regards operational failures to perform; here are just a few to demonstrate the point. An operational risk register may look like Table 7.22 detailing the risk event and key risk indicators.

Examples of high-level global types of key risk indicators that could be utilized within the operational area are as follows. Examples of global risks and indicators are shown in Table 7.23.

Other high-level KRIs that can be utilized in operational areas would be as follows:

- Quality indicators
- Workman's compensation claims
- Returned goods and services
- Warranty claims
- Demurrage charges
- Customer complaints
- Late deliveries
- Overtime hours
- Production declines
- Indirect labor hours
- Morbidity rates
- Recidivism rates
- Number of loss events

**TABLE 7.22** Risk Events/KRIs—Operational

| Risk | KRI |
| --- | --- |
| Drivers exceed 15 hour/day DOT limits/70 hours week | Drivers logs versus payroll hours |
| Intervention by regulators—Increase in WC claims | WC Claims Trend |
| Maintenance of trucks not done as required | Lack of entries to a preventive maintenance log |
| Contractor fatalities | Number of Incidents/M(O)SHA actions |
| Batch plant freezes up and nonfunctional | 0 production volume |
| Cold joint slabs—pour too slow | Number of re-pours |
| Concrete fails strength tests—core/swiss hammer | Number of failures |
| Customer call system not logged off properly | Customer complaints |
| Customer call system unresponsive | Excessive wait time |
| Injuries to others performing activities on our property | Incident reports to risk management |
| Lost loads | Failure to deliver notices from customers |
| Quality assurance failure | Increasing costs |
| Untimely calls to drivers on canceled jobs | Paid with no delivery |
| Liability for concrete spill/dump property damage | Expenses |
| Increase in litigation—personal injury | Lawsuits/incidents |
| Heat at job site not 280–300 degrees | Reshipment and reinstall costs |
| Order canceled after asphalt plant startups | Expenses with no revenue |
| Blending system inaccurate = bad mix | Shipments rejected |
| Decrease in production levels | Tons of output |
| Operating costs increasing | Total operations expense |
| Labor costs increasing | Total labor hours |
| Overtime hours increasing | Total hours of overtime |
| Personal injury/death—employee | Number of reported incidents |
| Personal injury/death—person on premises | Number of reported incidents |
| Products losing leadership position | Decline in primary product line volumes |
| Total dependence on limited products/applications | New road construction technology |
| Increase in litigation—personal injury | Lawsuits/incidents |

*(continued)*

**TABLE 7.22** (*Continued*)

| Risk | KRI |
| --- | --- |
| Excessive labor content in product cost | Labor $/unit produced |
| Excessive material handling expense | Material movement cost/unit produced |
| Site cannot be worked—material slide/cave-in | Clean up expenses/nonproductive labor |
| Failure of scaling system to interface with auto custom mix system | Manual activity/invoicing/adjustments |
| Breach of contract | Notifications of contract breach |
| Flyrock—Injury and damage | Payment by locations to complainants |
| Personal injury—third-party contractor | Number of reported incidents |
| Personal property damage | Number of reported incidents |
| Product liability—failure | Number of reported incidents |
| Product liability—personal injury | Number of reported incidents |
| Real property damage | Number of reported incidents |
| Competitive disadvantage | Loss of market share |
| Drop off in demand for primary product lines—economy | Volume decline in primary products |
| Geographic shift of the market away from locations | Volume decline in primary products |
| Transportation costs restrict entry to market and pricing | Transportation cost/ton |
| Customer confidence decreasing | Customer complaints |
| Negative community impact—bad neighbor | Volume of complaints—neighbors |
| Undesirable public behavior by employees | Arrests—actions by law enforcement |
| Increase in litigation—nuisance issues | Lawsuits/claims |
| Increase in litigation—small claims | Claims/incidents |
| Conveyors over highway transporting rock—new quarry | Number of incidents of material spills/damage |
| Increase in litigation—personal injury | Lawsuits/incidents |
| Accidents involving aggregate haulers with our loads | Number of incidents |
| Aggregate haulers not available for transport of materials | Missed deliveries |
| Customer dissatisfaction with products/services | Customer volumes/sales declines |
| Excessive rework of products required | Total reshipped units/total units shipped |

**TABLE 7.22** *(Continued)*

| | |
|---|---|
| Inefficient plant utilization/effectiveness | Electricity cost |
| Increase in litigation—personal injury | Lawsuits/incidents |
| Site cannot be worked—site is flooded/too wet to work | Clean-up expenses/nonproductive labor |
| Steel fabrication contractors—poor-quality work | Collapse or failure |
| Fraud/kickbacks on construction | Large volume # of change orders |
| Purchase card discount not received/applied | No records of discount received |
| Turnkey operations—failure to fulfill obligations | Lack of capital replacement as required |
| Local contractors selected as opposed to qualified low bid | Change orders—# volume |
| Low cost bidder selected—not pre-qualified | Change orders—# volume |
| Fraud can be perpetrated within vendor relationships | Channeling of purchases to one vendor |
| Gentleman's agreement used instead of contract | Channeling of purchases to one vendor |
| Inability of contractors to guarantee work/indemnification | Poor financial condition |
| Ineffective vendor rating system | High volume of adjustments in A/P |
| Insurance certificates not current | No central records of certificates—capital |
| Lease interest rates not fixed—interest rate acceleration | Increase in interest expense |
| Purchase cards/check requests bypass purchasing | Percentage of total purchases |
| Purchase cards not properly monitored | No detail transaction review |
| Purchasing activities are inefficient | Blanket orders as % of total purchases |
| Subcontractors work not controlled/guaranteed | Contract language |
| Third-party liability not indemnified | Litigation $/case |
| Turnkey operations—insolvency of third party | Certification of financial statements |
| Turnkey operations—third-party owner operates | Contract language |
| Vendors given preferential treatment | Channeling of purchases to one vendor |
| Vendors not effectively evaluated for stability | Bankruptcy, liens |

*(continued)*

**TABLE 7.22** *(Continued)*

| Risk | KRI |
|---|---|
| Volume discounts are not maximized with vendors | No central purchasing function |
| Financial/other exposure at end of lease | Costs to relocate operations |
| Operating leases improperly written to protect organization | Financial losses due to contract language |
| Operating leases not effective | Cost of operating lease versus ownership |
| Poor contacting practices—purchasing | Penalties paid |
| Poor contracting—capital expansion | Modifications and change orders |
| Poor contracting—third-party operators | Litigation $ to enforce contract |
| Poor contracting practices—subcontractors | Litigation $ to enforce contract |
| Inability to acquire more green areas of sufficient size | Cost/acre large tracts prohibitive |
| Reserves not sufficient to sustain market expansion | Product shortages—by market |
| Coastal—unanticipated sink hole develops | Consultant $s/hours to rectify |
| Diminishing site reserves/deposits | Decline in region/company-wide reserves |
| DNR/DEQ—repetitive violations | Increasing number of inspections/onsite days |
| Negative community impact—environment | Clean-up expenses/damage settlements |
| EPA/DEQ/DNR—groundwater impact | Fines/penalties/clean-up expense |
| EPA/DEQ/DNR air pollution—dust particles | Fines/penalties/clean-up expense |
| DNR/DEQ—noncompliance | Fines/penalties/clean-up expense |
| EPA—Superfund Legislation | Culpability under definitions |
| Environmental issues caused by lessees on our property | Incidents of spills/noncontainment |
| Site restoration—not performed or excessive | Cost of site restoration |
| Failure to resolve environmental issues | Increase in incidents |

- Legal expenses
- Unanticipated capital replacements
- Accelerating unit costs
- Loss of market share
- Significant concentration of all types of credit memos

**TABLE 7.23** Risk Events/KRIs—Global Operational

| Risk Event | KRI |
| --- | --- |
| Unsafe workplace | Number of lost-time injuries |
| Poor product quality | Volume of warranty claims |
| Untimely delivery | Customer complaints |
| Unresponsiveness at phone center | Abandonment rates |
| Ineffective R&D | Lack of market acceptability |
| Poorly designed advertising campaigns | Lack of anticipated results |
| Ineffective training | Low productivity |
| Machinery downtime | Low preventive maintenance costs |
| Unacceptable customer service | Declining customer base |

## Regulatory

As in Finance and Operations there are plenty of examples that can be offered up in regard to regulatory risk events, and as you would expect there is some overlap to be anticipated. A regulatory risk register might look like Table 7.24 detailing the risk event and key risk indicators.

Examples of high-level global types of key risk indicators that could be utilized within the regulatory area are as follows. Example of risks and indicators are shown in Table 7.25.

Other high-level KRIs that can be utilized in the regulatory area would be as follows:

- Workman's compensation claims
- Legal expense
- Number of open compliance issues
- Regulatory fines
- Regulatory penalties
- Frequency of regulatory intervention by type
- Disgruntled employees
- High rates of employee turnover
- Repeatedly exceeding mandated regulatory timeframes
- Regulatory hot buttons from Web sites
- Increase in compliance costs
- Cost of external assistance in compliance areas
- Volumes of HIPAA data on premises
- Number of employees impacted by Family Leave Act

**TABLE 7.24** Risk Events/KRIs—Regulatory

| Risk | Key Risk Indicator |
| --- | --- |
| DNR/DEQ—repetitive violations | Increasing number of inspections/onsite days |
| Negative community impact—environment | Clean-up expenses/damage settlements |
| EPA/DEQ/DNR—Groundwater impact | Fines/penalties/clean-up expense |
| EPA/DEQ/DNR Air Pollution—Dust particles | Fines/penalties/clean-up expense |
| DNR/DEQ—Noncompliance | Fines/penalties/clean-up expense |
| EPA—Superfund legislation | Culpability under definitions |
| Environmental issues caused by lessees on our property | Incidents of spills/noncontainment |
| Site restoration—not performed or excessive | Cost of site restoration |
| Failure to resolve environmental issues | Increase in incidents |
| Nonpayment of taxes | Fines/penalties |
| Overpayment of property taxes—inaccurate asset locations | Inaccuracy in asset listings—PPT Jurisdictions |
| Assets purchased in acquisition at wrong basis | Inconsistent valuation criteria applied |
| SEC—misstatement of financials for tax cushions booked | Cushions accrued versus used |
| State—Income tax not paid properly | Fines and penalties re: state taxes |
| Critical transactions not recognized for tax consequences | Inability to identify critical tax issues |
| Development data availability/accuracy | Inability to identify critical tax issues |
| Inaccurate calculation of time value of money | Interest expense and penalties paid versus interest saved |
| Tax planning risk model not effective | Actual outcome versus anticipated |
| Tax software not useful for purpose intended | Manual operations instead of using SW |
| Tax strategies overly aggressive | $ adjustments paid to taxing authorities |
| Disclosure of medical/drug information | Medical/drug information in personnel file |
| IRS—Independent contractors violation | Proportion of workforce that are IC |
| Environmental issues not properly evaluated at acquisition | Subsequent shutdown |
| No environmental audits performed on acquisitions | Environmental audit expenses |

**TABLE 7.24** (*Continued*)

| | |
|---|---|
| Purchase or acquire contaminated property | Fines/penalties/clean-up expense |
| Increase in litigation—environmental issues | Lawsuits/incidents |
| Effective risk assessment of ongoing operations not done | Open items not followed up on |
| Ineffective evaluation of acquisition candidate prior to close | Environmental audit expenses |
| Permit acquisition—Inability to obtain/costly | Applied for versus granted |
| Phase I environmental audits ineffective | Environmental insurance claim |
| Benefits not offered to contractors/temps who = employees | Federal guidelines for exempt employees not met |
| Classifications of employees not correct—Exempt and Non | Federal guidelines for exempt employees not met |
| OSHA/MSHA incident reporting inaccurate | Incidents versus reported discrepancy |
| Workers Compensation Claims—Cross-over to HB plan | Incidents versus WC claims |
| Litigation for regulatory violation | Increase in legal fees/special counsel |
| Denial, loss, or restriction of permits | Lost production days |
| Litigation for regulatory violation—Industry-based | Regulatory actions against competitors |
| MSHA—safety inspections required on equipment | Accidents with no equipment record |
| ADA—medical information present in employment files | Medical info present |
| ADA—Working conditions do not accommodate | Fines/penalties/rectification expense |
| Contract labor/temporary employees | Independent contractors meet IRS tests |
| HIPPA—Medical information not being held confidential | Medical info present |
| ADA—Segregation of medical information violation | Medical info present |
| ADA—Worker accommodation violation | Notices of violations/litigation |
| ATF explosives handling/reporting | Citations of violations from regulators |
| COBRA constructive notice of benefits | Fines and penalties |
| COBRA monitoring of eligibility | Part/ETO 18 m |
| EEOC—Discrimination against minority contractors | Notices of violations/litigation |

(*continued*)

**TABLE 7.24** (*Continued*)

| Risk | Key Risk Indicator |
|---|---|
| EEOC age discrimination | Average age of persons laid off or fired |
| EEOC hostile workplace (sexual harassment) | Number of complaints to human resources |
| EEOC violation—Hiring discrimination | Notices of violations/litigation/fines/penalties |
| EEOC violation—Promotion discrimination | Notices of violations/litigation/fines/penalties |
| EPA protected species violation | Notices of violations/litigation/fines/penalties |
| EPA Superfund cleanup violation | Notices of violations/litigation/fines/penalties |
| Family Leave Act denial of employment | Notices of violations/litigation/fines/penalties |
| FLRB—Unions and elections—Violations | Notices of violations/litigation/fines/penalties |
| Health benefits discrimination | Notices of violations/litigation/fines/penalties |
| HIPAA—Medical information confident | Notices of violations/litigation/fines/penalties |
| Local—Air quality violation | Notices of violations/litigation/fines/penalties |
| Local—Building code violation | Notices of violations/litigation/fines/penalties |
| Local—Fire Marshall violation | Notices of violations/litigation/fines/penalties |
| Local—Land use planning and regulations-permit loss | Notices of violations/litigation/fines/penalties |
| Local—Noise ordinance violation | Notices of violations/litigation/fines/penalties |
| Local—Special assessments unanticipated | Notices of violations/litigation/fines/penalties |
| Local—Zoning violation | Notices of violations/litigation/fines/penalties |
| MSHA noise standards not adhered to | Notices of violations/litigation/fines/penalties |
| MSHA diesel emissions std. not adhered to—Particulates | Notices of violations/litigation/fines/penalties |
| Overtime payment propriety | Overtime hour concentration with certain employees |
| Random drug screens—performance | Maintenance of drug screens on premises |
| Robinson-Patman predatory/unfair pricing | Pricing patterning |
| State—DNR effluent discharge violation | Notices of violations/litigation/fines/penalties |
| State—DNR—site restoration | Notices of violations/litigation/fines/penalties |
| State—DNR air quality | Notices of violations/litigation/fines/penalties |
| State—DNR water table pollution/impact | Notices of violations/litigation/fines/penalties |
| State—Sales and use tax | Notices of violations/litigation/fines/penalties |

**TABLE 7.24** (*Continued*)

| | |
|---|---|
| State—Hours and wages, breaks, and workers' rights | Notices of violations/litigation/fines/penalties |
| State—Unemployment compensation not covered | Notices of violations/litigation/fines/penalties |
| Sexual discrimination—Hostile work place | Suggestive material present on site—volume |

**TABLE 7.25** Risk Events/KRIs—Global Regulatory

| Risk Event | KRI |
|---|---|
| Unsafe workplace | OSHA violations/penalties |
| Discriminatory employment practices | Employee complaints |
| Untimely processing of claims | Low first-pass rate |
| Untimely processing of claims | SIC fines and penalties |
| Violation of grant reporting requirements | Loss of grant funding |
| Failing to constructively notify on COBRA | Excessive fines and penalties |
| Major environmental violations | Significant increase in the legal expense |
| Failure to file taxes promptly | Fines and penalties |
| Failure to file required reports w/SEC | Fines, penalties, delisting |

- Number of employees in the military
- Percent of employment base that are independent contractors
- Percent of employment base that are temporary employees
- Volume of hazmat material on the premises
- Volumes of explosive materials on the premises

## Technological

The same rules apply regarding the number and variety of risk events that can exist in IT/technology. A technology risk register may look Table 7.26, detailing the risk event and key risk indicators.

Examples of high-level global types of key risk indicators that could be utilized within the IT/Technology area are as follows in Table 7.27.

Other high-level KRIs that can be utilized in the IT/Technology area would be as follows:

- Turnover rates in technical IT positions
- Downtime

**TABLE 7.26** Risk Events/KRIs—Technology

| Risk | KRI |
| --- | --- |
| Servers at remote locations not overseen by IS | Downtime/loss of data |
| Inefficient utilization of IS/IT resources | IT cost per gigabyte of data |
| Required capital expenditures—Information Technology | Three releases behind on vendor software |
| Nonstandardization of processing platforms | Inventory of operating systems/platforms |
| Physical security over servers | Number of user control servers |
| Training of user department on system is deficient | Minimal or zero training expenses |
| Employees not deactivated after termination | File compare active employees to security file |
| Field techs share passwords with others | File compare for access/location/ attendance |
| Passwords not changed as required | Password effective time length |
| Security by job position—status not changed | Multiple accesses/employee |
| Sharing of passwords by employees | Follow compare for password use/ attendance |
| No tech support and ownership of interfaces written | Contract language regarding IP ownership |
| Ineffective help desk operation—Reporting | Coding inaccuracy in help tickets |
| Excessive modifications of software | Custom programming costs |
| Inability to integrate ERP effectively | Downtime/extended processing time |
| Inability to integrate application software effectively | Downtime/extended processing time |
| Inability to perform—Database administration | Job turnover stats—DBAs |
| Inability to perform technical support of application systems | Consultant reliance/fees/hours |
| Ineffective help desk operation—Assistance | Call time/abandonment rates |
| Ineffective application support programming | Failure on systems test/repeated user change requests |
| Ineffective system utilization | Required data not available timely |
| Intellectual property rights not secured— Systems | Loss of code/programming delays |
| Multi-vendor system strategy not effective | Time required to resolve problematic issues |
| Poor Contracting—Vendor developed SW | Cost overruns/delayed implementations |

**TABLE 7.26** *(Continued)*

| | |
|---|---|
| Poor implementation of vendor developed SW-users | Zero training expense/repeated helpdesk calls |
| Replacement of application system potential | More than three releases behind/high maintenance costs |
| Software Publishers Association (SPA)—Not in compliance with SW licensing copyrights | No oversight of utilization rates/licensing |
| Underutilization of systems capability and capacity | Percentage of capabilities actually utilized |
| Unreliable IS/IT Communications | Downtime of communication links |
| Data lost in transmission via communications links | Downtime comm. links/volume of data lost |
| Inability to perform technical support of operating systems | Job turnover stats—technical support positions |
| Ineffectiveness of Internet site | Hits versus transactions consummated |
| Intranet/Internet utilization operational impact | Customer/affiliate feedback/survey outcomes |
| Capacity does not meet requirements | Capacity analysis—utilization % |
| Inability to recover from outage/interruption | Recovery time increasing |
| Ineffectiveness of disaster recovery plan—Hot site | Promised recovery time versus test results |
| Ineffective anti-virus policies and procedures | Virus infection of environment |
| No fallback plan if servers fail | Recovery time/inability to recover |
| Network/system downtime/loss | Dropped communications freq. |

- Transaction processing time
- Number of suspended transactions
- Reporting deadlines missed
- Volume of confidential data to be managed
- Number of different technology platforms/application systems
- Percentage of business conducted on the Internet
- IT operating costs per GB/TB of data
- Number of new systems implementations undertaken
- Number of outsourced IT arrangements
- Percentage of business conducted at shared sites
- Number of emergency fix procedures invoked
- Failed tests of uninterruptible power supplies
- Loss of communication with point-of-sale terminals

**TABLE 7.27**  Risk Events/KRIs—Technology Global

| Risk Event | KRI |
| --- | --- |
| A compromise of critical sensitive data | Number of locations available |
| A compromise of critical sensitive data | Number of accesses granted to files |
| Loss of processing capability | Increasing downtime |
| Loss of processing capability | Very high percentage of capacity utilization |
| Ineffective helpdesk | Repetitive calls for same events |
| User dissatisfaction with a system | Excessive change requests |
| Ineffective front end edit and validation | Growing suspense file volumes |
| Inability to recover from a major outage | Recovery times/failure rates at hot sites |
| Ineffective systems implementation | Lack of usable or desirable data/productivity decline |

- Number of data integrity issues in data warehouse
- Inability to process critical transactions timely
- Number of systems that have historically not met budget criteria
- Turnaround time on required program changes

The previous discussion was for the purpose of energizing the concept of utilizing metrics for risk assessment. As can be seen by this exercise, the utilization of metrics can range from very high-level types of metrics to extremely low-level types of metrics and everything in between. The point is neither to overburden the enterprise with metrics nor to get into the minutiae of metrics in evaluating risk, but to demonstrate that virtually everything can be measured. The key exercise is to determine what things are worth measuring and then to utilize those as our risk criteria that we are going to track.

Depending on the business, there are limitless numbers of key risk indicators that could be employed. What has to be determined is which are the best key indicators for your particular business and establish those inventories for your usage.

In the next section we will not only talk about establishing risk registers; we will also utilize key parts of the organization from an administrative and operating standpoint as examples. These examples will then be accompanied by metrics of their key areas of concern that should be measured in each of these to actively manage risk effectively on a day-to-day basis.

## BUILDING A BASELINE RISK REGISTER

Risk registers are some of the most important elements of an ERM environment. Risk registers should be built for each and every logical business subset of the organization. The process of building a baseline risk register, one that is fundamental and easy to utilize, should be viewed as a straightforward process.

The first step is to determine what the primary functionality is of the logical business subset for which the risk register is being created. The second step is to define what the key outcomes are that are desired from the primary functionality of the business subset. The third step is to identify other risks that could prevent the key outcomes from occurring. Or, in a minimalist type of approach, take the inverse of the outcome, and utilize that as the critical risk. The fourth step is to identify KRIs, key risk indicators, for each of the risks, outcomes, or both depending upon your approach and incorporate those. The fifth step is to relate the key risk to the key mitigation technique, or in certain cases the related risk response, to ensure that the risk is properly controlled, limited, or responded to. The sixth step is to enhance the risk register with graphics displaying the risk or however one would choose to do so to maximize its utilization.

The risk registers can all be built with Excel spreadsheets, as they are very common and people know how to use them; then these can be embedded in the physical mapping of the enterprise. This practice will be discussed in the next section to highlight why this might be done and some of the key advantages of doing so.

Figure 7.3 is an example of a risk register and how it might be created for assimilation into an enterprise risk management scenario.

## EMBEDDING RISK REGISTERS AND KEY INFORMATION IN THE PHYSICAL MAPPING

The physical mapping of the enterprise is an essential part of making ERM successful. It will take discipline to put the map together and to include all aspects of the enterprise. However, not employing this discipline and expecting to have a successful ERM environment should normally be considered mutually exclusive. Without understanding where the organization operates, what it consists of operationally, and how it is physically structured, it becomes virtually impossible to effectively analyze risk.

| | Key Risk | Process Description | Risk Desc. Code | Risk Code | Key Outcomes | Risk Description |
|---|---|---|---|---|---|---|
| 78 | 1 | Insurance / Risk Management | 10.265002 | 2650001 | ensure that appropriate coverages are in place | gaps in insurance coverage are experienced |
| 79 | 1 | Insurance / Risk Management | 10.265002 | 2650002 | minimize insurance expense | insurance expense escalates vs. experience |
| 80 | 1 | Insurance / Risk Management | 10.265002 | 2650005 | utilize self-insurance appropriately | regular recurrence of similar or related risks |
| 81 | 1 | Insurance / Risk Management | 10.265008 | 2650003 | determine appropriate reserves for IBNR | self-insurance is underutilized / poorly utilized |
| 82 | 1 | Insurance / Risk Management | 10.265008 | 2650004 | minimize recurring risks | IBNR is not determined correctly |
| 83 | 1 | Business Development - M&A | 10.270002 | 2700001 | ensure that all models used are accurate | models are not tested or are found to be inaccurate |
| 84 | 1 | Business Development - M&A | 10.270002 | 2700002 | minimize the acquisition cost | Goodwill/excessive acquisition costs are evident |
| 85 | 1 | Business Development - M&A | 10.270002 | 2700003 | verify the accuracy of all assumptions used | assumptions are not verified as to accuracy |
| 86 | 1 | Business Development - M&A | 10.270002 | 2700004 | maximize due diligence effectiveness | due diligence is found to be lacking |
| 87 | 1 | Business Development - M&A | 10.270002 | 2700005 | verify accuracy of models post acquisition | models are not adjusted for erroneous assumptions |
| 88 | 1 | Plan Acquisitions | 10.275002 | 2750001 | determine the reserves of the potential acquisition | reserve amounts not accurately determined |
| 89 | 1 | Plan Acquisitions | 10.275002 | 2750002 | determine the condition of the plant | the condition of the plant is not accurately determined |
| 90 | 1 | Plan Acquisitions | 10.275002 | 2750003 | determine the efficiency of the operation | efficiency in the operation is not known / incorrect |
| 91 | 1 | Plan Acquisitions | 10.275002 | 2750004 | determine the production cost per ton | production cost per ton is incorrect |
| 92 | 1 | Plan Acquisitions | 10.275002 | 2750005 | accurately price the potential acquisition | price paid is excessive relative to value |
| 93 | 1 | Market Research/Analysis | 10.280002 | 2800001 | accurately analyze the market position | percentage of market is inaccurate |
| 94 | 1 | Market Research/Analysis | 10.280002 | 2800002 | maximize the business volumes | prices are too high |
| 95 | 1 | Market Research/Analysis | 10.280002 | 2800003 | forecast sales volumes accurately | sales volume forecasts are mistaken |
| 96 | 1 | Market Research/Analysis | 10.280002 | 2800004 | determine capacity to market percentage controlled | capacity determined is inaccurate |
| 97 | 1 | Market Research/Analysis | 10.280002 | 2800005 | maximize profit margin | prices are too low |
| 98 | 1 | Marketing | 10.300002 | 3000001 | create an effective marketing program | marketing program is ineffective |
| 99 | 1 | Marketing | 10.300007 | 3000002 | maximize revenue dollars with marketing dollars | revenue dollars generated are declining |
| 100 | 1 | Marketing | 10.300002 | 3000003 | maximize advertising dollars | advertising buys are poorly executed |
| 101 | 1 | Marketing | 10.300002 | 3000004 | maximize customer retention | customers are not retained |
| 102 | 1 | Marketing | 10.300002 | 3000005 | maximize customer relationships | customers do less business with the company |
| 103 | 1 | Marketing-Pricing / Sales | 10.301002 | 3010001 | maximize price per ton | price per ton is not maximized |
| 104 | 1 | Marketing-Pricing / Sales | 10.301002 | 3010002 | maximize ton sold | tons sold are slipping |
| 105 | 1 | Marketing-Pricing / Sales | 10.301002 | 3010003 | maximize marketplace position | position in the marketplace is suffering |
| 106 | 1 | Marketing-Pricing / Sales | 10.301002 | 3010004 | maintain high degree of customer satisfaction | customer dissatisfaction is increasing |
| 107 | 1 | Marketing-Pricing / Sales | 10.301002 | 3010005 | to expand customer base | customer base is contracting |
| 108 | 1 | Human Resources | 10.400002 | 4000001 | hire qualified employees | employees are not efficient and effective |
| 109 | 1 | Human Resources | 10.400002 | 4000002 | do appropriate background investigation | background investigation is inadequate |
| 110 | 1 | Human Resources | 10.400002 | 4000003 | minimize employee turnover | employee turnover is increasing |
| 111 | 1 | Human Resources | 10.400002 | 4000004 | control human resources expense | human resource expense for employees increasing |
| 112 | 1 | Human Resources | 10.400002 | 4000005 | maintain required staffing levels | vacancies remain unfilled |
| 113 | 1 | Employee Relations | 10.401002 | 4010001 | minimize union actions | union actions are on the increase |
| 114 | 1 | Employee Relations | 10.401002 | 4010002 | maximize employee satisfaction | employee dissatisfaction is increasing |

**FIGURE 7.3** Risk Register—Example

One of the great advantages of making a physical map is that it allows you to embed all of the key information relative to risk, controls, IT environments, or whatever other information you would like to readily access. By creating such a structure, you actually develop a central repository of all the critical information you need to run an ERM environment. This can be irreplaceable for effective corporate governance.

Within the mapping, the objects that would be embedded include all of the key data and information as well as illustrations and diagrams if required. This could be accomplished by populating Excel spreadsheets with this information and then embedding them in the mapped diagram. If the map diagram is created with Microsoft Visio, which nicely integrates with other Microsoft office products, a central repository of all risk, control, and governance information could be available at your fingertips for the use of all in the organization.

An example of what a physical map may look like is illustrated in Figure 7.4 with risk registers shown embedded in the map for ease of reference. Other illustrations are also embedded at the various locations such as IT environment diagrams and process maps.

By building a skeleton of the organization in the form of a physical mapping, you can construct something very similar to how the human body

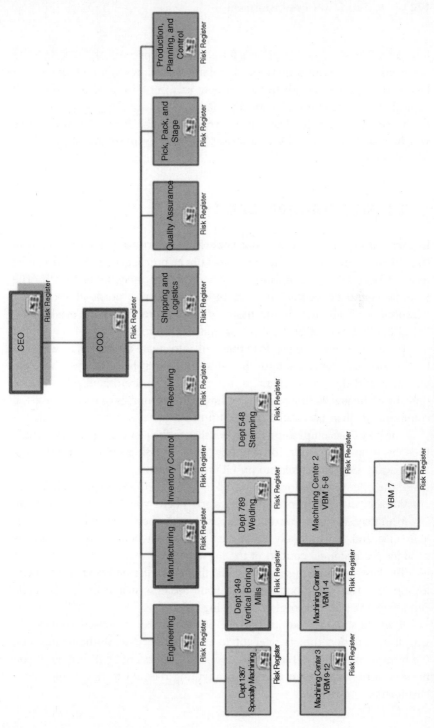

**FIGURE 7.4** Physical Map of Operations—Embedded Risk Registers

functions. The skeleton is the basis for all that is supported, the risk registers diagrams are the musculature, the data that flows up and down the logical data pathways are the blood flow and nervous systems. This is all capped off with how it is displayed visually, which are the physical features of the corporate entity. This means you can make it as sophisticated as you like, or just utilize the basics, as long as they meet the needs of the organization.

 ## THE MODULAR APPROACH

In those situations where it is not possible to determine the entire physical structure in one exercise, or where it may not be practical to do so in the short term or near term, organizations can employ the modular approach. The modular approach centers on the most critical risk areas of the entire organization. That then is the basis for setting precedents for establishing the ERM environment in the most expeditious manner.

What we're not trying to do in this book is to create a monster; all we want is a logical and systematic approach that is strategically laid out. If you have the resources and the commitment to undertake the entire organization at one time, by all means do it. If you do not have such resources or do not have the commitment, then bite it off a piece at a time.

One way of accomplishing this is by utilizing the modular approach, which then by definition centers on the key areas of risk with the intention of strategically aligning them into an ERM environment.

If the intent is to follow the logical approach set out in this book for the creation of your ERM environment, start where you have the best data. Unfortunately, the one drawback here is that the best data normally resides in finance, and, as we already established, that is not where risk resides, but it is good for the historical context of the impacts.

The best option is to search out the financial information that gives you insight into the operational areas of your business where the problematic conditions exist for purposes of managing risk.

It would stand to reason that one of the first key exercises would be to get all information that is relevant to customer service. Without question, the biggest risk you can have is no customers. Therefore by definition, if you have no other alternative, start with anything relevant to how happy your customers are.

In finance some of this information would be data such as:

- Credit memos
- Deductions or short plays
- Allowances
- Free goods or services
- Discounts
- Number of units shipped/services rendered

In operations some of the information and data would be:

- Customer complaints
- Volume declines
- Lack of orders booking
- Quality and defect occurrences
- Customer turnover statistics
- Inventory buildup

Once you have determined your critical areas of risk, you can start to put them in place one at time. The objective of the exercise would be to move on to the next area of maximum risk and utilize the best data available to build a methodology in that area and so on. You would simply progress stepwise from there but in a logical fashion.

The modular approach is really about building an ERM environment in some systematic fashion a piece at a time until the whole project is complete. This may be a preferable strategy when resources and/or commitment are limited or severely lacking. However, this is not the preferable way to build an ERM environment. For an ERM environment to be highly functional, approaching it in a piecemeal fashion may be counterproductive. However, given the alternative of not having an ERM environment at all, this is definitely preferable.

 **DETERMINING A FOCUSED OUTCOME GROUP (FOG)**

A method of approaching a modular ERM environment or, as an alternative, establishing focused risk analyses methodologies, you can construct focused outcome groups (FOGs). There are certain parts of the enterprise that lend themselves naturally to objective-based risk assessment.

These groups are naturals for analytically applied techniques and as such should be evaluated accordingly. Therefore, even if you run a subjective-based environment, although I hope not, you could intersperse FOGs within that environment as well.

There are a number of advantages that can be gained by utilizing metrics whenever possible even if it is not on a grander scale of ERM. Focused outcome groups are just that kind of situation. As an example, let's talk about call centers, which tend to be very risk-intense parts of the organization. Call centers fulfill a multitude of roles within organizations. Some of the functionalities that are normally housed in call centers are customer support and revenue generation.

Call centers provide the public face of the organization to the customer base in most instances. Think back on your own personal experiences with call centers. Did you have any bad experiences? Better yet, have you ever had a good experience that you were totally satisfied with? In many cases, unfortunately, the answer to the first question is *yes*, and to the second question is *no not really*. That is a dismal commentary on how call centers tend to be perceived by a very critical part of our business, our customer base.

In most instances call centers tend to be an outsourced arrangement, which literally means we have turned over a critical part of our business to somebody whom we have little control over. Therefore it is imperative that we manage the risk of these operations quite closely, as they can do extensive damage to the organization if not properly monitored.

The following is an example of call centers and the key statistics that may be measured to evaluate risk of these operations. When you have multiple call centers in place, you will have to evaluate the risk in a two-stage process. The first stage of the process is to do global analytics on all call centers for their primary outcomes or functionalities.

By performing the global analytics, the organization should be able to determine which of the call centers performs at the least acceptable level, with the lowest level of customer satisfaction. Once that has been determined, then the organization can analyze each of the metrics within those call centers that were shown to be most problematic, ergo the most risky.

By tracking each of the key metrics within the call center, you can systematically and methodically drill down to the specific point of concern. When you have arrived at this point, you will be standing next to the root cause of your problem. The analysis to be employed would be the following to determine a highly effective methodology of evaluating the risk in a call center.

Identify the key metrics related to the primary outcomes of a call center. The key metrics would be:

- Length of time on the call
- Time to answer
- Number of calls referred to a higher tier (level)
- Abandonment rates
- Employee turnover
- Customer satisfaction surveys
- Results of call quality monitoring

Once the key metrics have been identified, the data should be obtained and analyzed for each and every call center. An example is shown in Figure 7.5.

 ## NET RISK VERSUS RESIDUAL RISK

An area that needs to be discussed prior to launching into the analytics is some terminology related to risk and how risk is evaluated. In the audit profession, where I have spent the majority of my career, they have a tendency to utilize terminology that is very audit-centric as opposed to business-centric. A critical example of that pertains to risk assessment. The following is an expression that represents how auditors even in this day and age evaluate risk, strangely enough.

$$\text{Inherent Risk} - \text{Controls} = \text{Residual Risk}$$

What is even more interesting is how they arrive at the conclusion of residual risk. The process normally involves a scoring system in subjective-based risk assessment—that is, scoring and calculating with some magic formula. In other words, they score the inherent risk, or everything that could go wrong in a situation, five, four, three, two, one, or some derivative thereof. They then look at the controls that have been applied to the situation, and again they score at five, four, three, two, or one based upon the maturity framework for controls as espoused by the big consulting houses. Then, they make some behind-the-scenes calculations to determine the effectiveness of the controls at mitigating the risk. Finally, they arrive at residual risk.

This is all well and good, but it's still a bunch of opinions with absolutely no relationship to data or factual information in many cases, if not all. To me, of course, this does not employ common sense and is irrelevant to the exercise of risk assessment.

# Call Center Comparison

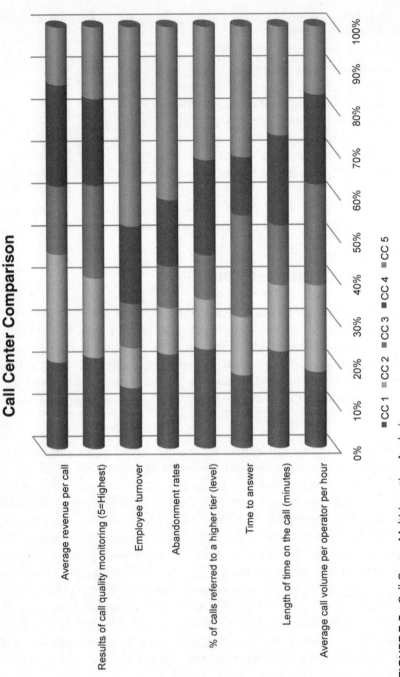

FIGURE 7.5   Call Center Multi-Location Analysis

In my many years of using analytics I have tried to apply them in the context of definitive common sense and logic. I also am a proponent of using business terminology as opposed to audit terminology. The one thing that I have never understood is why auditors talk to business people as though they were auditors; clearly they are not.

My approach to the same type of the previous analysis is to clearly use metrics in the context of how they are developed by the business as it operates. In other words, I do not substitute my own opinion in some artificial scoring system for the actual operating information of the business itself. After all, isn't the business what we're trying to risk assess and, in their case, audit? Therefore, the following expression is how I approach this subject matter, stated in business terms not audit terms.

$$\text{Gross Risk} - \text{Mitigation} = \text{Net Risk}$$

You might ask, *Why bother?* The reason is the evaluation of controls and their relevance to the mitigation of risk can be much more effectively arrived at by utilizing this methodology. Gross risk is, of course, everything that can still go wrong in the organization. Mitigation is not only controls, but also other appropriate risk responses that have been brought to bear on the risk conditions. Net risk, when utilized here in an objective-based risk environment, is the analysis of the movement of the outcome measures, KRIs, as they are generated by the process(es) under consideration.

If you are measuring the appropriate things and the outcome measures are moving in a negative direction, by definition your process is out of control, ergo risky. When the pattern of KRIs moves in a negative direction, then by definition your net risk is increasing. This is a highly effective way of evaluating not only the process effectiveness in achieving its outcomes, but also if it is operating in a controlled state of existence.

In all of the analytics discussed in this book, the previous expression should hold true. When the analytics show negative progression, no matter which one is employed, your net risk is increasing and your process is running in an uncontrolled state.

## BUSINESS RISK ANALYSIS TECHNIQUES (BRATs)

Another critical part of a data driven enterprise risk model is the selection of analytics to be used to evaluate the data. As noted earlier, the data and the form of that data is absolutely critical. It was noted that OR data, outcome focused raw data, is the best information to be utilized to evaluate risk. Likewise, it is imperative that the right analytic be used depending upon the risk condition that you are attempting to evaluate.

All analytics are not created equal and therefore cannot be utilized in every situation. There are very specific analytics that should be employed in enterprise risk management to maximize the effectiveness of the environment. We'll discuss a number of different analytics in this section, but they all share a very common trait; they are basic, straightforward, easy to understand analytics.

Why is this? It is because there is no reason to introduce unnecessary complexity into the risk analysis process. I have discovered over many years of doing this that complexity only breeds complexity, which runs counter to the whole theory behind this book.

## Trend Analysis

Trend analysis is far and away one of the simplest types of analytics that can be employed. It lends itself extremely well, however, to the analysis of risk and certainly to the evaluation of risk in a post-control situation. By looking at the analytics KRIs, it is quite easy to determine if a process is in control or out of control. As discussed earlier, what we are always trying to discover with risk analytics is whether the risk has been mitigated or not by the controls or other mitigation techniques.

Some of the unique characteristics of trend analysis are that it presents a good baseline history, if properly employed, of the organization and how it has performed in the past. This provides a sound basis for determining a predictable pattern of performance in the future in most stable business circumstances. In addition, when evaluating risk it provides a picture over time as to whether the net risk is increasing or decreasing. When the net risk reverses direction, whether that is positive or negative, you will know as fast as you can process the data.

By measuring a business over time and as it operates, it is easier to determine what the key indicators are saying about the business. Key risk indicators should be developed for every critical business process, not only to identify risk but also to identify potential efficiency and cost improvement opportunities.

Figure 7.6 demonstrates the evaluation of risk, using trend analysis in the banking sector. The subject matter of the graphic is lending and bad loans. Strangely enough I've been using this example for years and years in my seminars; little did I know that they were actually predicting the future of what

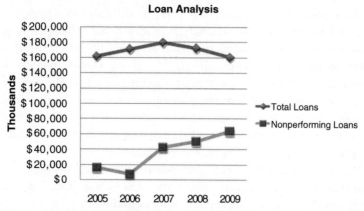

**FIGURE 7.6**  Trend Analysis—Example of Risk-Banking

would occur with the subprime mortgage meltdown. Please take a look at the example, and decide what it tells you about risk.

It can be seen in Figure 7.6 that there are two highly undesirable trends going on in this particular bank from a lending perspective. The top trend, which represents total loan portfolio on the graph, clearly depicts a reversal in the total loan portfolio. The bottom curve, which is nonperforming loans, or the waiting room for write-offs, has gained clear momentum to the upside.

Both of these curves are traveling in a risky direction, but worse yet they are converging on each other. The sad commentary here, of course, is that something has gone wrong in the lending process of the bank, and they are left with significant credit risk in their customer base.

This is a simple representation of a very serious situation. However, I believe it can be seen undeniably that if you put that in front of a board of directors sitting in a conference room, there is not a person in the room that would not see the risk.

## Pivotal Point of Change Analysis

Pivotal point of change analysis quite simplistically is abrupt movements in the data beyond which point the metrics move in an undesirable risk direction. The changes indicated in the data are indicative of underlying changes or conditions in the process or system, which could be undesirable. When plotted against a time axis in trend analysis, it can actually point out precisely where you should start looking for your root cause events and eliminates the guesswork from risk management.

Pivotal point of change analysis is a very useful tool in identifying risk. It is used in conjunction with trend analysis to spot those periods of maximum interest. The nice thing about pivotal point of change analysis is that it acts as an alert to the observer, immediately identifying change relative to the movement of the data. This is normally indicative of where the risk is either escalating or de-escalating depending on the circumstances. When employing metrics in risk analysis, it is imperative to understand what the movement of the data means. Pivotal point of change analysis is one of those key indicators: when you see the pattern, it is time to pay attention.

Those doing any type of risk management and analysis should take the time to identify the key analytics, which are going to help them to do their job much more effectively and efficiently. Failing to do this is simply going to make their job harder and make them less efficient at what they do.

Pivotal point in change analysis helps to isolate risk consolidation points, which are exactly where you should begin any type of root cause analysis. As mentioned previously, one of the key objectives of risk management is to identify root causes of unsatisfactory events and to eliminate them from the process or business. In addition, reviewing the analytics should give us clues as to what can be done or should be done to resolve the root cause conditions.

One bit of caution should be exercised when using this type of analytic. It occurs in the bottom trend presented in Figure 7.7. The bottom curve, which is the nonperforming loan curve, does not hold true to the analysis of pivotal point of change. The exception here is that the events that caused the loans to be nonperforming did not occur in those periods of abrupt change, but occurred

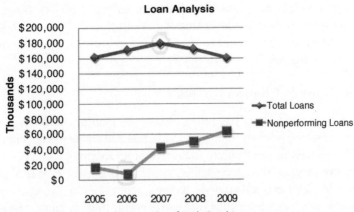

**FIGURE 7.7** PPC Analysis—Example of Risk-Banking

in an earlier timeframe. However, the point of change is still significant because all loans following the point of change can be utilized to determine a common thread of failure. This would be accomplished by step-down analysis that would trace the data through the various levels of the lending process and back to the loan officer.

## Mean Dispersion Analysis

Mean dispersion analysis (MDA) is probably one of the most useful of all of the analytics presented here in performing any kind of risk analysis work. One of the reasons is its flexibility. It can be applied to all types of situations in virtually all circumstances.

Mean dispersion analysis is used primarily for comparative purposes when you have multiple points of comparison that must be made to arrive at an intelligent decision relative to risk. In small, medium, and large organizations where you have multiple locations involved, this tool can be irreplaceable.

The fundamental premise of how it operates, in keeping with the theme of common sense and simplicity, is dispersion or variance from the baseline. The baseline is determined by one of two standards that are established.

If the organization has levels of achievement or standards of performance by which they operate, these can be utilized as the baseline for comparison. For example, if a retail organization will only allow 1.5 percent shrinkage in their inventory levels as a matter of corporate policy, that becomes a baseline for comparison of all of their retail outlets.

In those situations where a corporate standard has not been set or specified, a mean or average can be calculated for all of those locations and/or business subsets under consideration. Once the average has been established, each can be compared to that average to determine how far, how dispersed, they are from the mean. In this type of analytic dispersion from the mean, either positive or negative would be of interest.

For example, significant dispersion to the positive side from the mean could indicate a number of different things, some of which would be as follows. They may be what is referred to in many circles as "best practice" or "top of game," if you prefer being sporty, but they also could be lying through their teeth and perpetrating a significant fraud in how they are reporting. Anyone charged with the task of doing risk analysis and subsequent risk management would have to be extremely well versed in how to interpret these indicators.

However, once a knowledge base has been developed relative to what these indicators are—the common patterns, and how they normally perform—the information derived from them can be massive.

Mean dispersion analysis is used for comparative purposes and can be used to analyze anything from fast food outlets to call centers. It does not matter if the locations or business subsets under comparison are of different sizes. You would simply utilize ratio analysis to equalize the size of each one of the locations under consideration.

For instance, if you were comparing numerous manufacturing operations for risk in overtime, you would equalize them size-wise as follows. You would calculate overtime hours as a percent of total HRS paid to first identify the intensity by location. When you have determined the locations that have the highest intensity, you would then analyze them within their own operations. The purpose of this would be to isolate the points of risk where overtime is being concentrated. So in other words, you could analyze the overtime hours by shift, by machining center, and by supervisor. This would give you the ability to search for a number of different risks, not the least of which would be kickback schemes involving the supervisors and the workers.

Utilization of mean dispersion analysis allows you to focus the risk management resources where they can be the most effective. Identifying unacceptable root cause situations in the patterns greatly facilitates corrective actions that can be taken that will be meaningful and have high value added. This type of analysis can be utilized for thousands of different types of situations from efficiency and effectiveness to fraud. The key, of course, is that the outliers become the focus of attention once they have been determined. If employed, more effective resource allocation and overall business benefits will be possible.

## Threshold Analysis

Threshold analysis is a very versatile type of analysis. It would usually be performed when trying to analyze risk in the context of a predefined limit or other types of decision-making criteria. This type of analysis is extremely useful in validating that you do not have a fraudulent situation or that somebody is purposely manipulating an authority level. Threshold analysis is a very straightforward process as can be seen in the following example.

The risk you are trying to evaluate would be regarding all of those individuals who have the authority to approve contracts, for example, and their authority limit is attached to their user ID on the system within the contacting area. Say that the established limit of authority for everyone in that group is $50,000. If you want to evaluate the risk of fraud, or manipulation of the threshold, then you would simply download all of the transactions for a given period of time. Suppose you had downloaded all of the transactions, let's say for the period between July 1 and December 31. Then you could array them against the threshold for all transactions executed and see if the pattern displays anything undesirable.

Patterns that would be undesirable in this kind of analytic would be clearly a situation where a person has exceeded the authorized level but more importantly any cluster patterning just below the threshold. Cluster patterning just below threshold is indicative of people utilizing splitting techniques to defeat the threshold and to give them the ability to execute beyond their designated authority limits.

When people have the ability to operate over and above their authority limits and/or to split transactions thereby surpassing the limits, it puts them in a position of being able to extract favors and or kickbacks. They now have the ability to do things that may be lucrative to them in an undesirable and risky way. A key way of isolating risk and in many cases identifying potential fraud risk is through Threshold Analysis.

## Period-to-Period Comparative Analysis

Comparative analysis is the analytic that can put things into perspective, which otherwise may remain elusive. Comparative analysis is very commonly used in a number of industries to help develop strategies, analyze performance, and, of course, evaluate risk.

There are any number of period-to-period comparisons that can be performed. Some of the more common are as follows.

### Year-to-Year

Year-to-year comparative analyses are very common in the retail sector. For instance, retailers are very adept at comparing same store sales from year to year to determine how effectively they are performing in the marketplace. Also as we are all well aware it is not uncommon to do comparisons between years to see how much our retirement plans or stock portfolios have shrunk, or increased hopefully, as well.

### Quarter-to-Quarter

Quarter-to-quarter comparisons are actually some of the more standard types we see in financial reporting. We have all had the breathtaking experience of sitting in front of the tube watching CNBC and having our financial fate for the day decided when the quarterly reporting comes around. But there are many other things in many other businesses that should be looked at on this basis. Some items to be considered would be unit sales volumes, airline passenger miles flown, and so on.

In evaluating risk, quarter-to-quarter comparisons are valuable in that they move the risk evaluation timeline closer and closer to the point where action can be taken. One of the other areas of concern that is impacted on a quarterly basis is the number of required filings for regulatory organizations. Therefore, one of the areas for risk evaluation might be the timeliness of these filings or any other actions that were undesirable when viewed by the regulators.

### Month-to-Month

In looking at things in a month-to-month scenario, you start to shorten the time horizon to those things that are very relevant to how the business performs. When you have an unanticipated, significant downturn in activity from one month to the next, you start to look for all of the extraordinary factors that could give rise to such an event. Month-to-month comparisons are extremely helpful for taking stock in how the business is running for the purposes of making adjustments as required.

### Week-to-Week

The week-to-week timeframes for risk assessment get into the more minute areas of risk that are managed quite closely. You will truly see these much more in play in small to medium-sized businesses. The reason is that there is a need to manage cash, employees, and all other aspects of their business highly efficiently and effectively to maintain any type of competitive edge.

### Day-to-Day

In the any number of organizations, there is also the requirement to manage risk day-to-day. For example, hospitals manage bed count and patient census on a day-to-day basis due to the demands on staffing levels and also in relationship to case intensity. Many of the activities of other ancillary services of the hospital are tied to patient census. Some examples would be dietary, laboratory work, housekeeping, and so on.

Also you would see other areas of the hospital where day-to-day activity is critical to evaluate from a risk standpoint. For example, emergency rooms are constantly monitored for day-to-day activity and as you can imagine would have some predictable patterns.

Employing some common sense here, answer the following questions relative to risk. Which two nights of the week would you believe have the highest levels of activity in the emergency room? Which days and potentially nights of the week would probably have the highest degree of traumatic caseload concentration, barring something totally catastrophic occurring? It is probably not hard to conclude that the nights having the highest level of activity in the emergency room are going to be Friday and Saturday. The days and potentially nights are probably most likely to be Saturday and Sunday.

The evaluation of risk relative to the emergency room lends itself to common sense and data. The reason for the intensity of Friday and Saturday night, of course, is that more people tend to be out celebrating, in many cases over-celebrating and as a result end up incurring some kind of bodily harm. As regards Saturday and Sunday, the intensity of traffic on the roads is much higher due to the fact that many more people are driving as opposed to being at home or working in an office. In addition, you also have athletic events that are taking place, which lend themselves to injuries as well as those who view themselves to be athletes with the occasional weekend outing.

The point being made is that by looking at the actual facts and statistics it is much easier to predict the risk that there will be greater intensity in the emergency room during those timeframes. As such, staffing, equipment availability, and certain types of medical supplies must be present and in some cases in abundance.

The other obvious factors that play into this risk scenario are the key outcomes of the emergency room. How many people that were wheeled through those doors eventually walked out the door of the ER or the hospital? When the morbidity rates start to escalate, something is desperately wrong, or the intensity has shifted dramatically. Either of these cases demands instant action and that required changes be made to mitigate these undesirable outcomes.

Another real fact of life in emergency rooms, which also increases risk and must be monitored, is a utilization of these facilities as walk-in clinics. When this occurs, it obviously occupies extremely important facilities and talented caregivers. If this practice starts to interfere with the ability to deal with real emergencies, something has got to change. This pattern should be constantly analyzed and alternate facilities be established to deal with this type of care.

Period-to-period comparisons can be highly useful, but they must be closely scrutinized to ensure that they are reflecting the information that is desired. Period-to-period comparisons are most useful where the data is consistently measured, the business has been established for a period of time, and the fundamental product/service lines have not been altered in any way.

Other key issues that come into play are seasonal fluctuations, changes in the data being compared, and fundamental business changes such as reorganizations, centralization, and decentralization.

The key to utilizing period-to-period comparisons as an indicator of risk is clearly stability of the organization. In highly stable environments, these types of comparisons can be tremendously valuable in the types of risks they can evaluate and the information and insight they provide.

Some generic examples of data that can be compared would be as follows:

- Receivables by aging category
- Inventory concentrations:
  - Raw materials
  - WIP
  - Finished goods
- Sales by product line
- Gross margin by product line
- Mean time between failures
- Total units produced
- Claims processed

There are literally millions of them that can be utilized. An example of one that would be critical to the retailing industry is shown in Figure 7.8.

When looking at same store sales from year to year, an organization can start to analyze events that are taking place in their market area. A good example would be cannibalization of their own market by their predatory practices of establishing multiple outlets in defined market areas. The same types of comparisons could then be done by department within the retailer, by product line, and so on.

### Stratification

Another extremely useful tool is stratification. The key thing in performing any type of risk analysis is being able to recognize undesirable patterning. Data stratification allows for the grouping of similar items for analysis. Once the data are grouped, they can illustrate quite clearly concentrations of risks that were not evident before.

The key thing that must be remembered in this area, however, is that data discipline is absolutely essential for this to be successful. What you would find

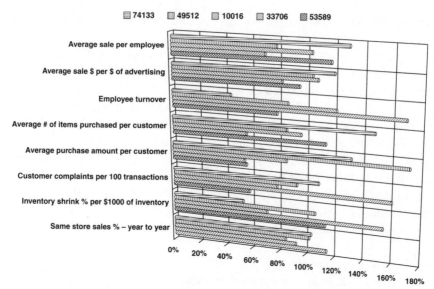

**FIGURE 7.8**  Comparative Analysis—Retail Outlets

more often than not in most companies and organizations is that their data discipline is badly lacking, and effective stratification would be severely hampered, if not virtually impossible to accomplish.

In many of my seminars I jokingly refer to the helpdesk as the helpless desk, and virtually everybody in the room laughs because they understand the problem. There are so many times when people come away from the helpdesk feeling not helped it is almost inconceivable that it would even be referred to as the helpdesk.

That aside, the issue that I am referring to here is the proper categorization of helpdesk tickets by reason code. This is absolutely essential to understand the pattern of issues that are confronting the users, so that appropriate analysis of the risk points can be done and the problems rectified. Unfortunately, if you were to analyze the statistics with any degree of regularity, you might determine that in fact a very high number of the codes used for the work tickets fall into two categories: miscellaneous and other.

This is another example of useless information gathered within a corporate or organizational structure. There must be absolute and strict discipline on how work tickets are coded, each and every time, to the appropriate reason codes, so that the problems can be analyzed and rectified. If this discipline is not installed and not taken seriously, the user community will become increasingly frustrated, and the degradation of service will intensify. The result will be increasing cost of operations.

Data stratification allows for the grouping of similar items to perform enlightening analysis. This is extremely important, because in many situations the data is not well organized for such analysis.

A good example of this would be the following. If most organizations were to respond honestly, I would be willing to bet that nowhere in their accounts receivable or customer database have they cross-referenced every customer that belongs to a common holding company. As a result, they have no idea how much of their business can be negatively impacted should they disenfranchise a member of that group. This is just one of thousands of examples that could be brought to the table.

Once critical data are grouped, the benefits become obvious:

- Totals become significant
- Types of data can be recognized as useful
- Concentrations of risk can be determined
- Issues previously unrecognized become apparent

Some common types of data that can be useful if stratified would be the following:

- Transactions by dollar size
- Transactions by date
- Transactions by customer
- Critical codes by data type
- Volumes by product line

This is the tip of the iceberg of things that can be stratified. However, within your own organizations you will find numerous examples of the areas where stratification can be irreplaceable as an analysis technique. The key is to properly identify which codes or data are indicative of risk and pursue them to maximize their information content. An example of stratification analysis is presented in Figure 7.9.

### Ratio Analysis

Another very commonplace analytic, but one that is extremely useful in the evaluation of risk, is ratio analysis. Ratios can be utilized to depict relationships

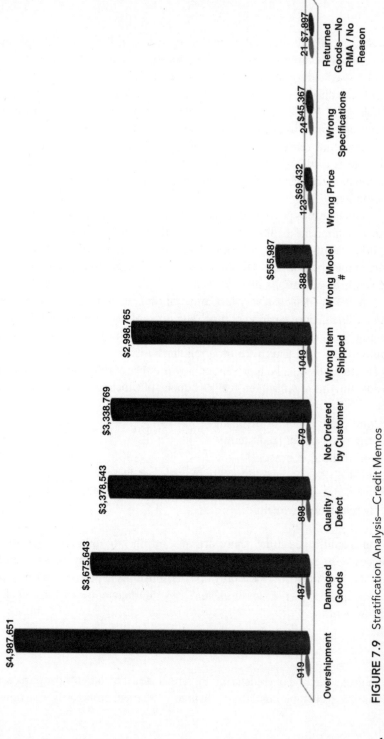

**FIGURE 7.9** Stratification Analysis—Credit Memos

189

between critical indicators of risk in the organization. They can also be utilized to common-size various parts of the organization for comparative purposes as was discussed earlier in mean dispersion analysis.

It is not difficult to generate ratios; what is difficult is to realize what they are telling us. When used properly, ratios can identify very significant and highly undesirable trends in the risky areas of an organization.

Operational ratios are exceptionally good indicators of the fundamental health of the company. An unfavorable movement in the inventory turnover ratio can be extremely helpful in analyzing process failure in critical areas of the organization.

Financial ratios provide multiple points of utility, and they can tell us a lot about our financial health as an organization, but they also are extremely insightful about operational issues. Operations are what drive the success or failure of the organization. The financial results are of course a reflection of the success of the operations and vice versa.

Figure 7.10 depicts a very fundamental ratio, days in accounts receivable (DAR), trended over a period of time. The upward progression in the graph is depicting a negative trend in the net risk position. This is not a trend that any organization would like to see on a regular basis.

Figure 7.10 could be representing any number of risks that may be taking place within this organization. A few examples of which would be the following:

- Inaccurate billing or invoicing
- Overextension of credit terms
- Poor collection practices
- Outside risk-financial instability of customer base
- Fraud risk—there is no customer at the other end of the transaction and therefore no payments

As would be assumed there are any number of different types of risk that could be taking place, which would be indicated by this patterning of the days in AR. Also, this is only one of thousands of very useful ratios that can be applied to risk analysis and risk management within the ERM environment.

## Profiling

Profiling is a method of predetermining areas of risk in data for the purposes of isolating unacceptable conditions and managing them proactively, real time or,

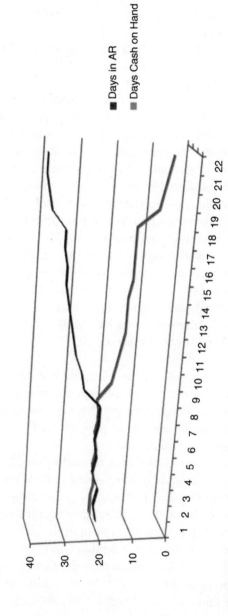

**FIGURE 7.10** Ratio Analysis—Risk Example

at worst, near time. By building profiles, risk management personnel can focus their attentions on those key areas that can bring the most harm to the corporation or organization. Profiling does involve some effort to correctly construct the tool, but once created it will be invaluable in its ability to manage risk in a timely manner.

Profiles are normally designed in such a manner that all issues are raised to the appropriate person on an exception basis only. In other words, profiling will not require the risk manager and/or risk assessor to constantly be looking for a certain risk condition. The profile should recognize the risk condition automatically and raise it to the attention of the appropriate risk manager/ assessment person. The inherent message here is that when an exception condition is raised it must be acted upon. The profile should be designed in such a manner as to not make reactions by key personnel elective but mandatory.

Profiling can be employed in any number of business circumstances and also has clear application in others where societal benefits can be attained. The best example of that is screening for terrorism suspects by profiling patterns of behavior. Some of the things that would clearly be included in these profiles would be countries visited, length of stay in the countries, group affiliations, personal acquaintances, travel habits, travel frequency, prior incidents—to name a few. Profiling can be accomplished in near time or real time automation, which must be adapted to the circumstances.

A couple of basic examples for applying profiling for risk assessment and risk management purposes are as follows.

*Wire Transfers*    Wire transfers are an obvious application for profiling from a number of different aspects. One of the keys is timeliness, and the need to respond and then take action as required. There are numerous laws that are in effect worldwide trying to control the flow of cash in and out of certain countries and to and from certain groups.

One of the best ways to do that is to establish profiles to preclude the sending of cash or to facilitate the movement of cash from those countries which may be deemed hostile. For instance, any movement in and out of those countries would be subjected to extreme scrutiny before any transactions would be finalized. Profiles could be built that would isolate any such transactions by geographic source or destination, financial institution, bank routing code, and so on. Any transaction determined to meet any of the unacceptable criteria would immediately be truncated. The nice part about it is that this can be fully automated and not rely on manual intervention for any of the activity.

*Money Laundering—Cash Deposits*    A historical profile can be built based on daily or other types of frequent activity. For instance, the deposit patterns of customers of a bank can be tracked by the cash in activity that takes place on their accounts on a daily basis. In other words, you can build a historical profile to determine if cash deposits are just below reportable thresholds and are distributed among various branches on the exact same banking date. When unacceptable patterns have been detected, a profile can be built to isolate those customers and bring them to the attention of the appropriate regulatory bodies or law enforcement officials.

*Retailing—Distribution and Warehousing*    Profiling can be a big player in the area of risk assessment but also in the area of maximizing opportunity. It is no secret that Wal-Mart has been highly successful in retailing, and much of that success has got to be attributed to their superiority in the area of systems and data analysis. With the vast amount of online data that Wal-Mart preserves on an ongoing basis, it is relatively easy to build profiles of typical consumption patterns by its customers.

Having these profiles in their possession allows them to distribute products to their stores much more efficiently and effectively, reduce shelf life and spoilage, turn their inventories, and maximize their profits. The type of competitive advantages that they have gained by employing these methodologies is massive and has facilitated their ascension to the top of the retailing industry.

Risk analysis and management has two sides: risk and opportunity. All the tools, methodologies, techniques, and data that we have talked about here can be used to evaluate and assess as well as manage either of these.

Figure 7.11 is a simple example of profiling analytics that could be used to evaluate customers in the context of what types of risk may be posed to the organization by the patterns that are made evident.

Customer concentration of:

- Discounts
- Allowances
- Credit memos
- Deductions
- Free products

### Data Patterns—The Fraud Factor

In deference to my esteemed colleague and very good friend, Leonard Vona, founder of Leonard Vona and Associates, a highly talented and sought-after

Customer REAL Profitability Profile

| Customer # | 12356 | 48976 | 98732 | 00178 | 01569 |
|---|---|---|---|---|---|
| Total Sales for the Year | $12,345,768 | $44,447,890 | $58,234,567 | $98,765,124 | $101,987,006 |
| Total Credit Memos | $ 38,765 | $ 876,054 | $ 8,589,729 | $22,387,690 | $ 11,697,650 |
| Total Adjustments | $ 12,546 | $ 2,897,650 | $ 2,956,478 | $ 3,452,678 | $ 4,678,945 |
| Total Discounts | $ 2,567 | $ 13,546 | $ 6,543,762 | $ 9,887,654 | $ 8,879,654 |
| Total Allowances | $ 1,298 | $ 229,876 | $ 2,812,326 | $ 5,985,235 | $ 6,796,543 |
| Total Deductions (Short Pays) | $ 0 | $ 12,095 | $ 3,218,760 | $ 8,871,234 | $ 5,123,987 |
| Total Cost of Sales | $ 6,456,892 | $21,908,765 | $29,452,009 | $46,324,897 | $57,980,976 |
| Total Discounts, Allowances, Adjusments Etc. | $ 55,176 | $ 4,029,221 | $24,121,055 | $50,584,491 | $37,176,779 |
| Total # of Units Sold - Product A | 8,746 | 18,345 | 23,769 | 39,897 | 45,834 |
| Total REAL Profit Per Customer | $ 5,833,700 | $18,509,904 | $ 4,661,503 | $ 1,855,736 | $ 6,829,251 |
| Average Unit Margin - Product A | $ 667.01 | $ 1,008.99 | $ 196.12 | $ 46.51 | $ 149.00 |

FIGURE 7.11  Profiling Analytics—Profitability Profile

forensic accounting firm, I will not purport to be an expert in fraud, which I am not. However, over my long audit career I have learned a few things about fraud and how to recognize it.

One thing that has become crystal clear is that fraud can be detected only when it is manifesting itself in patterns. The patterns can be detected only by employing analytics and large-scale data analysis. There is no other way to be successful in uncovering the risk of fraud.

As a result of Sarbanes-Oxley, I know people dread the term, a very interesting dilemma has been put upon the auditing profession. One of the key standards that is employed in work relative to SOX is the PCAOB,s Audit Standard 5. It says in so many words that auditors must, during the audit, be vigilant for fraud in those areas that might give rise to fraud. That is no small task and cannot be accomplished given the tools and techniques specified in the standard. The primary types of testing specified in the standard are walk-throughs and sampling. I will not belabor this point any further, but these methodologies will never detect fraud except by pure happenstance or sheer unadulterated luck.

But more to the point is that fraud is a huge exposure to virtually all organizations. A lot of people may not be aware of the points of exposure, but they are numerous. I think one of the ones that were most blatantly obvious in the latest banking scandal is executive compensation. Executive compensation in most instances has become the root of all evil with respect to corporate deception and less than above-board dealings with their shareholders and the public in general.

The patterns that indicate executive compensation may be an area of primary fraud concern have hopefully become exceptionally clear to everyone and do not warrant reiteration. But just a final thought on this, the next time you are watching CNBC and you hear the quarterly or annual results, consider this. If the commentator says "they exceeded the analyst expectations by a penny" or "they were directly in line with analysts' expectations," ask yourself is anybody really that good in the real world?

Because fraud always manifests itself in patterns, it lends itself nicely to risk assessment using data and analytics. In areas where risk of fraud is extremely high, it behooves the organization to employ analytics to mitigate these exposures to the greatest degree possible. Detailed next are a couple of areas where fraud is quite high in the normal course of events but is quite minimal in regard to the areas where fraud is possible and is perpetrated daily.

There are two industries in which fraud is pervasive and unfortunately has become so commonplace that a day-to-day occurrence is an accepted part of the environment. These two industries are healthcare and construction.

Healthcare as an industry is subjected to fraud on a massive basis. Why is that? Think about this in the context of how the marketplace is truly defined. This is the only marketplace in the world where the following qualities exist, at least as it was operating at the time this work was written.

It is the only marketplace in the world where the primary consumer of the services desires the highest quality healthcare, does not know what to consume, when to consume it, how much to consume, why it is necessary to consume it, how much it should cost, and does not pay for it directly in most circumstances.

Worse yet, a huge portion of the population remain uninsured in terrible economic times. If they need care by whatever deceptive or other means, somebody's going to ensure they get it. This may be another family member who is insured through their employer, a very common practice indeed.

The providers of the services in order to remain economically viable must sell as much as possible, at the highest price tolerable, and want to provide the highest quality of services possible. They must also in most cases overbill the consumer or other responsible party for the services rendered to private pay and insured individuals to make up for the shortfall in reimbursement from government programs.

To compound the provider's problems, virtually none of them have cost accounting to know how much each treatment is actually costing them, and whether they should even be in that part of the marketplace. Add to this, for those institutions that are 501(c)3 tax-free institutions under the Internal Revenue Code of the United States, they are mandated to provide healthcare to the indigent. Whether those patients are economically viable or not is irrelevant; if they enter the institution, they must be cared for.

Those that pay the bills want the consumer to minimize consumption, with the risk of much higher consequences down the road and minimize the payment to providers to support a bottom line. But minimization of the payments, of course, exerts downward pressure on the quality.

I find it most entertaining when you watch the town hall meetings that have taken place on the subject matter of healthcare in this country. The irate citizenry sparked by the special interest groups of the insurance industry: through their selectively implanted operatives, railing against the reform of the healthcare system.

Not one of them understands anything about this environment. It is very scary to see how little people in this country actually know about what goes on and how out of touch with reality they really are. It is scary to the point of being sickening if not downright depressing.

Even worse yet, perhaps I should run out and buy one of the wonder drugs the pharmaceutical companies are always pitching on TV with all those unsavory side effects, like oily discharge! What do you think; do I need a second opinion?

Moving forward, two key areas of risk that impact many organizations can be evaluated utilizing the following metrics:

1. **Health benefit claims.** To evaluate the exposure brought to self-funded health benefit plans
2. **Change orders on construction contracts.** To review those areas of virtual guaranteed exposure in any large-scale construction contract

*Health Benefit Claims*   One of the biggest risk areas of most companies and organizations these days is undeniably health benefits for their employees. Another known fact but poorly monitored and scrutinized is that fraud is extremely high in the area of health benefits. Fraud can be perpetrated and is perpetrated on organizations by any number of parties that are actively involved in the administration of health benefits. These parties can be providers, employees who consume the health benefits, and third-party administrators who are unscrupulous.

Health benefits provide a fertile field for profiling that would greatly enhance the ability to control the exposures that any organization undertakes, most particularly in those that are self-insured, which is virtually all organizations of any size.

The importance of risk assessment and risk management in this area via profiling is that the gains that could be a realized cannot be overstated. Profiling can be a powerful tool in combating fraud in these arenas, and is absolutely essential for pattern analysis.

There are a number of different profiles that can be built for analyzing health benefit claims for fraud. What has to be determined is what are going to be the points of emphasis and where is the organization going to explore for fraud. The profiles that are built will have to be specifically focused on known fraud conditions that have been evidenced in the past, whether inside or outside the organization.

These profiles can be built historically from the data or information that the organization receives or can be one-off profiles given unacceptable occurrences of certain events. Illustrated in Figure 7.12 is an example of profiling to determine unusual consumption patterns by employees in a self-insured health benefit plan of an organization. This historical profile, developed over a six-

Fraud Risk Historical Profile—Insurance Card Sharing

**Company Address: 55 E. Monroe St, Chicago**

**Provider #'s (Doctors)**

11278965 OBGYN-A

54322879 OBGYN-B

| Provider Locations | Miles from Company | | |
|---|---|---|---|
| Chicago-A | 0.1 | | |
| Hoffman Estates-B | **25.6** | | |

| | Profile of Employee | Avg. Profile for Other Employees | Profile Variance |
|---|---|---|---|
| CPT-4 Code Class | OBGYN-PreNatal | OBGYN-PreNatal | |
| Dates of Service - Total Times - Standard OV-A | 13 | 11.5 | |
| Dates of Service - Total Times - Standard OV-B | 21 | | |
| Total | 34 | 11.5 | 22.5 |
| Employee # | 24563 | | |
| Total $ Claims Through Birth | **$54,500** | **$23,750** | **$30,750** |
| # of hours absent for physician appointments | 15.5 | 16.5 | |
| Average hours absent per office visit | **0.46** | **1.43** | |
| Average annual claim $/employee/Family Coverage | **$107,750** | **$43,950** | **$63,800** |
| # of family members covered/average # covered | 4 | 5 | |
| Average annual claim$/family member | **$26,938** | **$8,790** | **$18,148** |

**FIGURE 7.12** Profiling Analytics—Example of Fraud Risk

month period, is then matched up against the average of all employees' consumption within the plan, viewed in isolation as being excessive consumption or matched against their attendance profile, or a combination of the above. Profiles can range from extremely simple to highly sophisticated; however, as cautioned before, the simpler the better.

In this case the pattern utilizing very simplistic provider numbers for example purposes is a case of sisters sharing an insurance card to have coverage while both of them are pregnant. Of course, the self-insured plan is then covering both the employed sister and her sibling who should not be covered. In this case it was discovered that the noninsured sister had a premature baby who incurred over $300,000 of the total charges.

*Construction Contracts*   Change orders in construction contracts as mentioned earlier are a key area to review. When they are excessive, change orders are a virtual certainty for fraud exposure on any large-scale construction contract.

If you are attempting to manage fraud risk in construction contracts, you must first monitor the bidding process. One of the popular misconceptions about minimizing risk in the bidding arena is the use of sealed bids. This is erroneous as regards any type of assurance in mitigating fraud. The reason is that those facilitating the bidding process can easily call the contractor and the contractor will tell them what was bid on the job.

The process that then takes place is that person, who in my mind is considered the pivot point, takes that information and facilitates a winning bid for the chosen contractor. The pivot point means it is a person on both sides of the transaction. They are part of the bidding process and subsequent to award are also the ones who are authorized to approve change orders.

All price information is fed to the designated winning contractor, who is the last to bid, with the lowest price and submits the bid just before the closing deadline. They are then awarded the contract in most instances, begin the project, and start to submit the change orders. The change orders are normally established on the basis of time and materials and not fixed price. The underlying agreement between the contractor and the pivot point is that the pivot point will get 10 to 15 percent of the change orders as they are approved and paid by the organization.

In addition, much of this is facilitated by another fraud scheme known as the merry-go-round. This is where you have a limited number of large contractors in a region. The scheme would work as follows. Let's assume for this example you have four contractors: A, B, C, and D. They conspire to make A the low bidder on the next contract and B, C, and D are then hired as subcontractors on the contract. A can submit virtually any change orders required since A is the winner of the bid by default. The person on the inside of the organization that facilities the contracting also benefits.

The next major project that is bid B wins, and A, C, and D are subcontractors. However, in this situation the minimum bid has gone up securing higher compensation for all four participants to the detriment of the organization itself. The change orders flow, and on and on it goes escalating each project cost higher and higher into the clouds.

The key in profiling this situation is to focus on the change orders, the frequency, and the dollar amounts, along with the terms. Also you must be able to determine if the bidding process is really fair and equitable. These are extremely good indicators of risk not only because they can identify a potential fraud situation, but they can also identify a process that is ineffective. There are only two major reasons why change orders would exist in any construction contract: fraud or the project was ill defined from the outset. If it is the latter of these reasons, then you have a process that is highly ineffective and needs to be corrected immediately. That would certainly be something that you would want to become aware of if you are trying to manage risk in a large organization with heavy construction requirements.

 ## UTILIZING LOGICAL DATA PATHWAYS TO FOCUS ON ROOT CAUSE AND RESOLVE IT

Logical data pathways (LDPs) constitute the blood flow and nervous system of the corporate body. The human body would not last long without a nervous system or life-sustaining blood flow. The same thing is true in the corporate environment; an organization is nothing without its data. Logical data pathways are the means of transporting information from the source of the data to the destination, for which it is intended.

As will be seen in the next bank lending example, the information flow is vertical, starting at the location that generates the loan and travels upward to the organizational headquarters. This flow of information is nothing more than the source-to-destination flow. By inference, you should also be able to follow the information from destination to source, in other words in reverse order.

The ability to do this creates a great tool for enterprise risk management. By virtue of this structure, we are able to follow the information from the destination back to the root cause of the problem if in fact risk is indicated. By

# Loan Losses LDP™ % of Losses–Bolded

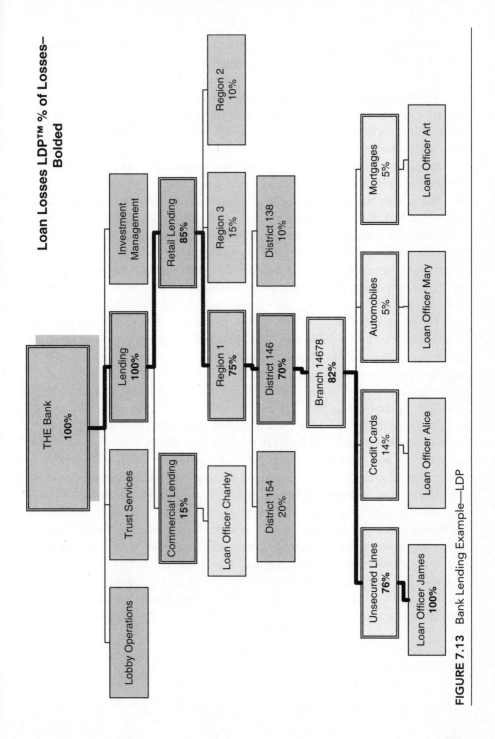

**FIGURE 7.13** Bank Lending Example—LDP

utilizing common information that should be available in every organization, ERM, the BRAIN of the organization, should be able to evaluate the bodily functions on a continuous basis.

The whole purpose of this type of methodology is to approach logically the subject matter of enterprise risk management in a manner consistent with how we live our daily lives. In other words the body of the ERM environment mimics our own human anatomy and how we function daily.

In Figure 7.13 we are tracing the logical data pathway of information from the point of loan generation to corporate headquarters. By reversing the flow of the data, we are able to center on a point of significant risk to the organization. Along the logical data pathway, we are simply following the warning signs based on percentage of concentration of bad loans strewn along the pathway. The key to accomplishing any of this is not rocket science but simply having the discipline of presenting good sound data to the organization. If that is the only minimal requirement and is not being accomplished currently, what is wrong with this picture?

The other nice feature of this approach is that it detects data integrity errors as they occur. Knowing that you have data integrity errors in some of the primary information flows of your organization is a huge discovery but also a significant risk. As alluded to in Chapter 1, data, data everywhere but no information, is a very common occurrence in many large but also medium- to small-size organizations.

As shown in Figure 7.13, given a good flow of information, it is not difficult to isolate and determine the root cause of the operational problem—risk. In keeping with sound practice in enterprise risk management, that is the whole purpose of the exercise. That is where the management portion of ERM comes into play. It does no good to isolate the risk if you are not going to manage it or do something about it. Logical data pathways provide the tools and the methodologies to get to the point of resolution. In this case the branch loan officer for whatever reason has been permitted to lend money in a haphazard and risky fashion. This has had the impact of jeopardizing not only the branch but also has significantly escalated the credit risk of the entire institution. Granted as you move down the pathway the percentages get smaller, but the concentration of risk is still the key factor to be isolated and dealt with.

CHAPTER EIGHT

# The Future Evolution of the Model

 **ERM FOR THE TWENTY-FIRST CENTURY**

When setting expectations for the enterprise risk management (ERM) environment, it is important to understand the necessity for change. If there is one area in the organization that must be dynamic and constantly fluid, it is enterprise risk management. As we move forward further into the twenty-first century, the frequency of change is going to be impossible to comprehend. At no other time in history will technology, and knowledge gained through technology, change more or be more influential in how our organizations and the world as a whole runs.

The key to success in enterprise risk management is to stay on top of change. More correctly stated, the mission of ERM is to predict change before it happens. The mission statement of ERM must always say, "Our mission is not to remain the same." Therefore, from the first day in which ERM becomes an operational part of enterprises, they must be moving in the direction of where they want to be in the future. This chapter will talk about a number of things to be considered by the people who are responsible for enterprise risk management as they set off down that road.

**SYSTEMS STRATEGIES**

The very first thing that the Chief Risk Officer (CRO) and/or head of ERM must realize is that systems are the key to the future. Therefore, it would be very prudent to closely align themselves with information technology and the Chief Information Officer (CIO). They must become an integral part of all new system development efforts that are being brought to the table for the organization.

The purpose of this is to ensure that every new system that is brought into the organization or created within the organization is done with a risk emphasis as part of its inherent design. This effort must be initiated from the outset and clearly communicated to those that are critical to new system selection, design, and functionality. Whether they build the systems internally or are going to be involved in the selection criteria from the world of the vendors, the message must be consistent, and it must be uniform.

As discussed in Chapter 1, we can no longer afford to be implementing substandard systems in our organizations. If discipline and strategic thought process are not invoked each and every time that a system is being considered, we will simply install another system that is inadequate to run a business today.

Here are some casual observations about risk relative to systems implementation and about how implementation is done today. In very few organizations that I'm aware of is there active involvement up front by two critical groups within the organization: namely, ERM and internal audit. In fact, in most cases internal audit is nowhere near the system until it has already been implemented. This, of course, is totally wrong. In order to have a knowledgeable internal audit function, they should be actively involved on the front end of all systems to ensure that all business risks have been considered and that appropriate controls and security have been included in the design to mitigate those risks.

At the same time, enterprise risk management must be in consultation with the primary users of the system. The purpose is to ensure that they have identified their key business outcomes for the processes to be operated and supported by the system. Then by definition if they have identified key business outcomes, they should also be identifying the key metrics or data they will use to evaluate these objectively. By being involved up front in the process of enterprise risk management, they can ensure that the relevant risks have been properly taken into consideration and that there is a means of measuring them.

In the following sections, we will bring this emphasis formally into the structure of how an organization should develop sound system criteria. The ideal situation is to put in place an entire strategy for making every system that is created and/or purchased risk-centric. A manner of accomplishing this will be discussed in the following sections.

 ## DESIGN CRITERIA AND SPECIFICATIONS

For every system that will be implemented in an organization there must be a fundamentally sound set of design criteria and specifications. For those organizations that are actively seeking a highly effective enterprise risk management environment, an integral part of those design criteria and specifications must be making the system risk-centric.

What does the term *risk-centric* really mean? Literally, it means that the system in its fundamental design, tooling, specifications, capabilities, and even the type of data gathered by it are centered on risk for the part of the business supported by the system. To accomplish this, the user or primary owner of the system must truly understand the concept of business risk and how it must be accommodated by the system. This is where the enterprise risk management people must center their efforts in every new system development project. They must sit down and educate the individual risk owners not only in the risks they own every day, but also in how they can effectively track and manage them by the data they gather and the system's capabilities.

 ## DESIGNING RISK-CENTRIC SYSTEMS FOR EFFICIENCY/ GOVERNANCE: STEP BY STEP

Creating a risk-centric system should not be a task or a chore. Risk-centric systems should have been in existence in every major organization since the concept of a system was invented. Unfortunately, the historical landscape of systems implementation is littered with misconceived ideas of what a system should be to run a business. The popular mantra in the past has been to define the business requirements, find a system that closely approximated these, and then modify it accordingly to meet the criteria. What is missing from the equation, of course, is providing a real methodology for overseeing the business from a risk and governance perspective.

Now that it is fashionable to consider the concepts of risk and governance, everyone is rushing to the table to try and incorporate them in corporate initiatives, but still in most cases practitioners are failing to do so. In the following sections, we will demonstrate that it does not need to be difficult to create risk-centric systems that will give you a much better run business and a higher degree of corporate governance.

## Truly Understanding the Business

The very first step in designing any kind of effective systems environment is to really understand the business or business subset, which it is to support and/or operate. This may seem like a very basic concept, but it is often misunderstood and done poorly. It must take into account a number of different aspects of the business to ensure that it is designed properly.

For instance, a system that is specifically dedicated to the provision of customer service has got to have all of the features necessary to facilitate that goal. It clearly must be extremely timely, which means fast processing; it must be highly accurate; it must be highly flexible to accommodate all situations; and so on. Therefore, by definition, when a system like this is to be brought into the organization, very significant discussions need to be held about all aspects of customer service. Every service to be rendered, every condition that could arise, every code that must be entered, in other words everything that is necessary for successful customer service experience, must be discussed and accommodated.

If the system is going to establish the public face of the organization, for instance, on the Internet, great care has got to be taken that it is 100 percent accurate and provides a pleasant experience for the customer. So whatever the purpose of the system may be, in order to align it with a risk-based approach we cannot just assume that everything is business as usual; our efforts must be strategized to be accomplished. Unless we have run the business perfectly in the past, anything else will be less than adequate. There is no substitute for knowing the functionality of the business when designing the system.

## Defining the Primary Risk Events

Once we have a thorough understanding of the business, the next thing that needs to be addressed is defining the primary risk events. Depending on how sophisticated you want to make the risk environment, this could be a multi-stage exercise of risk analysis. Later on in this section, I will provide an example of a limited multistage risk analysis for a systems environment.

However, if you want to maintain a very straightforward and basic type of risk approach, the following is a strategy to invoke. First, understand the primary outcomes of the business or the relevant business subset. These are sometimes designated as business objectives; however, some business objectives are not always defined as outcomes and therefore are useless in risk assessment. In isolating primary objectives, care should be taken to identify only those things that are most critical if you want to limit the extent of metrics that are going to be incorporated in the environment. Therefore it is imperative that this exercise be performed very judiciously to ensure the maximum benefit from a minimum amount of content.

## Defining the Critical Data

Once we have established the key outcomes of that subset of the organization, the focus then asks what data is required to manage these risks dynamically. The data must have the appropriate qualities in order be effective as a key risk indicator. These qualities are that the data should be outcome focused and raw (OR data). This will require some time and effort to ensure that it has these characteristics, however, it is time well spent as the future of the organization depends on it.

First think about what sorts of data are normally gathered in the organization and how they could be modified to meet the requirements of risk assessment. If possible, we want to utilize known data elements. We should not go out and create things that do not need to be created. Many times we find that data we are already gathering, if utilized appropriately, could satisfy the criteria. However, if appropriate data has never been gathered or is poorly handled, then it should be abandoned and new metrics determined. There is no reason to waste time trying to fit a square peg into a round hole only to get a badly distorted result. The data must fit the task of risk assessment.

## Identifying the Data Capture Methodology

Provision should be made within the design of the system to capture and house the data that will be utilized for risk analysis and risk management of the business subset. The objective here is to make the capture of data as painless and fluid as possible. This is not possible in all circumstances, but in most cases with the technologies available today data capture will most likely be accommodated with some degree of ease.

There are many types of medium that can and are employed for the capture of data. The most important thing to be remembered is that we must capture the right data elements, not just any data element. Therefore whatever technology and or methodology is employed it should only be selected if it will capture, as efficiently as possible, exactly what we are intending.

In most cases the data that is going to be utilized will be forwarded from some other systems environment, be captured digitally, or be input through some front-end edit routine. The key for those items that are coming in through the edit routines is to make sure that the edits are appropriately designed to preclude data with form and content that is not as desired.

## Designating the Critical Risk Data Fields in the System

It should be emphasized that the data fields that house the critical data for risk assessment and management must be clearly identified and understood by every user of the system. Why is it so important? The reason is because many times when new systems are brought into an organization people are not properly trained on the systems and as a result do not understand the criticality of certain features. One of the most commonly overlooked concepts is the emphasis on the fields that must be populated with data and the importance of doing so. Without this emphasis, most people are going to take the lazy way out in populating data on a system. In other words, they will use the easiest alternatives and not feel compelled to do what is necessary.

A good example of this is the following. In creating a risk model for a major organization, one of the key of risk factors from a cost perspective was the consumption of electric power. During the exercise of building the model, that became a very big point of contention with the accounts payable personnel. The reason was that they would have to make a few more keystrokes to populate the field that was already present in the Enterprise Resource Planning (ERP) environment indicating the units of power actually consumed. They were adamant about the fact it was not their job to populate that field and that they only needed to capture the amount due to the utility company for purposes of paying the bills.

Of course, this is ludicrous. If power consumption is a critical cost factor that plays heavily into risk, it must be captured. The cost of a couple of extra keystrokes by accounts payable personnel should never be the deterrent to capturing the data that is required. Such occurrences are exactly why systems with so many capabilities are so inadequate in today's organizations.

An integral part of this exercise is to ensure that the data that is selected for risk assessment can also be utilized to evaluate the effectiveness of the control environment both from operations and design standpoints. What is the point?

The point is that if you are judicious in how this is done, you can establish highly efficient environments that can run virtually everything in the enterprise from a governance standpoint. It is imperative then that the right data be captured and made available to support these critical functionalities. So do not fail to designate the appropriate data fields, and make sure they are populated!

## Building in the Appropriate Tools and Techniques

Once the risk-centric data has been determined and has been captured, the other key component that must be present is the appropriate tool or technique to analyze the data. It should be clear that in order to be effective, dynamic, and fluid for the facilitation of real-time risk assessment, the tools should be automated. These types of tools, when built directly into the systems, are called system-centric data-centric tools. These types of tools will be discussed later in this chapter and must be very seriously considered in structuring an ERM environment for the twenty-first century.

The other part of this is the techniques, which boil down to the analytics. As discussed in a previous section, there are hundreds of different types of analytical approaches that can be taken, but we must select what is most appropriate. In selecting an analytic technique, we must pay attention to the longevity factor and the elimination of any type of distortion. What is implied here is to stay with very fundamental analytics that will deliver reliable results on a consistent basis, irrespective of the business conditions.

For instance, in Chapter 7 we talked about comparative analysis on a period-to-period basis. But, as emphasized in that discussion, this type of analytic is subject to misinterpretation where the business is known to be cyclical or undergoes frequent change. When you are selecting an analytical technique to be employed in risk assessment and management, you should go with whatever is low- or virtually no-maintenance. Therefore, analytical techniques such as these types of comparative analysis should be used sparingly, if at all. It is not that they are not relevant in certain circumstances, but another alternative may be a better choice.

## Determining the Timing of Reporting

By inference from previous discussions, if you are going to go to the trouble of building-in these types of tools and techniques, it would stand to reason that you would like the reporting to be virtually real time. That is not the only alternative, but in those critical risk situations where time is of the essence it may be the best alternative. In designing the system then, consideration must be given to not only the timing of the reporting but also the form.

It is a well-known fact that, historically, exception reporting has been generated for years and years and years. However, this type of reporting was in many cases ignored and not acted upon. This is not the type of precedent that we want to follow going forward. Therefore, any type of reporting that is going to be associated with this type of tooling must be real time and highly effective.

As a result, one of the things that will be discussed later is the utilization of secure e-mail to deliver these types of results almost instantaneously to the appropriate parties. As we all know in this day and age, information is king, but stale information is useless. For example, in a rapidly rising stock market it does no good to know what the stock sold for one minute ago; it is totally irrelevant and has no bearing on an intelligent business decision.

The key to risk management report timing then is "the sooner the better— don't delay or you are going to pay!"

## Presentation of the State of the Enterprise

Just like the state of the union or the state of the state, the state of the enterprise from a risk perspective is absolutely critical to senior executives and the board. However, unlike these other types of informative sessions, this information cannot be delivered on such an infrequent basis. Also, unlike these other types of updates, key risk information should not be delivered orally or by audio means.

The information regarding the state of the enterprise to gain more risk perspective must be presented in a timely and businesslike fashion. For purposes of risk reporting, you should always use analytics that are as current as possible, in a format that is easily consumed by senior executives and board members. For that matter, risk information should be delivered in a format that is easily consumed by virtually everybody in the organization. That format is visual, not audio. In certain risk situations, for instance, a call to 911 regarding something that is happening at that very moment, audio delivery may be the only viable format. However, from an enterprise risk management perspective to deliver the big picture of what is really going on, where it is happening, how intense the impact is and so on, visualization is the only way to communicate.

By default then, the tools built into the system to communicate the risk must have the capability of raising visually the red flags as to the status of risk. These tools will provide the senior executives and the Board of Directors with the capabilities to manage risk on a dynamic basis and respond as soon as practical to the situation.

The critical reason why this is so important is to make sure that communication actually takes place. As we know, the old idiom regarding communication is that it has not taken place until the other person understands. The relevance here is that people at the top of the organization are visionaries not audiophiles. Visionaries see, they don't hear well; therefore give them the picture, and they will grasp it quickly; tell them a bedtime story, and you will lose their attention instantaneously. If you want action show it, don't tell it!

## Establish the Flow of Information to the ERM Environment

Once the system has been outfitted with the tools and information necessary, then provision must be made for how this information will be transferred to the ERM environment automatically. It is imperative that information flow to ERM with no intervention on the part of the user. If the transfer of information involves any type of significant activity on the part of the system user, the risk is extremely high that it will not take place. The reason for this is that in most situations the users already have enough on their platter of things to do without having to feed another environment with information.

Therefore, the ERM personnel must be actively involved in the design of the system to ensure that the information they require to effect change and effectively manage risk is forthcoming timely. This may imply in certain situations that there be designated personnel within ERM who are charged with all of the tasking discussed in this section. The reason why this may be necessary is that most businesses are undergoing some kind of major systems change on a constant basis. If designated personnel are not established for this type of function, ensuring that our systems environments are risk-centric will be hit or miss and totally haphazard.

The timing of the information flow to ERM is one of the most critical aspects. It is extremely likely that critical information that is received may have to be brought to the attention of the Board disclosure committee immediately, for publication in some instances. Therefore, in this part of the exercise, compatibility of format, content, and visual presentation capability should be clearly emphasized.

It is implicit, as in any system exercise, that all of these capabilities be thoroughly tested and determined to be functional prior to the system being implemented. Making a system risk-centric must always take place in Phase 1, as we all now know what happens to those things that are relegated to Phase 2.

##  DYNAMICALLY INTEGRATED RISK EVALUATION (DIRE)

Dynamically integrated risk evaluation (DIRE) is a methodology of utilizing systems and systems capabilities to evaluate risks. In its very embryonic stages, this science or methodology has been around for some time. I personally have been employing these techniques for many years. However, such tools have been scattered and haphazard in their implementation.

The whole thought process behind this type of approach is to have systems do what they do best—process data. It is still amazing, in virtually all organizations, how much heavy lifting of data is still performed by people. With creative techniques in how systems are designed and implemented and with the incorporation of appropriate tooling, a lot of this manual effort could be avoided. The point here is not to downplay the importance of human intervention, but too much human intervention actually slows down the process and compromises the results.

Technology and systems as designed today have immense capabilities to simplify the oversight and governance of organizations. The problem is that these issues are not given high priority when the systems are created. As a result, we end up trying to govern our organizations physically instead of logically. Almost all enterprises today are simply too big to do it this way anymore. We have to start to incorporate the realization that systems are built to generate and manipulate data, and that is what they should be used for. By utilizing the techniques discussed in this book all organizations can actually generate full-blown governance methodologies that will help them run their organizations better and cheaper, and give them a competitive edge over their counterparts.

The types of tools illustrated in the following sections are not rocket science. If they were, they would not be included in this book. The importance of a key business tool lies in its simplicity.

##  TRIGGERS AND MOMS

The first two tools, Triggers and MOMS, are very similar in functionality. The first one, threshold triggers, is the generic name for a tool utilized to evaluate risk thresholds. The second tool, Metric Oversight Monitoring Systems (MOMS), essentially has the same functionality. The implication of the acronym is that you can't get away with anything when MOMS is watching. Both of the tools are centered on the evaluation of risk using metrics and in their implementation tend to be data-centric and system-centric. This implies by definition that they tend to be incorporated directly into systems by design. They utilize the capability of the system to automatically perform governance 24 hours a day, 7 days a week, 365 or 366 days a year.

Both of these tools rely upon data generated historically for the determination of the threshold of risk and the triggering mechanism, which will invoke notification automatically. In other words, to establish the risk threshold the process owners or system users would look at the historical pattern of information relative to a certain risk event. They would use that proven information to determine what their risk threshold, or threshold of pain, is for that particular functionality of the system. That then becomes the first part of the tool, which would then be established as a reference point for the system. The second part of the tool is the triggering mechanism. The triggering mechanism is normally established in relation to how much risk, or risk tolerance, is acceptable within that particular functionality of the business or system.

Once the MOMS threshold of risk as been established and is accepted, and the triggering point has been determined, they are then established as reference fields for the system to be evaluating against. These reference fields are locked down by security and are not allowed to be modified in any way without the explicit permission of the ERM organization, the senior executives, and/or the board of directors as appropriate.

A MOMS mechanism should be established in each and every primary module of the environment that directs key organizational activities or executes critical transactions. These triggers become key oversight mechanisms for the evaluation of processes or systems as required. One of the great governance features of this is that it is independent of control of the process owner or the system user. In other words, risky events or unsatisfactory results cannot be swept under the carpet without appropriate notification somewhere up the line.

The MOMS would operate as follows:

- The risk threshold is established.
- That trigger point is determined.
- The fields are populated and implemented in the system.
- The fields are properly secured so that they cannot be altered.
- The business is conducted as normal within the process or system.
- When the threshold trigger point is breached an e-mail notification is generated.
- The instantaneous e-mail notification should be multiparty. It can be any or all of these depending upon the seriousness of the risk event:
  - Process owner/systems user
  - Internal audit
  - ERM organization
  - Senior executive
  - Board of Directors
- Root cause determination is undertaken.
- Corrective action is appropriately taken and the trigger reset.

As mentioned previously, these threshold triggers can be and should be put in any and all critical modules of all software systems implemented in the organization. This can run the gamut from physical security to logical security, from fixed assets to financial reporting, from cash management to legal activity. There is really no limitation as to where these types of tools can be utilized effectively.

Detailed next is a simplistic example of how threshold triggers could be implemented. In the interest of keeping the example straightforward, I will utilize a common financial scenario. In this scenario a very commonplace, but very critical, everyday occurrence is illustrated. Figure 8.1 is an accounts receivable aging analysis shown in an Excel format. It shows the normal buckets of aging that are represented in these types of processes. It also shows the threshold trigger that was established and secured for this function. The risk threshold or threshold of pain is set at 60 days, and the triggering point is established at 27 percent of total outstanding receivables.

As accounts receivable is processed, if the amount of receivables outstanding over 60 days exceeds 27.1 percent an instantaneous notification would be triggered to the preidentified parties. The process would then involve a designated response from either the key executive, internal audit, or the ERM organization as shown in Figure 8.2.

##  REAL-TIME PROFILING

Embedded Audit and Risk System (EARS) Real-Time Profiling is the further migration of the profiling concept discussed in the analytics section. EARS, as utilized in a data-centric system, is what will be illustrated here. EARS is used for the purpose of isolating risky events within a computerized processing environment. The thought process here is to create a profile utilizing past experience to trigger immediate response or oversight when required. The profiles can either be historical profiles that are built over a period of time, given a set of transactions or system events, or can be profiles developed to isolate unacceptable conditions immediately.

This type of tool is also embedded in the system by inference and as such is capable of instantaneous feedback whenever a triggering event is encountered. These types of tools are used in circumstances when delays in corrective actions are simply unacceptable. Common applications of these techniques are encountered by businesses and individuals on a daily basis. In sophisticated banking organizations, these types of profiles should be developed and employed in two key areas as appropriate.

Accounts Receivable Aging

| Threshold Trigger | | Days | % of A/R | | | | | | |
|---|---|---|---|---|---|---|---|---|---|
| | | 60 | 27.10% | | | | | | |
| | 0–30 | 31–60 | 61–90 | 91–120 | 120+ | Total | 61–120+ | % of Total |
| Customer1 | $ 3,000.00 | $ 2,478.00 | $ — | $ 354.00 | $ 1,546.00 | | | |
| Customer2 | $ 2,768.00 | $ 1,820.00 | $ 126.00 | $ 1,239.00 | $ 214.00 | | | |
| Customer3 | $ 3,456.00 | $ 1,765.00 | $ 1,257.00 | $ — | $ 345.00 | | | |
| Customer4 | $ 1,278.00 | $ 3,590.00 | $ 1,287.00 | $ 1,326.00 | $ 762.00 | | | |
| Customer5 | $ 6,734.00 | $ 1,250.00 | $ 1,238.00 | $ 1,298.00 | $ — | | | |
| etc. | | | | | | | | |
| Total$ | $ 17,236.00 | $ 10,903.00 | $ 3,908.00 | $ 4,217.00 | $ 2,867.00 | $ 39,131.00 | $ 10,992.00 | 28.09% |

Trigger Is Active

**FIGURE 8.1** MOMS Excel

215

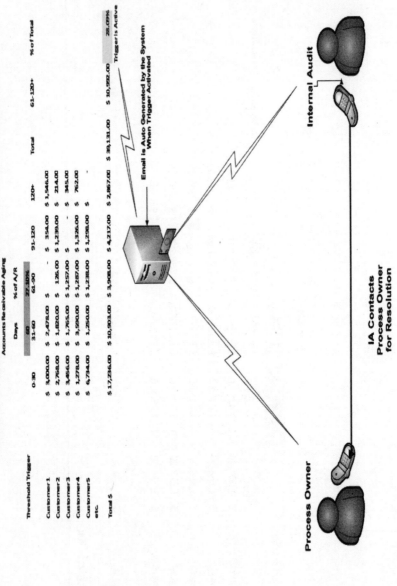

FIGURE 8.2 MOMS Flow

The first key area is wire transfers. It is imperative that a bad wire not make it outside the bank. As a result, these tools can be implemented to ensure that, given certain criteria, the wire is properly reviewed and authorized before it leaves the premises.

The second key area is credit card administration. Every fraud unit of every major credit card issuer depends heavily on EARS or similar types of mechanisms to identify unusual spending patterns by their clients. By building-in a historical profile of how we consume goods on our credit cards, these units are able to determine with a high degree of predictability what we will do. If we step outside our normal pattern then the system automatically triggers an intervention by a fraud investigator.

For example, I started to do seminars in Las Vegas, after not being in Las Vegas for years. I presented my credit card at the hotel the first time I went there, and shortly after it was swiped I received a phone call from my wife. She said the credit card company just called and asked if you were in Vegas. They further inquired as to whether you were at a specific hotel. Once she was able to affirm that I was, the inquiry was over.

These types of tools are unbelievably efficient and effective, in that the fraud investigator really only has to talk into a headset and make the inquiry. The system does all the heavy lifting relative to processing the data, identifying the exception condition via the profile, and dialing the phone. Think for a minute how long it would take to do this simple action if it was done without the benefit of this type of tool. In reality, it could never be accomplished in any type of timely fashion. And time is of the essence when fraud is involved.

It is unfortunate that we have refined and implemented these tools in many situations for this functionality but we have not made the same types of tools available for overall enterprise risk management and governance processes. Therein exists the one great point of failure. There is absolutely no reason why with appropriate discipline and effort these types of tools cannot be integrated throughout the entire enterprise. There is plenty of technological capability. The failure to use these tools truly lies in the failure to employ vision and foresight.

Figure 8.3 shows a simplistic EARS example of how it might be seen from an overall conceptual view.

The most critical point to be remembered about these types of tools is to keep them straightforward and understandable. In addition, these types of tools can be implemented in virtually every platform that is being utilized by organizations of any size today.

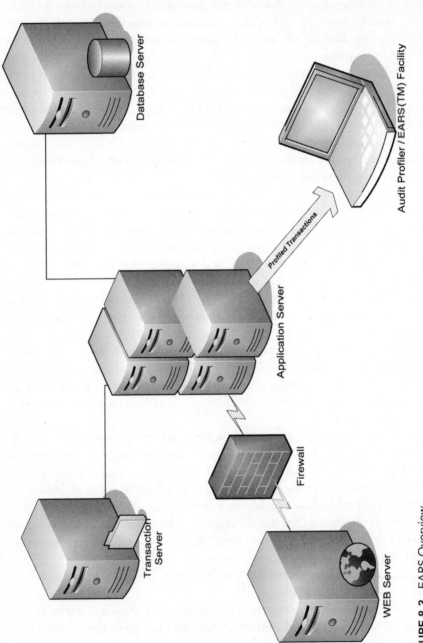

**FIGURE 8.3** EARS Overview

In this section risk evaluation and assessment has been discussed in the context of system-centric/data-centric tooling. This can however be implemented in a more primitive or evolutionary stage in the context of data-centric/system-dependent types of tooling. If this is the only alternative, it still may be far superior to the other option of not having it at all.

 ## SETTING STANDARDS FOR FUTURE EVOLUTION

In setting the standard for the future evolution of the ERM environments and systems in general, it is time to start setting the bar a lot higher. For years now, corporate executives have been shortchanging their shareholders by shoddy systems strategies that are keeping most organizations in the Dark Ages. All of this has been done in the context of trying to meet the short-term expectations for the next quarter's performance.

I'm not sure when people are going to figure out that this is counter to their best interest. Unless it is the stated intention of most corporations to have a useful life of years instead of decades why do they keep thinking short-term and hamstringing the organization? Do they really want to set themselves up for failure?

It is time for shareholders to demand better performance from their Boards of Directors, their CEOs, CIOs, and the rest of C-suite. The Achilles' heel of most organizations is their simple lack of meaningful and useful data and information. The reason they do not have it is because of the lack of vision on the part of the people just listed and their overwhelming desire to enrich themselves instead of the organization.

As part of the ERM organization implementation, it should be a stated strategy to improve all systems' quality methodically and continuously both in current time and in future times. In other words, whenever a new system is raised, it must be done right and it must be risk-centric.

CEOs, CROs, and CIOs should be held directly accountable by the Board of Directors for the ongoing creation of risk-centric systems. Any organization that is serious about doing enterprise risk management on any type of global or enterprise scale must make this mandatory. Shareholders should be conscious of the fact that their organizations are running systems that are substandard in every way and as such are subverting shareholder value.

The popular belief that next quarter's results are what build shareholders' value over the long term is ridiculous on its surface. What is sorely lacking in what we've seen as massive corporate failures is the effective utilization of data, or the lack thereof, to manage risk on a day-to-day basis. The best interests of the shareholders and society in general have been sacrificed and sacrificed time and again at the altar of greed on behalf of the senior executives and the board. It is painfully obvious from both a public perception context and the inability to perform consistently and effectively that executive compensation is out of control. This is the biggest risk, next to the lack of data that is reliable and usable, that most organizations have.

Therefore, the key strategy that must be implemented is to reward executives based upon the types of visionary systems and overall governance methodologies that they put in place instead of next quarter's bottom line and the attached bonus compensation. Clearly, the focus has to shift to a technology-centric strategy that is clearly defined and highly effective.

I can almost hear the grousing from here: *We just don't have the money or that is just too expensive.* Yet there is always money to pay bonuses and to do other things that do nothing to ensure the longevity of the company. It has reached a point now where this problem is so rampant in corporations around the world that we can no longer afford not to solve it. How long will it be before the next major meltdown occurs, the one we don't recover from for years?

The necessity to establish a course of action that will achieve top-of-game governance with the utilization of best-of-class systems is a plan that is long overdue and sorely needed. By incorporating the concept of automating ERM with the implementation of every new system we can build an extremely powerful environment in which to run all organizations even if it is one system at a time.

CHAPTER NINE

# Related Topics and Special Risk Situations

 **MANAGING RISK/AUDITING REAL TIME**

One of the key things that should emerge from a highly functional enterprise risk management (ERM) environment that is based upon an automated platform as discussed in Chapter 8 are some economies of scale that are lurking beneath the surface. Data-centric ERM has the potential to bring more value to the table, much more value, than any initial ongoing cost of automation could offset.

One of the critical rules I have always operated by is this: if no good business reason to change something exists, then don't do it. I do not want to pontificate on the virtues of data-centric ERM or advocate its adoption if it does not provide business value. There is no reason to spend money on a business process or information system if the rewards are not going to be greater, far greater, than the expenditures.

The same holds true with enterprise risk management. If it is just going to be a figurehead organization sitting on the org chart looking important—curtains for the windows as many would say—don't make the investment. It is a funny situation that we have slipped into in the world of business in which many people like to talk about all the latest things and use the buzz words of the day but in reality haven't done a thing. The problem with most of the buzz words they are employing is that people don't have the slightest notion of what they really mean or how to truly implement them in any kind of workable business context.

The implementation of a highly automated enterprise risk management environment should beget many more business advantages at the point of its inception. Some of the cost advantages and economies of scale that can be gained by implementing data-centric ERM will be discussed in more detail later in this chapter. However, suffice it to say that if there are not real business advantages gained and measurable as a result of implementing such an environment, then it has not been implemented correctly, or the design was deficient from the outset.

There should be any number of significant advantages gained by implementing a data-centric environment for managing risk. One of the most basic is running a much more efficient and effective business.

Let's explore some fundamental examples to see if this is true in the context of day-to-day business operations.

Let's look at a manufacturing operation. Suppose that we are noticing over time that the amount of unanticipated scrap that is being generated at a facility is accelerating at a significant rate. The global risk indicator brings this to the attention of operating management. The risk metrics that they are maintaining on the shop floor provide a logical data pathway to the point of failure. By following the metrics, it has been determined that the problem is not the result of bad machine setup or instruction sets. It is also determined that tooling is correct and has been properly utilized in all instances. It is also determined that we are using journeyman labor on the machining center where the majority of the scrap is being generated.

The one common element of risk is the raw material component itself, and those that are failing are all from one specific vendor. By utilizing this information, it is easy to center on the source of the risk. It is clear that the vendor is sending us substandard material. It could be either that the metallurgical content is defective or the material has not been made to the proper specifications and tolerances. By utilizing the logical data pathway, we are able to isolate the problematic vendor and the related raw material component. Why is this important, and why would we want to know?

Anyone who has worked in a manufacturing environment understands quite quickly that when material fails in production it causes an avalanche of aligned risks that start to take place—each one with its own attached cost factor. The following are some of the costs that are incurred when the material from a vendor fails:

- Production must stop while the material is removed, negatively impacting productivity (**indirect labor cost**).
- Other jobs relying on this component to be produced will have to be rescheduled (**rescheduling costs**).
- Additional time will have to be made on the production schedule to accommodate the reintroduction of this job order onto the shop floor (**additional rescheduling costs**).
- The direct worker must now clock out and move to indirect coding for the idle time (**lost production cost**).
- Another job not involving that material must then be moved to the machining center (**material handling costs**).
- That is, of course, after we have had to issue it out of stock (**issuance costs**).
- The item must be removed from the production floor and taken to shipping to be returned or sold to a scrap vendor (**material handling costs**).
- Assuming the sale to the scrap vendor, we must then invoice it to the scrap vendor (**invoicing costs**).
- We then must make sure we collect the money due on the invoice to the scrap vendor (**accounts receivable and collection costs**).
- Purchasing must then generate another order for the same material (**material acquisition cost**).
- The material must be received when shipped (**additional receiving costs**).
- The material must be transported from receiving to inventory control (**material handling cost**).
- Inventory control must then record it on the stock status (**handling costs**).
- The material must then be reissued to the shop floor (**reissuance cost**).
- The material must then be staged and loaded on the machine (**production setup costs**).
- The order must be brought to the point of completion prior to failure (**additional production costs**).

In the preceding listing is a representation of the types of cost that get built into organizations when fundamental risks are not properly managed in day-to-day operations. What is most frightening about this situation is that this is not at all unusual. If this goes undetected for any period of time, and that vendor continues to introduce poor materials into our operations, the day-to-day costs continue to escalate.

I could recite example after example after example of these types of occurrences in virtually any industry and/or organizational structure, but the simplicity of the message is clear. Most organizations feel that on a daily basis they do an exceptional job of managing risk; however, if they looked deeply into their operations and their organizational structure, they would get a rude awakening at just how poorly they do, in fact, manage risk.

A fundamental premise that can establish an organization's propensity to manage risk is where they fit in the pecking order relative to other companies of their same size and characteristics. If the CEO looks you in the eye and says, "We don't have any risk around here. My people are managing it effectively every day," start looking around. If you are able to determine that that same company that is so proficient at managing risk is actually number six in their industry and not number one, it can only be concluded that somebody is mistaken. It would appear at that point that the corner office is out of touch with the front-line operations.

If an organization is effectively managing their risk every day, they would be number one in their industry or respective grouping, wouldn't they? Why would they not be?

 ## MONITORING CONTROLS WITH METRICS

Monitoring controls is now fashionable and has been made so by the guidance finalized in 2009 from COSO. I have been monitoring controls with metrics for many, many years as part of the exercise of evaluating risk using metrics. Approached logically and with common sense, controls should be part and parcel of the same exercise of evaluating risk on a continuous basis.

As mentioned earlier, my colleague Dave Coderre has written a global technology audit guide (GTAG) on continuous auditing. One of his key points made in that highly progressive publication is that continuous risk assessment is absolutely essential to the accomplishment of continuous auditing. By inference, whenever continuous auditing is employed, it is normally centered on the subject matter of controls. By logical deduction then, why would you not monitor controls using metrics if you are using metrics to perform continuous risk assessment?

I originated the theory early in my audit career that there had to be a better way of validating controls than slogging through a sample of transactions that is so small in relationship to the volume that it is virtually meaningless. One of the great frustrations is that the sample when drawn judgmentally by an auditor cannot be defended on the face of pure logic with any operations personnel. Therefore, by virtue of its ineptness the exercise is useless, but it puts a good curtain on the window by saying "it's been audited." As a result I abandoned that practice early on.

It was clear to me from looking at risk using metrics that not only could I evaluate the risk of a process, but I could also evaluate the status of the controls in that process. The key to all of this lies in developing the right metrics to evaluate each and every part of the enterprise. As discussed earlier, when you concentrate on the outcome of a process and find the metrics to measure it you are clearly in touch with the key risks of the process.

The reason is because the inverse of the outcome is the key risk of the process. Then, by logical extension, if that is the key risk of the process, you look for those controls directly related to those key risks or outcomes, and you will have identified your key controls. By further extension of the same logic, when the metrics that measure those risks are performing erratically, the controls are not functioning at an acceptable level or are totally nonfunctional. A simple example to illustrate this is shown in Figure 9.1.

From the trend lines, it is painfully obvious that there is a tremendous amount of risk taking place in this particular process, namely the billing, accounts receivable, and cash collection process. What is shown is a prolific upward spiraling of the days in accounts receivable contrasting with a death spiral downward of the day's cash on hand.

Looking at those two trend lines, one can easily conclude that some of the key outcomes in this process are not being realized. Namely the collection of

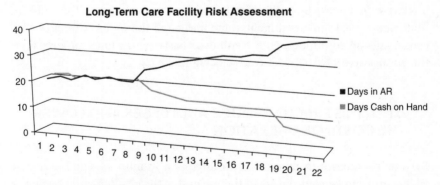

**FIGURE 9.1** DAR/DCOH Example

cash and the effective management of receivables as critical outcomes are simply not occurring. We also know for a fact that whatever controls are in place in this process have already had their impact on the process. The data itself shows that the controls that are in place in the process are wholly inadequate or are nonfunctional.

This harkens back to the net risk inherent risk discussion that was presented in Chapter 7. In this situation we are looking at the net risk of this process rapidly escalating on two different fronts.

Contrary to popular belief, it would simply not be sufficient in this situation for a financial auditor to go into this process and advise the firm to increase their bad debt reserve to properly state their financials. Yet undeniably this is precisely what would happen in this circumstance. The metrics, however, are crying out about the massive operational risk that is present in this process. but improvement will also bring to the table one of the greatest advantages of utilizing data for the evaluation of risk and the evaluation of controls—the ability to eliminate or severely reduce testing of the controls. It is painfully obvious by the trends of the data in the net risk position, post-control, that the controls are not working or are ineffective in design. What will be gained by further testing the controls only to conclude the obvious? What has to be done in this situation is to turn attention to why the controls are not working and what needs to be corrected to bring this process back into a working state.

Yet in this situation I feel comfortable in stating that every audit firm out there would still be pulling their samples for testing only to conclude that an increase in the bad debt reserve was necessary. That is a financial issue that can be arrived at in two seconds without any testing, but that is nowhere near the business issue that is the real risk to the enterprise.

What needs to be determined is what is wrong with the underlying billing process, so that it may be rectified by eliminating the root causes of the problem. That would yield some real audit value instead of the useless exercises that consultants all go through on a continuous basis, which unfortunately then the business pays for with zero value being realized.

 ## UTILIZING ERM TO REDUCE AUDIT FEES AND LOWER THE COSTS OF OPERATION

By utilizing metrics to monitor controls/risks a number of significant cost advantages can be gained. One of the greatest is the elimination of testing of transactions by the external and internal auditors. Can you imagine how much the audit bill could be decreased if you could eliminate testing by your externals? That is precisely what can be accomplished here. You can literally eliminate transaction testing from the landscape and all costs that are wasted and associated with it.

In addition, instead of having your internal auditors concentrated on performing useless sampling, they could be pursuing the real meat of the matter. The real issue here is the root cause of the increasing risk, as evidenced by the metrics, and how it can be eradicated. When the root causes are discovered and appropriately dealt with, you will get real productivity gains, the controls that are failing will be detected and corrected, and in this case you can forestall the failure of a business unit. All of this can be accomplished while increasing your cash flow dramatically.

This example is meant to put in perspective the real-life business gains that can be realized by employing this type of ERM. Data-centric enterprise risk management can actually reduce your cost of operations by doing away with unnecessary activities that are being performed on a quarterly and annual basis year in and year out.

I was warned by a relatively high profile individual, after he concurred with the effectiveness of this approach, that I was in the process of trying to push a boulder up the mountain. The people living on top of the mountain are, of course, the large firms that have no interest in a methodology that will lower their fees or their billable hours. Essentially what he told me is that as I'm pushing the boulder up the mountain there are thousands of people standing on top pushing the boulder back down.

It is no secret to me that by taking this approach I am bucking the trend, going against the establishment or swimming upstream. This is not the first time that I've been told, "Duckert, you are a maverick"; "Duckert, you don't understand how it works around here"; or the ever-famous "Duckert, you're not a team player." If that is the case and it has never bothered me in the past, why would I care if I am shoving a boulder up a mountain?

What I'm actually trying to accomplish is to restore some sanity to the whole practice of auditing, risk management, and corporate governance. Something has to change to ensure that the shareholders' money is not wasted on frivolous activities that have been evidenced time and time again to be useless. You don't have to look back far into the timeline to figure out that something is rotten in Denmark—no offense to Denmark because it's a beautiful country, with fabulous people, and I think the world of it. Every one of the major corporations that failed in the recent financial crisis all had opinions issued on their financial statements as required by law, and I would be willing to bet that the majority would have been unqualified opinions just prior to the time that they ceased operations forever.

If highly effective governance can be accomplished by building a risk model internal to the organization that can be utilized to minimize or eliminate unwarranted testing that simply wastes money and yields no benefit, while delivering high value business results, why would any organization not do this?

Any visionary organization that is seeking to reduce its operational cost and to ensure that it is highly effective in governing its organization should very seriously consider data-centric ERM. It is the vehicle that can accomplish just that. It is time to make the move toward effective corporate governance that is cost-effective and provides real business returns of numerous types.

For the others that would choose to ignore what is in the best interests of their organization both near-term and long-term, the tar pits are waiting. Give my regards to the saber-toothed tigers, I have always admired them.

 ## MERGERS AND ACQUISITIONS: LET'S BUY SOME MORE RISK

There are a number of options that can be utilized to increase market share. You can invent must-have new products, you can create a niche that nobody else controls, or, of course, you can always buy your way in. If you are not going to be able to expand your organization by organic growth due to lack of creativity or simple inability to do so by marketing or other means, get out the wallet.

If utilizing your wallet or your stock value, for example, is the pathway to be pursued, you had better be good at what you do. The battlefield of mergers and acquisitions (M&As) is littered with the remains of those that weren't good at what they did. The big caution, or better yet red flags, should start waving the minute the M&A phrase is uttered. Why?

Because for a number of years one of the percentages that has been bantered about as to the failure rate of mergers to meet all of their initial required criteria is northward of 85 percent. That in anyone's view is a gigantic rate of failure and would definitely qualify as risky on anybody's Richter scale. It would be huge if it was even 50 percent.

Let us start from the beginning and list of some of the most significant risk events that take place that should immediately put people on notice that the chances of failure are huge and you are about to become a statistic.

## Selecting the Target

Identifying the organization that on the surface appears to be the ideal fit for our organization isn't exactly easy and may even be highly speculative. What are some of the reasons that could account for this?

Who has certified their financial data, and have they under any circumstances fallen victim to the undue influence of the owner who is seeking to sell? I'm not questioning the integrity of each and every accounting firm, but there have been sufficient instances in every firm (large and small) where things have fallen through the cracks. That having been said, do you want to be the organization that buys someone who is on the other side of that crack?

■ **Key Risk:** Financial statements are not properly stated and/or are intentionally misrepresented.

### Key questions to be answered:

■ How will you positively assure yourself that their financial results as stated do in fact accurately reflect their performance as an organization, both current and historic?
■ If this is not done, how will you protect yourself contractually with right of recovery if you miss something in due diligence or if it is misrepresented by an outside party?

## Due Diligence?

The reason for the question mark in the subheading of this section is asking is due diligence ever done? In most instances it is not only due, it is certainly overdue. One of the most critical points of failure in many merger and acquisition scenarios surrounds due diligence. In many instances, due diligence is insufficient, poorly done, not done, or the results are totally ignored.

What I always find amusing is that every internal auditor I've ever taught has reacted uniformly whenever queried on the subject matter of due diligence. They either have two days to do something while trying to remain unnoticeable on the acquisition candidate's premises or the reality of it is, in virtually all instances, that they are nowhere near the place until the acquisition has closed. I have never been able to understand what goes on in the minds of senior executives who pursue this type of thought process. This conclusion can only stem from two fundamental circumstances: (1) Their internal auditors are extremely sharp, and executives don't want to hear what they have to say on the record and then act in defiance of it, or (2) the executives have almost no confidence in their internal auditors and believe them to be totally inept. If that is the case, they should fire the whole lot of them.

- ▪ **Key Risk:** Due diligence is not performed because the CEO has already decided the M&A is going forward.

### Key questions to be answered:

- Who will be held accountable for causes of failure that could have been discovered in due diligence?
- Will the responsible executive be held accountable and subsequently penalized for the failure? If not, why not?

## Unanticipated Events

There are a number of unanticipated or unforeseen events that can take place—these are commonly referred to as risks. An example from a colleague would illustrate this fact exactly.

According to my colleague, a close family member of hers was actively involved in business development for a major corporation. His job was to identify and isolate potential merger and acquisition candidates, in this case an acquisition. The targeted company was highly successful and in a very compatible field of products, which were, however, unique. The strongest asset of the company was a highly charismatic and dynamic owner who created all the products and established the customer base from scratch.

This person's family member pursued the owner of this corporation to sell the company to their organization for approximately five years. After five years of relentless pursuit, the owner acquiesced and agreed to sell on the condition that all monies would be exchanged at the closing with no delayed earn out provisions. The track record of the company was solid, and so this was agreed to. The purchase price of the company was approximately $400 million, and the date of closing was set. The owner of the corporation was 46 years old.

The closing took place at 10:00 A.M. and, since much of the preliminary work had been performed in advance, was concluded by 11:00 A.M. with all monies transferred. The owner of the business just acquired died at 1:30 P.M. that afternoon with no provision having been made for key man insurance. The subsidiary lasted approximately eight months before it imploded and disintegrated rendering the $400 million investment useless.

- **Key Risk:** All the critical components of the acquisition have not been properly considered in terms of risk and the risk mitigated appropriately.

### Key questions to be answered:

- What are the critical components of this acquisition that make it succeed or fail?
- Have we properly identified the key risks and taken the appropriate mitigating actions? If not, why not?

## Inability to Integrate the Acquisition into the Organization

There are many reasons why an acquisition cannot ever be properly integrated into the organization. Some of the more common ones that cause nightmares in this arena include culture clashes, inability to integrate business processes, and the ever-present inability to integrate systems. For purposes of this discussion, I will use the one that is most common to everybody—the inability to integrate the systems. The cost of accomplishing this task is always severely underestimated because there are hidden surprises around every corner.

Let me relate a couple of actual incidents that occurred subsequent to the acquisition date of two subsidiaries of two different companies. Both of these involve the double whammy of first of all acquiring somebody and secondly having to deal with a totally outsourced IT arrangement.

In situation one, the organization acquired a subsidiary that had out-sourced its IT and was 3 years into a 10-year contract. As related to me by someone involved in the meeting, a meeting was scheduled between the company and the outsourcer. The subject matter of the meeting was the desire to exit the contract for the purposes of bringing all systems under one roof in the parent organization. This is a very sound strategy and facilitates a much greater control of your data and information systems.

In the meeting conducted at the outsourcer's facility, there was only one member of the outsourcer's team present. When the appropriate introductions were concluded, the CIO of the acquiring company told the outsourcer that they wished to exit the contract. At that point the outsourcer asked if in fact they had read the contract to which they responded affirmatively. But the CIO recognized something was wrong and asked directly what exactly the out-sourcer was referring to. The outsourcer said the clause that relates specifically to data ownership, which caught everybody by surprise. The contract terms stated that the outsourcer owned all data that they processed on behalf of that organization and as a result the stated price for their data was $50 million. The price was subsequently paid, and the data was released. However, it represented a significant increase in the cost of the acquisition.

Situation two was strangely similar to situation one as they were in the similar position relative to their contractual arrangement with an outsourcer. The key difference was there was no buyout provision for the data, but there was a more insidious type of situation going on. A meeting was held, and it was agreed that the outsourcing arrangement would be terminated. A date was agreed upon for the systems and data to be returned to the acquiring parent company.

Unfortunately, the contract that was in effect made no mention of the format in which the data and systems must be returned. Clearly the fundamental assumption would be that digitized media would be utilized. Instead, the outsourcer did total data dumps on paper media and returned it on pallets wrapped in plastic. According to the person who was discussing this situation, they were unable to raise the systems or restore the data in a timely fashion, and the subsidiary disintegrated due to the inability to run the business.

- **Key Risk:** All underlying arrangements especially related to critical functionality such as IT are not known or fully understood prior to acquisition.

### Key questions to be answered:

- What are the critical underlying arrangements that do exist for critical support units or parts of the business?
- Have we properly identified the key risks related to these and made provisions to properly safeguard our interests and operate the business from day one?

## Eliminating the "Us versus Them" Syndrome

It seems that there is no way to get around it, but workers' loyalties are going to remain with the original employers who saw fit to provide them a livelihood. Those types of loyalties and bonds are extremely hard to break, and in many cases that never occurs. You then end up with "us versus them" and a fractionalized organization. The unfortunate part about this is the impact on operating costs, which can be monumental. This is exacerbated when there is a culture clash as well.

- **Key Risk:** Anticipated synergies will not be realized due to the inefficiencies that occur as a result of uncooperative labor forces.

Key questions to be answered:

- Do we understand the culture and the nature of the labor force that is going to be acquired with this company?
- What will we do to countermand a negative impact on the organization due to personnel attitudes and work habits?
- What types of definitive actions are we prepared to take, and how might problems negatively impact the acquisition?

## Making a Private Company Sarbanes-Oxley–Compliant

A number of acquisitions are actually privately held organizations, and in many cases they are being purchased into publicly held companies. The issue that immediately becomes front and center is the limited amount of time that you have to make a private company Sarbanes-Oxley–compliant. You must think about the impact on your quarterly reporting when you acquire a company that has significant control deficiencies. This may trigger an 8-K disclosure and if proper assurance cannot be gained could be extremely uncomfortable for the certifying executives.

- **Key Risk:** All of the activities that must be undertaken to make them Sarbanes-Oxley–compliant are not properly anticipated or investigated prior to acquisition.
- **Key Risk:** The control systems in the acquired company are significantly deficient, and the acquired company represents a large percentage of the combined operations.

Key questions to be answered:

- Do we understand all the critical financial and operational issues that they have on their agenda?
- How material will they be to our organization in the context of timing for compliance with the law?
- Do we have a clear grasp of the fundamental control structure that they have in place (both manual and automated) that will impact the financial reporting cycle for 404 purposes?
- Have we planned the closing date in such a manner as to not short-cycle ourselves relative to being able to become compliant?
- Have we dug sufficiently into their history to ensure that they do not have any financial and/or significant operational skeletons hiding in the closet?

These are some of the areas that can be looked at in the context of mergers and acquisitions relative to risk that are clearly only the very, very tiny tip of the iceberg. Acquisitions involve a tremendous amount of dedication and knowledge to the task of making them successful. These types of undertakings are not for the faint of heart or for those operating on a shoestring. You must have very deep pockets and thick skin to be successful in the merger and acquisition business.

## OUTSOURCING: WHAT YOU DON'T KNOW COULD KILL YOUR ORGANIZATION

Outsourcing—where should we start with this minefield of risks? We have so many to choose from, and that is what makes this subject matter great from a risk perspective. There are so many areas that can be discussed in the context of risk relative to outsourcing that it is almost overwhelming. It is even scarier how poorly it is managed in a very large percentage of outsourcing arrangements.

In the following subsections we will discuss a number of different risks that take place in outsourcing—all of which or any one of which could be fatal to an outsourcing arrangement if improperly managed. Let's start by putting one of the key facts in all of this right up front in the discussion.

There are a lot of people in corporations and other organizations who believe once they outsource something and it leaves the door or leaves the premises, their problems are over. What they don't realize is their problems are just beginning. There is one true fact about outsourcing that a number of corporate executives fail to realize. That fact is you can outsource anything you want, but you can never outsource risk! This statement bears repeating therefore here it is again: *you can never outsource risk!*

Outsourcing has been purveyed by the snake oil salesmen of the consulting arena to be the panacea for all corporate ills. Unfortunately, it brings on many more ills than it cures in most instances. What the purveyors have not brought to the attention of a lot of senior executives is that thinking that somebody else can run your business better than you do is somewhat misguided. If not misguided, it is certainly a commentary on themselves and their executive skill sets.

Whenever critical parts of organizations are handed over to an outsider or third party, you have lost a certain degree of control over its operation and its quality. The one key, however, is that whenever something goes wrong they are coming to see you. Your customers, your employees, or your vendors do not care who the outsourcer is; all they know is they are supposedly doing business with or are employed by you. As a result, you will bear the brunt of any and all undesirable consequences when supposedly the problem days were over. The risk never goes away, and that plays into each and every thing that you outsource.

In regard to enterprise risk management and the necessity to monitor and manage risk in outsourcing, this cannot be overstated. There must be a high degree of attention paid to any and all types of outsourcing arrangements within the confines of the ERM environment. Some of the high areas of risk that need to be considered (besides the ones to be discussed next) are preserving our corporate image, impact on those most greatly affected by the outsourcing, and the ability to oversee the arrangement long term.

We will now commence the discussion on some of the key risks that need to be noted in the critical stages of any outsourcing arrangement. We will start at the beginning of the process and work our way toward the end.

## Analysis of the Decision

The very first point of critical risk takes place at the decision to undertake outsourcing in the first place. There are some good reasons to outsource. A couple of reasons include lack of available skill sets in critical functionality by any other means and inability to locate suitable replacements for key talent sets due to lack of succession planning. If you look back and think about things logically, that is exactly what gave rise to the outsourcing industry in the first place. When organizations started panicking about the year 2000 and the world coming to an end at 12:01 A.M. is when outsourcing got kicked into high gear.

Because a lot of major systems were still written in some of the more archaic languages (at least in today's terms) like COBOL, to make changes everybody started seeking out COBOL programmers. Most of the COBOL programmers had written their last lines of code long before the advent of the year 2000 and were long gone, much to the dismay of these panicking entities. Luckily, I say somewhat facetiously, they were able to isolate the talent source outside of the United States, and that was the start of things. All of a sudden a new major corporate initiative and industry were formed, and the consulting houses were off to the races.

The talented systems engineers from other countries stepped up to the challenge, much to their credit, and dealt with that situation admirably.

However, a highly undesirable outcome of this same situation started to develop below the surface and went undetected until in many cases it was too late. As young people started to look around at job opportunities, fewer and fewer of them were enrolling in the IT programs at major universities because IT began bleeding jobs by the millions. Why would a very bright individual who was paying top dollar for her education want to go into a field where many career paths within that area of study only presented the following two opportunities? One opportunity was the ability to live and work in some country halfway around the world, the second opportunity was to take a job with a huge amount of job instability with an unsure future. You would certainly want that for your child wouldn't you?

What has now occurred is a self-fulfilling prophecy thanks to, in a great part, the brilliant strategy of outsourcing. We have eliminated a very vital set of talents in this country, eliminated massive amounts of jobs, which we could sorely use right now, taught other people in the world how to beat us at our own game, and are in the process of giving away one of our last great strengths as a country, intellectual property. This, of course, is irrespective of the other tangent effect of fueling other highly competitive economies to our own with our money. What a strategy, dang we're good. But I digress, you have my humblest apologies.

Many of the following reasons for outsourcing and making the decision are actually all the wrong reasons when you look at them logically:

- Economic benefit to the organization is one of the big ones you hear kicked around all the time—we're going to cut costs. Statistics will be cited later on in this chapter that will prove categorically that this is incorrect. The other fact is you don't solve a short-term cost problem with a long-term strategic initiative. That simply doesn't make any sense.
- "Everybody else is doing it and we must do it to remain competitive" (better known as but not often referred to in these circles as the lemming theory). All of the rest of our competitors are heading in that direction so let's follow them, right off the cliff. Everybody else is doing it is a very poor reason to do anything once you reach the age of reason.
- The "it doesn't make any sense for us to do things that are not our core business" argument. All of a sudden some misguided business genius (I use the terms very loosely) determined that everything that wasn't "core" should go away. Without digressing into a massive conversation over each and every aspect of this, I would simply refer you back to the core diagram, Figure 3.1. Remember when I referred to the critical support units or CSUs,

one of those being IT. Take about a minute and apply some common sense. What, if anything, runs in your organization without your IT environment being hot and functional? Nothing. When you start getting into this layer of the organizational structure, you are cutting pretty close to the bone of what holds everything together. But cut away if you must, until eventually the core rots or you sever it from its ability to operate.

- And last but not least, "I don't want to tackle it because it's too politically volatile" reason. Outsourcing has now become a way of life and the answer to all corporate problematic situations that nobody wanted to tackle internally. The easy out for executives who do not want to wrestle with the politics is to simply say in the best interest of the company we are going to outsource this to cut costs. But again as mentioned we will see later that this simply isn't true.

The last point to be made in this section (you will see later on when we look at the Ventoro study statistics) is that lack of preparation and improper decision making are what causes a large percentage of these arrangements to fail.

## Appropriate RFP Design

A key point of risk relative to outsourcing is to ensure that the request for proposal (RFP) is properly designed and specified. The RFP forms the basis for the contract and the arrangement that will eventually be struck with the outsourcer. In addition, for anything not specified in the RFP you will not be able to hold the outsourcer accountable for those criteria.

If an outsourcing arrangement is destined to fail, there are four key areas in which the risks are extremely high when that part of the process does not arrive at the appropriate outcome. Poorly defined RFPs are the second key area of risk of failure relative to outsourcing. Poor decision making is the first.

There are a number of very specific things that must be noted in the RFP. A few examples include forecast of future activities that are going to impact the arrangement, critical deadlines that must be met, and how critical data will be forthcoming from the arrangement. The critical data will be absolutely essential to managing the risk in these types of scenarios, as physical presence is not an option in most outsourcing arrangements. Therefore, the only hope of having effective oversight in long-term management of the arrangement is going to be logically. Without highly tailored risk-centric data that can be obtained almost at will, you will not be able to be successful in these types of endeavors.

Therefore if the RFP is poorly designed, you are immediately on the road to a less than ideal outcome from any outsourcing arrangement.

## Appropriate RFP Review and Selection

Some other relevant risks must also be looked at in the process of reviewing RFPs and also selecting the vendor. Every organization must be cognizant of the types of risks that can creep into this process and may in fact undermine its validity.

To avoid the risk of launching into a long diatribe of everything that can go wrong here, let's just pick one critical issue of risk. That risk issue is controlling the RFP responses back to all that were originally sent out to perspective vendors. The key reason for doing this is to learn a number of things relative to the riskiness of our RFP. For instance, we would like to know that everybody responded to the RFPs that were sent. This ensures that a number of undesirable risks have not taken place.

One such risk is to exclude a prospective vendor from consideration because somebody in the process simply does not mail them a packet or mails it too late to respond. This could be interpreted as biased or prejudicial and may get you litigated. A second risk is there are a large number of nonrespondents to the original solicitation. This could be indicative of a number of subrisks. First, a large portion of the prospective vendors were excluded to drive the business to a preselected candidate. Second, a number of qualified vendors did not respond to the RFP indicating that it may be poorly designed or impossible to execute with any type of cost effectiveness. That then gives rise to another risk worthy of consideration: what about those who did respond? Are they lying through their teeth and really aren't capable of doing the job? Those are just some of the reasons why you want to track the RFP responses and make sure the process has integrity.

## Appropriate Contract Design and Protective Covenants

On this subject matter you could go on virtually into infinity, and I simply am not going to live that long. As a result we will severely constrain this discussion. The key point is that this is the third critical area of risk where an outsourcing arrangement can be doomed to failure. As mentioned earlier, the RFP process is absolutely essential to setting good contract terms, but at the end of the day it is what is in that contract, unless the RFP is included by reference, that governs. In fact, that is one of the best provisions you can put into your contract is to ensure that the vendor understands that they will be held accountable for each and every capability responded to in the RFP.

There are literally hundreds of things that are extremely important, but let's just discuss the "right to audit" clause and the "acceleration of penalties" clause. The "right to audit" clause gives you the ability to send your internal auditors onto the premises at any time, at no cost, with open access to systems, processes, and physical facilities. These are just some of the privileges that should have been included in that clause but in many cases have not been. What results is a toothless clause with virtually no enforceability. Standing on the outside looking in with no right to change things in an outsourcing arrangement is a poor place to be.

A second very basic clause is the "acceleration of penalties" clause. This simply means that every time we have an unacceptable occurrence relative to inability on the part of the outsourcer to meet service level agreements (SLAs) or statements of work requirements a penalty should be levied. However, these penalties must be escalating; otherwise you run the risk of never being able to resolve an issue. It may become clear to the outsourcer, for instance, that it is cheaper to simply pay the penalties and not fix the problem. If this situation is having major repercussions that are undesirable on your customers, vendors, or employees, this may be totally unacceptable. At times, you must be able to significantly impact the wallet of the outsourcer to get their attention.

## Risk Profiles for the Arrangement

Another area that is unfortunately neglected when outsourcing parts of the organization is that they never build the concept of risk profiles into the arrangement to allow for appropriate oversight. Risk profiles should be developed for each and every part of the outsourced functionality and utilized to evaluate the performance of the outsourcer. These should be designed to be able to determine whether the desired outcomes are achieved or not. These profiles many times should actually be designed within the RFP to establish the expectations early on with the outsourcer.

When this is not done, there is little or no consistency in the oversight of the functionality of the outsourcer. The problem is that when people change places in the oversight function, or are replaced by new people, without these types of tools available there is no point of reference. It is extremely difficult at best to try and gain any kind of continuity when these types of fundamental processes are lacking. Risk profiles would normally be tied to the desired outcomes of the process, and the metrics developed accordingly so that they can be monitored logically. The lack of appropriately designated risk profiles is one of the biggest risks that can take place due to its negative impact on the ability to manage the outsourcer.

## Appropriate Risk Metrics for Monitoring the Arrangement

The point has already been clearly made relative to the necessity of well-developed risk metrics. One key thing to bear in mind, however, is that even if you do not do enterprise risk management objectively, outsourcing is one area that demands this type of methodology. There is no other way to effectively monitor a remote location other than with the use of data and doing it logically. If there is an area of risk that must be done in this fashion, this is definitely it.

The risk metrics developed should tie into the SLAs that have been established for the outsourcer. These can then be used to effectively measure their performance in a fair and unbiased manner. Besides taking great care in developing the risk metrics, extra caution must also be taken relative to how they are going to be measured and by what means.

In many areas of customer service that are historically outsourced, timeliness of the ability to oversee what is occurring is of the essence. Therefore, the risk metrics must be properly focused, and the means of producing them and reporting them must be real time or near time. If this is not the case, the organization starts to assume a very large risk from the standpoint of customer service, which may become in some cases intolerable.

There are numerous studies and information sources that support the fact that outsourced call centers are not increasing their levels of performance—they are actually degrading over time. The Customer Satisfaction Index by the CFI Group showed that customer satisfaction had declined by 20 percent between the years 2008 and 2009. Further, first-call resolution for onshore call centers is 26 percent higher than for offshore call centers. More importantly, the call center statistics also reflected that when connected with an offshore call center, potential customers were three times more likely to defect and not buy from that company again.

The appropriate risk metrics must be in place and must be utilized to monitor the activities of all outsourced arrangements. One of the observations in the Ventoro study to be referenced later is that the lack of appropriate outcome-focused metrics and the right measurement criteria of same is a key failure point in outsourcing.

## A Good Set of Baseline Metrics Going In

Tied into the previous discussion is the necessity for developing a good set of baseline metrics before the outsourcing arrangement is ever activated. Baseline metrics are those measures of activity that we have confidence in relative to effectively running the business that were, or should have been, employed when we ran the business. Baseline metrics should be developed for every part of an outsourcing arrangement. This can run the gamut from customer service to the number of accesses granted to our critical datasets and systems.

Another observation of the Ventoro study is that most executives have no idea what their baseline metrics should be, and have never had a good method of measuring the effectiveness of their business. In the majority of outsourcing arrangements, attention to baseline metrics is simply lacking or nonexistent, which again establishes a pattern for certain failure. Let's use a simple example to illustrate the point.

Assume we have a supercritical system that is responsible for doing everything that is imperative to the success of the business. If we do not take a reading of what the baseline metrics are for accesses to that system, in other words everybody that has access and at what level, what do we now do when it is outsourced? If the outsourcer has taken over the security functions and can essentially assign any accesses they would desire to, how would we know who could get into our system and what they could do there?

As an example, what may be part of the outsourcing contract is the ability to provide 24/7 support for that supercritical system. In order to accomplish that, what if the outsourcer takes the liberty of opening up our supercritical system to every one of its technicians all around the world for unlimited access at any time? Without the baseline metrics of how many accesses were granted and in what capacity, with the ability to compare that information to post outsourcing data, how would you know? It would certainly be a major point of concern, if not an unacceptable business risk, that has just been thrust upon us by the outsourcer without our knowledge. No baseline metrics, no idea that it ever occurred!

## Designing Appropriate Service Level Agreements

Service level agreements are pretty standard fare for any type of outsourced arrangement. But ensuring that the SLAs have been properly designed to our specific business is a significant risk. The outsourcer may have canned or predetermined SLAs that they employ in other similar clients, but they may be irrelevant as applied to our business. Therefore, it is imperative that the SLAs track directly to our business requirements.

The SLAs must be reviewed in significant detail to ensure that they are appropriate for the task at hand, namely running our business. It is pretty clear that bad SLAs can keep you in the dark on unacceptable problems in the business. This can lead to significant backlash that is headed straight for your company doors should the negative impacts become too great.

A key area of exposure in this area is the situation in which the measures that determine satisfactory or unsatisfactory SLAs may be poorly developed or ill-fitted to the task. Here is an example of how this can occur.

A client of mine, by whom I was engaged, subsequent to many of their outsourcing decisions, decided to outsource all of their transportation needs, which included delivery of product to their customers. In my absence they set a service level agreement that called for 99 percent accuracy in deliveries on a monthly basis. That may appear stellar on the surface, and wouldn't it be great if this was achieved every month? Not so fast, the one percent that inevitably was not done right on a monthly basis was the company's largest customer. How does it sound now, risky or not risky?

A generic example in the area of IT would be as follows. What if the outsourcer guaranteed you 98.6 percent uptime on all of your networks on average? That may sound terrific, but what if you had one supercritical network that supported every critical function of your business and 60 noncritical networks? All of the noncritical networks had very high percentage uptimes, but your supercritical network is only up 54.5 percent of the time. But when you summarized all of the uptimes together it came to 98.9 percent. They exceeded the service level agreement as stated, and earned a bonus for doing so. How do you feel about it? Risky or not risky, we all know the answer to that one, don't we?

## Having a Good Oversight Methodology and Technological Support

To round out the earlier discussion, this is the fourth major area of risk that if poorly done is definitely going to doom your outsourcing arrangement to the abyss of failed endeavors. There are a number of risks associated with this functionality of outsourcing as you can imagine, so we are only going to consider a couple at best.

The first key area of risk is committing the money to have highly talented people with extremely good working knowledge in the area that they are overseeing. This normally means a high-level manager, director, or supervisor who is intimately familiar with the function that has been outsourced. What is most curious is that most organizations think they are going to save tons of money by getting rid of all these highly paid people. That assumption is total fiction, because without those knowledgeable people you cannot oversee this arrangement.

What inevitably happens is organizations don't make these full-time positions, and the oversight dramatically suffers due to lack of attention. Or, it starts out well, but there is no succession plan, and highly talented people do not desire to do this type of functionality forever. As a result, they lose interest or get promoted, and they bring in a substitute who has absolutely no knowledge of what's going on. There are no risk profiles or underlying process in place that provide stability, only poor metrics with no historical context all in the hands of people who know nothing about what they're doing. This is of course a recipe for disaster.

The second key risk is how and where to establish the oversight, and how to ensure the ability to restructure or retract that arrangement. There are two key ways in which to establish oversight from a location perspective. The first is to retain the employees on your own company site, captive oversight (CO), and then equip them with the tools and techniques they need to do oversight remotely. The other option is to actually station employees at the outsourcer permanently or what could be referred to as on-site oversight (OSO).

The first model of captive oversight is only going to be as good as the technology and the data given to them to perform this functionality. They must have open access to all data they require at any time they desire to have it as part of the arrangement. They must have properly defined metrics that are clearly risk-centric and clearly related directly to the primary functionality of what is being overseen.

Also, they must have the technological platform that allows them to extract the data, manipulate the data, and analyze the data in any form they need to perform their oversight. The more automated this process and the more real time the data, the more effective they are going to be. If any of these things are lacking, you will basically hamstring their ability to do their job, and their enthusiasm for performing the oversight tasks will wane quickly.

The OSO model is one of the riskiest that can be established in outsourcing. If this is the initial oversight functionality that is established, you had better have a contract provision that allows you to revisit that, retract it, and establish the captive oversight model if required. The reason for this is that once an organization sends skilled individuals out to the outsourcer it is like cutting them loose from the mother ship and sending them to another planet. In other words, if you live with Martians long enough, you begin to think like a Martian or as a more familiar phrase goes, "When in Rome do as the Romans."

It is a predictable pattern that the loyalties of these people will switch to the outsourcer somewhere between the sixth and eighth month of their residence. At that point, your oversight is essentially gone, and you will be very lucky if they don't start defending the outsourcer against your claims.

## Multiply Your Outsourcing and Multiply Your Risk

The more things you outsource, the more you multiply your risk, but it is not a straight-line linear relationship. In fact, your risk multiplication can take on exponential proportions. As discussed, it is very common for organizations to outsource multiple functions, not just one. When executives get on a roll, anything that is not core has got to go. Let's use an example that I developed for a client of mine, which illustrates this point precisely. It is called the Baseball Diamond of Risk (BDR). Referring to Figure 9.2, here is how it sets up. The manager (MGR) represents a process owner or department head that still remains with the company. This person is the only one still gainfully employed by the organization.

Playing the catcher's position is Human Resources (HR). HR, the first functionality that is outsourced, is responsible for all human resource activities throughout the entire organization. The organization occupying first base is the outsourced pension fund administrator (PEN). They are responsible for managing numerous pension plans for the organization and its various employee groups. The organization occupying second base is outsourced benefits administration (BEN). They are responsible for managing all benefits for the organization. We will skip the shortstop because well it just doesn't fit the game plan. Playing the third base position is the outsourced payroll (P/R) function.

Now just for grins I have put IT as an outfielder in left field because they are very far removed from the rest of these with respect to normal functionality. But of course as you may have imagined, IT is already outsourced as well. The point of this illustration is just how convoluted risk can get when you have multiple organizations running critical functionalities and they are all outsourced. Worse

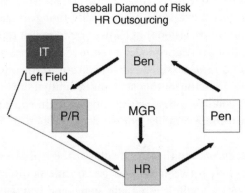

**FIGURE 9.2**  Baseball Diamond of Risk

yet, they all have to interact constantly because they all play important roles in the health, well-being, and job satisfaction of our employee base, which is one of our most critical assets.

Okay, let's start the ball game. The manager pitches the ball to an employee for strike three and says you're out of here. The employee at this point has a number of choices assuming the game is over for them and so is their playing career with this team. They can go quietly out of the ballpark and disappear over the horizon. They can raise a ruckus, kick dirt on the shoes of the manager, and file a litigation action, or decide to go down into the clubhouse, hide out, and dream up what kind of nasty things they can do for payback. Each of these activities raises a certain specter of risk for the organization from the necessity of notification for COBRA benefits, to having to wind up the legal team to defend another purported wrongful discharge, not to be confused with the oily discharge mentioned earlier.

Meanwhile back at the ballpark, the manager now must initiate the termination notice for the employee who just left the team. That notice must alert HR that this person is gone and that they should take the appropriate actions for termination. It would be the hope then that HR has the contact points for every one of the other players on the baseball diamond. In other words, they must notify the pension managers if involved, so that the appropriate pension actions can be taken if required due to the employee's years of service to the team. HR, or somebody, must notify the people that are responsible for benefits, wherever they exist, that this former team member must be removed from the roster as appropriate.

Then HR, or somebody, must notify payroll that this person is no longer eligible to be paid and what type of severance and/or vacation payouts, and so on to which they may be entitled. While all this is going on, somebody must also notify IT that if the former employee has any type of security clearances, they must be deactivated and cleared from any and all systems now. For instance, we would not want that player down in the clubhouse to be a former operating systems programmer and still have access. That could get ugly, to say nothing of risky.

What is the point of the baseball diamond scenario? It is meant to express the complexity of how risk must be managed in a multioutsourcing situation. That is why I mentioned before that enterprise risk management must have its eye very clearly on the ball on the outsourcing arena. This is without question one of the most risky areas that most organizations possess, and it can be devastating if not properly overseen. Can you imagine—if you had massive turnover on a regular basis—the times people could drop the ball and things that are absolutely essential simply wouldn't be done? The propensity to be in violation of major regulatory requirements and the subject of significant litigation is virtually assured.

Just simply proving that all of the interactions are working correctly on an ongoing basis for every employee in this scenario, irrespective of trying to oversee all of these areas appropriately, would be mind blowing. Without an extremely sophisticated, highly automated methodology used to evaluate this, there would be few, if any, guarantees that you are not hanging out in a thousand different directions from a risk standpoint.

 ## DEBUNKING THE OUTSOURCING MYTHS: THE VENTORO STUDY

Everything in this section that will be discussed will be referenced to a critical part of the Ventoro study. The Ventoro Preliminary Findings and Conclusions Report was issued around October 2004 and can be found at www.ventoro.com under the research and publications tab. What an interesting coincidence that this is about the same time, if not exactly the same time, that the COSO/ERM model came out. What a shocker—a framework for managing risk that may really work and probably some of the best information I have ever seen for managing outsourcing risk emerge at essentially same time. Since the Ventoro study was dated as a 2005 study, now some people might say well that's a little dated—perhaps so in a pure temporal sense. However, I have no doubt whatsoever that the findings then would be no different now except that they may reflect a much more negative trending.

Why would I make such an assertion? A colleague of mine who works for an outsourcing firm who specializes in locating economical labor sources for their clients told me they have had to change sources 12 times in the last 15 years. In addition, there are only so many skilled workers to go around; as a result compensation equalization is rapidly accelerating in a number of labor markets globally. It all comes back to the famous premise of supply and demand. The supply is not there, the demand is rising, therefore the compensation rises. High tide raises all boats.

The Ventoro study is an extremely good document for anyone who is entertaining the notion of outsourcing offshore or offshoring their operations. The fundamental difference between the two is outsourcing offshore you hire a firm that specializes in outsourcing in a different country. Offshoring your operations is when you go in and establish your own organization and hire all of your own people in another country.

I will introduce a number of graphics from this study to ingrain the message that outsourcing is wrought with risks if improperly done or done for the wrong reasons. All of the graphics appearing here in this chapter are from that Ventoro study and are the results of their excellent work. In connection with the graphics shown, I will then make some of my own observations and commentary relative to the risk or information that is being depicted and why these things should be critical to the ERM environment.

Figure 9.3 depicts the participants in the study. There were 5,232 key executives that were polled from North America and Europe. This is a very representative group of informed individuals. In other words, this was not 10 people in Yale, South Dakota (no disrespect to Yale—my mother was born there!).

It is significant that it is a nice cross-section of information of experiences that relate directly to the risks that can be encountered in this arena. It is also significant that it should be the key executives who are the decision makers in these areas and therefore would know better than anybody the pitfalls that can be encountered. This broad perspective of risk can be invaluable to the ERM environment in getting centered on what is really important.

This graphic is important, in that it indicates that there are still a lot of people waiting out there to make this kind of decision, even though outsourcing has been in existence for any number of years now. However, it can also

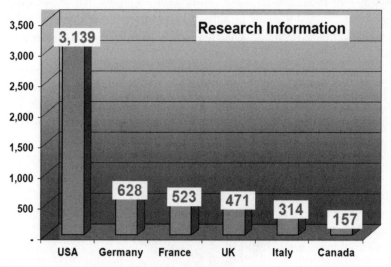

**FIGURE 9.3** Research Participants

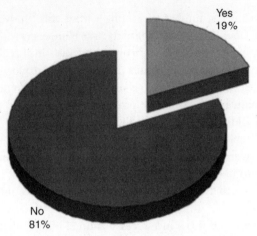

**FIGURE 9.4** Percent with an Outsource Strategy

reflect that in organizations of certain sizes outsourcing is not such a pressing issue, which then raises another interesting question. If we're going to try and stimulate job growth in this country, what kind of fiscal policy do you establish to foster job growth?

Based upon this and Figure 9.4, you could conclude that the small to medium-sized businesses should get a tax break and those that are shipping the jobs offshore should actually be subject to a tax for the privilege. A risk that would certainly have to be considered here is whether that type of tax policy will become a reality.

As you can see in Figure 9.5, again it is undeniable that the Fortune 1000 group has actively embraced outsourcing as a strategic initiative. This raises another very interesting question. If you look at the graphs that will be following (from Figure 9.8 on), why are we seeing what we see? If these

**FIGURE 9.5** Fortune 1000 Firms with Offshore Strategy

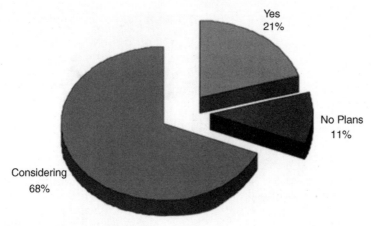

**FIGURE 9.6**  Next-Year Strategy

are supposed to be the best and the brightest organizations, the results they are experiencing don't seem to substantiate that they are the best and brightest by any stretch of the imagination. The risk clearly being depicted here is if they continue with this strategy, which as indicated by Figure 9.6 they will, does this bode well for the future? In other words, is it a sound strategic initiative, and will their cost structure be positively or negatively impacted?

Figure 9.6 shows that 68 percent more executives were considering and were already planning an outsourcing strategy for the following year. This implies by definition that outsourcing will continue to expand. The risk issue that is being raised is how many of these organizations will succumb to the same mistakes that have been made in the past? From an ERM perspective, this should ratchet up the consideration they give this risk if they are in a firm where this is being considered.

The overwhelming majority in Figure 9.7 were definitely going to be spending more money in the year after the study on offshore outsourcing. This means by definition that they are placing more corporate assets at risk in an area where as cited in the study they cannot calculate a return on investment due to their lack of baseline information. If this is still true today, which would be highly likely, it would seem to be an extremely large financial risk to be investing precious corporate resources in those areas where a provable return is virtually an unknown.

Figures 9.8 and 9.9 are two of my favorites of all of the graphics presented in the Ventoro study. These are the key decision points as to why this type of strategy is undertaken in the first place, and as a result they are the key areas of

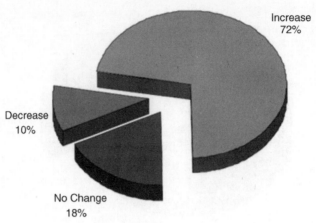

**FIGURE 9.7** Change in Offshore Spending

Copyright © Ventoro 2004, page 13.

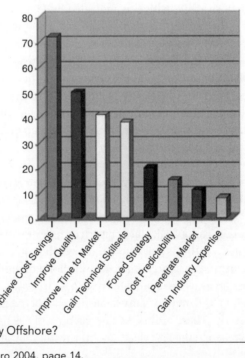

**FIGURE 9.8** Why Offshore?

Copyright © Ventoro 2004, page 14.

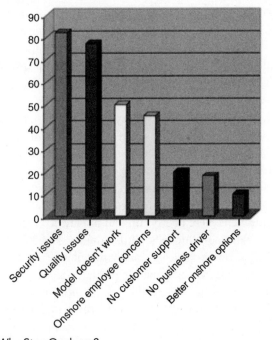

**FIGURE 9.9** Why Stay Onshore?

risk that must be considered by enterprise risk management. Clearly in 70 percent plus of the cases presented in Figure 9.8, the primary reason for embarking on this strategy was to save costs. What is extremely alarming with the graphic is that the second-most-prominent reason is to improve quality for roughly 49 percent of the respondents. A couple of big risks come jumping out from this particular graphic.

The first big risk is that there is this blind assumption that they will save costs by invoking this strategy, and the sheer number of respondents believing it says it's essentially guaranteed. Yet the likelihood is excellent that they have not anticipated all of their costs or included them in the analytics to determine if this was the right choice. I would be willing to assert with little or no risk that one of the key costs that was excluded in virtually all of the cost studies was the cost of exiting the arrangement.

Most executives and other people involved in this process do not understand that they are going to leave this arrangement at some time in the future. It is not going to last forever, and by definition when you leave, you will have massive transition costs or pay a significant fee for the privilege if it's premature. These costs are virtually never factored in, and as such these expectations are totally unrealistic. The other portion of the expectations that is unrealistic is the percentage of cost savings that are going to be experienced. In very few, if any, instances are the percentages expected ever realized.

The second big risk is the quality issue. This is saying that executives actually expect their quality is going to go up by shipping this function out to somebody else who has never performed it before in our circumstances. If one were to look at this applying common sense, this also says that whoever made this decision clearly was running an organization where quality was not important. I do not know about you, but to me that seems to be a damning commentary on the senior executives. That would also go along with other observations in the study, which clearly stated that executives had no idea how to measure the functionalities within their own organizations before they outsourced them. This implies that their organizations were poorly run and displayed a lack of discipline.

Figure 9.9 is extremely interesting from a number of different perspectives that impact risk. The number one reason not to embrace the strategy of moving offshore is security. That is an extremely important consideration, but there will be an interesting twist on this further on in one of the other graphics. Depending upon how you interpret it, this is a very visionary executive saying it is not worth the security risk to take this action because they are concerned about the offshore firm or personnel. Another interesting question is how many of them foresaw the risk, which is actually the bigger risk that exists in their own organizations? This risk is quite the opposite of what you would logically conclude. This risk will be illustrated later.

The second key point of observation is that just as in the previous graphs, the second-largest reason (approximately 77 percent) not to do it is quality. This also implies that whoever responded accordingly feels that the risk is extremely low in their current operations and that they must be running a fairly tight ship. That is actually quite refreshing and would be interesting to see if the statistics of those organizations actually substantiated that belief.

The third and most interesting of all that I will discuss here are those respondents who said the model does not work (approximately 48 percent of the respondents). That may be indicative of a population that has done some intense homework and isolated all the key risks that are inherent in these arrangements. Those people probably have an extremely good set of insights into how their organization actually operates. They have risk-assessed the situation and have resisted the call of the Sirens of outsourcing.

How much needs to be said about Figure 9.10 from a risk perspective? The commentary on the effectiveness of the assumptions versus the reality of the world of outsourcing could not be more conclusive. The first bar saying that 27

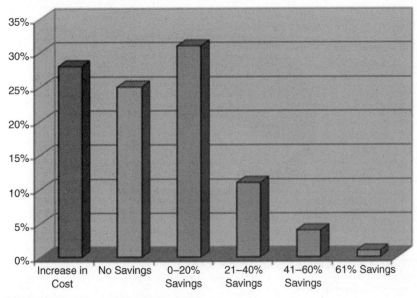

**FIGURE 9.10**  How Well Is It Working?

percent roughly actually spent more to outsource than it costs those organizations to operate it themselves is absolutely comical. These organizations incurred more risk, and the point clearly is they did not do their homework, did virtually no research, had no idea what they were doing when they ran it themselves, and didn't know whether they should outsource the function or not, but they did it anyway. How much are these companies actually paying these people to make these business decisions? That is a pathetic commentary on corporate governance.

The next bar at 24 percent basically says that they broke even. However, it is highly unlikely that they broke even when you factor in all of the costs incurred, the process and system disruption, and every other type of dysfunctional activity that was undertaken to accomplish this. Wow, talk about chasing oneself around the block; what an exercise in futility!

Add both of those bars together, and the number is 51 percent who either spent more for the privilege or at best broke even, but as I mentioned that is highly unlikely. Let me see, I seem to recall from Figure 9.8 that the number-one reason for doing this in the first place was to save money—obviously in these cases it is not happening.

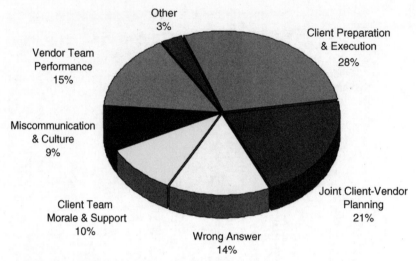

**FIGURE 9.11**   Offshore Outsourcing Root Failure

One of the critical risks that ERM must then undertake is to make sure that all significant assumptions relative to major strategic corporate initiatives are sound and proven. When you couple this with the dismal success of mergers and acquisitions, which was discussed earlier, it does not take a rocket scientist to figure out that something's wrong with the guidance system of these organizations.

There are a number of things of interest to be noted in Figure 9.11. It is very clear that 28 percent of those that fail are due to client preparation and execution. They don't understand why they're doing it, and they don't know how to execute. Another 21 percent of the root failure causes are because of joint client-vendor planning. Poor planning, indicative of total lack of preparation, is responsible for this second-greatest set of causal events. Another 14 percent say that what was done was the wrong answer. This percentage is indicative of poor research and again not understanding what they are doing.

Add this all up, and this means a whopping 63 percent of all causes of failure are because of ill-prepared misguided efforts.

All of this information points very clearly to what we discussed earlier, which is that organizations that go into outsourcing offshore many times do it for the wrong reasons and they don't plan well at all when they do it. Worse yet, they don't take the time to determine if it is a valid strategic initiative. Much

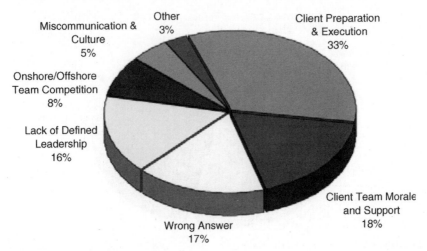

**FIGURE 9.12**  Offshoring Root Failure

of this may be prompted by consultants as well, which again goes back to our discussion of the blind leading the blinder.

As shown in Figure 9.12, offshoring root failure causal events follow a very similar pattern, and again there are undeniable indications of the client not being able to prepare themselves adequately and not able to execute this strategic initiative in 33 percent of the cases. Failing because you are not prepared adequately is a dismal statistic and speaks volumes about the direction that the organization is getting from its senior executives.

In addition, the teams that they formed are clearly not adequate to the task, have low morale, and are receiving inadequate support in the areas in which it is required in 18 percent of the cases. Further, Figure 9.12 illustrates that 17 percent say that it was the wrong answer, clearly pointing out they did not properly research their strategic initiative before executing it, or in most cases executing themselves. Add all of these numbers up, and this totals 68 percent of failures due to ill-preparedness, little or no research or understanding of the subject matter, and improper execution.

These damning statistics go back to the points that I was making earlier in this section. If you are not prepared, if you don't do your homework, if you don't execute a proper RFP, if you don't execute a good solid business contract, if you don't have baseline metrics, you're going to fail!

Of all of the graphics presented in the Ventoro research study, this is my favorite by far because it destroys one of the greatest urban myths about

**FIGURE 9.13**  Where Are the Savings?

Copyright © Ventoro 2004, page 22.

outsourcing. Going back to Figure 9.10, which we talked about earlier, if you ask the question "Where all the savings?" you can stop right there, and it would still be a great question in almost 52 percent of the cases. However, referring to Figure 9.13, the very first common misperception that the savings are actually going to come from labor savings or salaries and wages is blown out of the water. Nothing could be further from the truth—only 9 percent is the result of the employee cost, and you would think that that is the scary part.

As shown in Figure 9.13, that is not nearly the scariest part. The scariest part is the largest percentage of savings category on the graphic is 46 percent for internal process improvement. Do you realize what a commonsense, literal interpretation of that result would be? It would mean that you could take some total quality management methodologies (TQM) that were in this country in the 1940s, thanks to such notables as Deming and Crosby, apply those same methodologies today, and solve all of the problems noted here without leaving your own building in 46 percent of the cases.

These data point to another alarming and annoying conclusion about outsourcing. A number of these outsourcing strategies are undertaken simply because nobody wants to play the internal politics, and nobody wants to take an active interest in resolving the root causes of problems in their companies. They don't want to manage, they just want to be paid huge sums, and then they want to make it somebody else's problem. The fallacy in their logic, of course, is that it remains their problem.

**IP Theft Source**

Offshore Team 33%

Onshore Team 67%

**FIGURE 9.14** IP Theft

Copyright © Ventoro 2004, page 102.

It is clear that vendor execution is only responsible for cost savings of 45 percent. In my mind this raises the immediate question of where is the real gain? While giving up control of critical parts of our organizations, you still retain all the risk? I must be missing something; unfortunately, no I don't think so.

According to the research conducted by the Ventoro group, any firm executing an offshore strategy has a 1 in 10 chance of incurring Intellectual Property (IP) theft. It is alarming that there is at least a 10 percent chance that you going to lose some of your IP, and as we all know, the chances of loss are much higher in certain countries. But the scariest part is what is depicted in Figure 9.14.

The chances are twice as high that you are going to lose IP to internal employees as opposed to offshore personnel. The reason for this is that they feel they are being abandoned by the company. Whenever that feeling sets in, self-defense is the only logical strategy to pursue, which is what they do.

This surfaces another huge area of risk and exposure whenever outsourcing is undertaken as a strategic initiative. Just as discussed earlier in this chapter, utilizing the OSO, on-site oversight model, those people who are charged with overseeing the outsourcer but are resident at the outsourcer also feel this same form of alienation.

In the area of risk in outsourcing, it cannot be overemphasized that loss of critical employees during that time, after it becomes known that outsourcing is

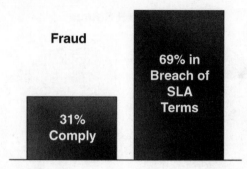

**FIGURE 9.15**  Fraud Rate

on the agenda for strategic initiatives, is imminent. Any highly or semi-skilled employees who believe they are within the areas that will be affected by outsourcing are going to immediately start heading toward the exit unless they are retained by some very lucrative arrangements.

Normally, the best strategy for retaining personnel is to select those that you want to retain in advance, come up with a lucrative package to make them stay, and put them in responsible positions overseeing the outsourcer. This does, of course, run counter to the whole theory of thinking you are going to save a lot of money—because you are not. If you do not do these things, however, you run the bigger risk of losing all of your qualified personnel. If, in fact, the outsourcing arrangement never goes forward at that point, this would be catastrophic.

If you are looking to be defrauded in outsourcing, you have come to the right place. As shown in Figure 9.15, the statistics overwhelmingly state that you will be defrauded in these types of arrangements. Step right up to the table, your seat is waiting for you, or, more correctly phrased, your seat is waiting to be handed to you. In virtually 70 percent of these cases, you will be defrauded, meaning the vendor will be out of compliance with your SLAs or statements of work. So in an extremely large portion of the circumstances it is not a question of whether you will be defrauded—you will—it is just a matter of severity.

The only things that will mitigate these types of occurrences are good sound metrics and highly qualified oversight of the contract. Organizations that do not have these in place are twice as likely to be defrauded as those who do. It just makes good business sense to put the right processes in place, but this also gives you a baseline to measure your success or failure in the outsourcing arena.

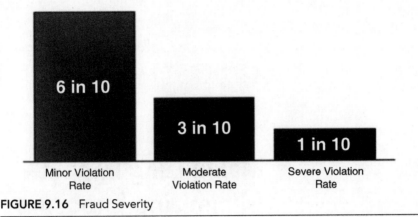

**FIGURE 9.16** Fraud Severity

Figure 9.16 rounds out the discussion of fraud relative to offshore outsourcing strategies. As shown in Figure 9.16, 6 in 10 of these are minor violations, 3 in 10 moderate violations, and 1 in 10 is severe. It is important to realize that in many cases the outsourcers have encountered operating costs that perhaps they did not anticipate or they are looking to shave a few corners to make a bigger profit. Whatever the case is, it comes right out of your pocket. That is where their hands seem to be permanently attached like an undesired extra appendage.

This concludes thoughts on these issues for this chapter. I will now move forward to our closing discussion in Chapter 10.

# CHAPTER TEN

# Maximizing Impact— Minimizing Exposure

 ## WHO OWNS THE RISK MANAGEMENT PROCESS?

In establishing an enterprise risk management (ERM) environment, one of most critical questions is this: Who owns the risk management process, and how are the duties divided accordingly? Let's make some clarifications initially so that everybody understands precisely what is being discussed here. The ERM environment, risk management process, and everything that constitutes it can be very simply divided up from a responsibility standpoint.

Let's start with the first fact that the chief risk officer (CRO) does not own all of the risk of the enterprise. He is responsible only for the risk of not properly reporting significant risk events in a timely fashion to the appropriate parties.

The first things that must be owned are the business and/or organizational risks. Business/organizational risk are the risks that confront the organization every day and are owned by everybody in the organization in the respective levels at which they operate. In other words, everybody throughout the entire organization owns risk just because they come to work every day and collect a paycheck. But just for the sake of discussion, let's give a very simple example.

Bank tellers have a tremendous amount of risk that they deal with every day, yet strangely enough they are the least paid position in most banks. The bank teller has primary responsibility for pleasing the customers and retaining their patronage. They are the front-line people who build or destroy the image of the bank every day by the relationships they form and constantly enhance with the customer base or by the ones they ruin. They handle all the cash transactions coming over the teller line and must balance every day. In the context of regulatory violations, they should be the first ones that would notice undesirable patterns of behavior with persons or companies within your customer base.

In other words, if there was a company or a person who was constantly trying to wash money through the bank by avoiding the lawful limits of reporting, these types of practices should be noticed by the tellers, and the proper persons should be informed. But if the tellers are not diligent or if they are not inspired to be diligent, these things will go unnoticed. They also set the tone for whether the customer is going to be interested in buying other services of the bank that are being offered, especially if as a result they are going to have to have more interaction with those tellers.

It doesn't make any difference if you are teller in a bank or a worker on a high voltage line trying to restore power—you own your own set of risks and certain risks of the organization as well.

The second part of the ERM environment that must be owned is the ERM functionality itself. That means, of course, the infrastructure of gathering the risk information, setting the risk responses, determining probability of occurrence and impact, discovering the root causes of risk, and the timely reporting of same. All of the noted responsibilities belong to the CRO or ERM head in the case where a CRO does not exist. This person is responsible for every facet of the ERM functionality and must be held accountable for any shortcomings encountered within that discipline.

So there is a clear division of responsibilities within the enterprise risk management. Everybody within the organization is a risk owner. The head of ERM is responsible for the process of bringing significant risk events to the attention of senior management and the Board of Directors.

 ## INVOLVING THE STAKEHOLDERS: CREATING A CRITICAL BUSINESS TOOL

To be successful, enterprise risk management must involve virtually every key person in the organization. This is true because if those people within the organization who are key to its operating capabilities do not embrace ERM, then ERM will never become a viable part of the business on a day-to-day basis.

In implementing ERM, it must always be approached as an environment that is owned by everybody for their own mutual benefit. Enterprise risk management should not be something that is thrust upon the persons in the organization and then subsequently undermined by their failure to embrace the concept.

However, in order to ensure success, the ERM environment must be truly built as a business tool that earns a return on the investment that is deemed acceptable by the organization. If done properly, there is no reason why ERM would not be sought after by each and every key member of the organization, not just tolerated as another one of those useless corporate initiatives.

That is why I advocated that it be incorporated into every aspect of the environment and that it be data-centric to yield the maximum benefit with a minimal amount of resources required. In addition, if properly implemented, it will be a tremendously valuable exercise in proving that the data integrity of the organization is intact and functioning as intended.

Everyone in the organization should want to actively participate in it because it has proven itself highly successful in those areas that have embraced it as the quintessential must-have business tool.

 ## EXTENDING THE IMPACT: MAKING IT A COMPANY ESSENTIAL

One way to extend the impact of the ERM environment and to make it highly effective in the twenty-first century is to make it an organizational essential strategy (OES). An OES is a defined strategic emphasis that must be undertaken each and every time that a major change to the company infrastructure is undertaken.

The literal interpretation would mean that you cannot establish a new business process, nor can you build and implement a new system, without employing the appropriate risk emphasis as required to facilitate the functionality of ERM. Every organizational essential strategy should be mandated to be included in the design and execution of every critical infrastructure modification.

If these types of mandates are not put in place, there will be no uniformity of purpose as the movers and shakers of the organization will not be compelled to focus on risk as a major part of their responsibilities. The identification and management of risk within acceptable tolerance levels should be part and parcel of every goal or objective established throughout the enterprise. It would be even more effective if it was established as a key part of every executive's and key manager's compensation packages relative to amounts received, bonuses paid, and promotions earned.

If ERM becomes an interwoven part of the fabric of the enterprise, then it has a chance of attaining a high degree of success. If it is viewed as simply a bolt-on attachment occupying space on an already crowded engine block, then chances for success are extremely slim.

## STRATEGICALLY LINKING KEY RISKS AND KEY CONTROLS: CREATING A HOME

As stressed earlier in this book, it is essential to recognize the undeniable link between key risks and key controls. Wherever there is a key risk in the organization, there must also be a key control to perform one of two critical functions. The first critical function is to help mitigate or completely eliminate any highly undesirable risk condition from the organization. The second critical function would be to trigger an appropriate risk response in those situations where the risk does manifest itself within the organization.

Essential to the ultimate success of any organization is the need to understand the importance of ERM as the driving force of all strategic initiatives undertaken within it. ERM must be thought of as the Holistic Oversight Management Environment (HOME) and must become the overlord of all management and governance of the enterprise. All other initiatives become logical symbiotic subsets or layers of the environment with the responsibility of taking information from ERM and feeding back critical information that may not be known to ERM. Such things would be unknown or emerging risks, changes in existing risks, modifications of potential impacts, known impacts, and changes in probability of occurrence to enhance ERM effectiveness. A visualization of what is being discussed here is shown in Figure 10.1.

ERM provides the only logical total environment to incorporate everything required for good sound organizational governance. As discussed earlier, without utilizing ERM as an anchor point for all governance, risk, and control (GRC) concepts, the organization will end up with a highly fractured and dysfunctional governance environment, which is counterintuitive at best. *Common sense would say that makes no sense whatsoever.* We do not need 2, 3, 4, 5, or 20 different little groups, all looking after the same or similar subject matter within one organization.

A structure that is organized in that fashion will lead to haphazard information flow and massive duplication of effort, resulting in a high degree

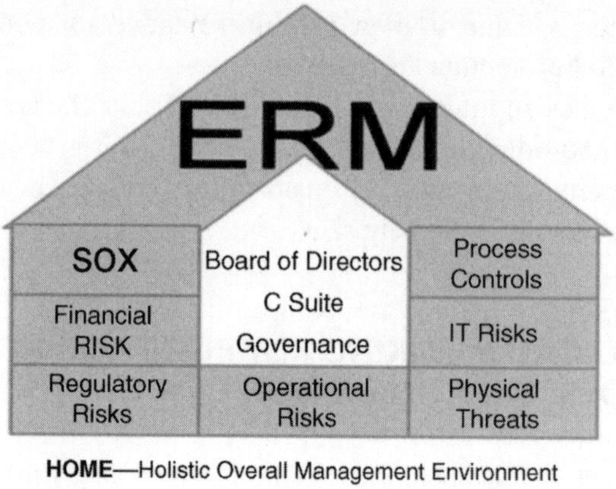

HOME—Holistic Overall Management Environment

**FIGURE 10.1** HOME

of inefficiency and excessive cost. There is absolutely no reason not to incorporate all governance functionality into one totally integrated, highly functional enterprise. The exception to this statement, even though it should have a symbiotic relationship with ERM, is internal audit.

Internal audit is a very important part of the overall governance structure when it is properly focused and the department leadership is strong and visionary. However, it cannot be incorporated under the oversight and control of the ERM environment. The reason is that it must maintain its independence and its objectivity as a result of the way in which its audit charter is structured by the audit committee.

The internal audit group must risk-assess and audit everything in the enterprise, which includes ERM. The group cannot be totally unbiased or impartial if they were to audit enterprise risk management while reporting into the function. Hmmmmmm! That sounds as if it would be a problem if internal audit reported anywhere but administratively to the CEO with a direct line to the Board of Directors–Audit Committee. Oh well, that is a problem for another day.

Internal audit must be able to independently review the process and reach conclusions relative to its efficiency and effectiveness for the purposes intended. What must be required is that it fulfill its mission to accurately identify, manage, and report timely on the status of all critical risks existing within the enterprise.

# BUILDING THE DREAM HOME: AUTOMATING EVEN YOUR SOX

In the everyday world of going to the office, I do not know what big advantages would be gained by automating your socks in the process of getting dressed. But when we talk about automating SOX in the context of making Sarbanes-Oxley much less painful to comply with, that should certainly spark some attention around the old water cooler.

One of my other tricky acronyms, DREAM (Data-Centric Risk Evaluation Assessment and Management), should be the ultimate goal to which every ERM environment aspires. In discussing the subject matter in Chapter 8, I identified threshold triggers and MOMS as two critical tools that should be incorporated into the future strategic initiatives of each and every ERM environment that exists. The incorporation of these tools goes hand in hand with the up-front immersion of the ERM environment into the new systems development efforts of the organization.

By applying these types of tools and activities to the world of IT, all organizations can make monstrous strides toward highly effective governance in the twenty-first century. As mentioned earlier, the one great differentiator between highly successful organizations and all of the others with whom they compete is their highly effective employment of advanced automation and technology.

It can never be overstated that behind every successful organization is a highly disciplined, highly automated environment that facilitates its operations day in and day out without exception. DREAM HOME is nothing more than an ERM-based governance infrastructure combining one of the greatest assets you have, your data, with a resource that in this world is definitely plentiful and comparatively cheap, computing power. Bringing these together into a data-centric risk assessment and management methodology to make you a super-power within your industry or competitive segment certainly warrants some significant strategic attention.

A high-level representation of what a DREAM structure may look like is shown in Figure 10.2.

The concept of a DREAM HOME may look overwhelming at first, but it is something that can be obtained strategically by each and every organization with careful planning and visionary forethought. The only thing that is holding back any organization in this country, or for that matter the rest of the world, from accomplishing these types of things is senior executives who are not visionaries. It's like any other fundamental issue—it all goes back to tone at the

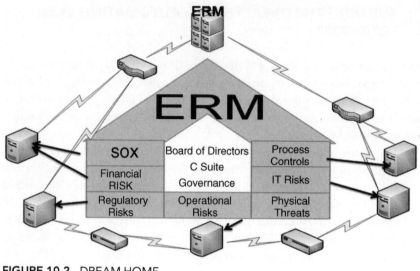

**FIGURE 10.2** DREAM HOME

top. If their longest view of the world is the end of next quarter, an organization has no ability to build for the future. These types of concepts are meant for companies that intend to be around for the next 20, 30, 50, 100 years, and beyond.

If you look at those corporations that are truly great, and unfortunately there are not many, those are the ones that will see the need for the tools and get them built. They will see also the return on that investment multiply year after year while they bypass their competitors and start dominating the marketplace. Risk assessment and management is all about being able to predict the future, seeing the risks before they are upon us, and taking the appropriate action to avoid the need for crisis management. These types of tools turn from reactive when they first come into existence as a result of having to establish a historical baseline, to proactive and predictive once that line in the sand has been drawn.

The problem that plagues subjectivity-based risk models, which is essentially what everybody is still using today, is that they are now and always will be grounded in guesswork and supposition instead of data and facts. They will always have to be repopulated with guesswork and scoring every time a risk assessment is desired. They will never ever attain the plateau of being data driven, flowing, liquid, and able to predict the future based upon building historical context dynamically.

Without this capability such ERM environments will never be able to see the future, which is the whole objective of enterprise risk management in the first place. Therefore, if you cannot see and predict the future, which requires looking forward, then by process of elimination you must always be looking backwards. That is the equivalent of driving a car by looking in the rearview mirror.

Only the truly great companies know that you have to look out of the windshield to drive a car!

# About the Author

G REGORY H. DUCKERT, MBA, CPA, CISA, CIA, CRISC, is a Certified Public Accountant, Certified Information Systems Auditor, and Certified Internal Auditor. Mr. Duckert was educated at the University of Wisconsin–Madison and obtained an MBA in Accounting in 1989, a BBA in Accounting in 1978, and a BA in Economics in 1971. He is also the CEO and Founder of the Virtual Governance Institute. The Virtual Governance Institute specializes in consulting with major organizations regarding progressive twenty-first century methodologies for the construction of data centric enterprise risk assessment and management models including Financial, Operational, Regulatory, and IT areas of concern that yield high business values. He also consults with his clients in all areas of auditing including continuous audit/consulting platforms.

In addition, in depth hands-on consulting is also performed in the areas of operational analysis and process improvement methodologies. He has developed extensive risk assessment metric inventories for evaluating risks in all organizational areas including operations, IT application systems, IT operations, regulatory and financial areas. During his audit career he has championed progressive, high value, high impact audit techniques to ensure the maximization of the audit product delivered.

Mr. Duckert is the only non-governmental person ever invited to address the Permanent Undersecretary for Military Affairs of Parliament and the Defense Audit Board of the Ministry of Defense–United Kingdom on the subject matter of risk. He also is involved in the building of or consulting on the creation of Data Centric Risk Assessment and Management models on a continuous basis.

Mr. Duckert is also a Senior Consultant for MIS Training Institute and a lead instructor in their audit practice area on an independent contractor basis. He has also authored and taught numerous IT/audit/consulting seminars and workshops which are currently or were previously offered in the public and private venues.

His professional works and publications include the following: Process Flow Auditing; An ERM Approach to Building Annual Audit Plans; From Auditor to Consultant, Developing Essential Competencies; Data Driven Auditing: A Business Approach; Using Risk Assessment to Build Individual Audit Programs; The Business Risk Lab; Auditing the Manufacturing Process; Acquisitions, Mergers, and Divestitures; Auditing Healthcare Institutions; Auditing for Quality Improvement; Auditing Health Benefits; Sarbanes-Oxley: Roadmap to Compliance; COSO-ERM Utilizing the New Framework for SOX Compliance; Auditing Outsourced Operations; Establishing Enterprise Risk Assessment and Management Environments; Continuous Auditing: A Data Centric Approach; Establishing a 21st Century Audit/Consulting Function; Data Mining: An Essential Auditing Competency; Risk Boot Camp; Risk Based Internal Auditing; Auditing the ERM Environment; Dashboard Metrics for Auditing/Risk Management; Building Continuous Risk Assessment Models; and The CEO's 10 Key Question Handbook for Their Direct Reports.

# Index